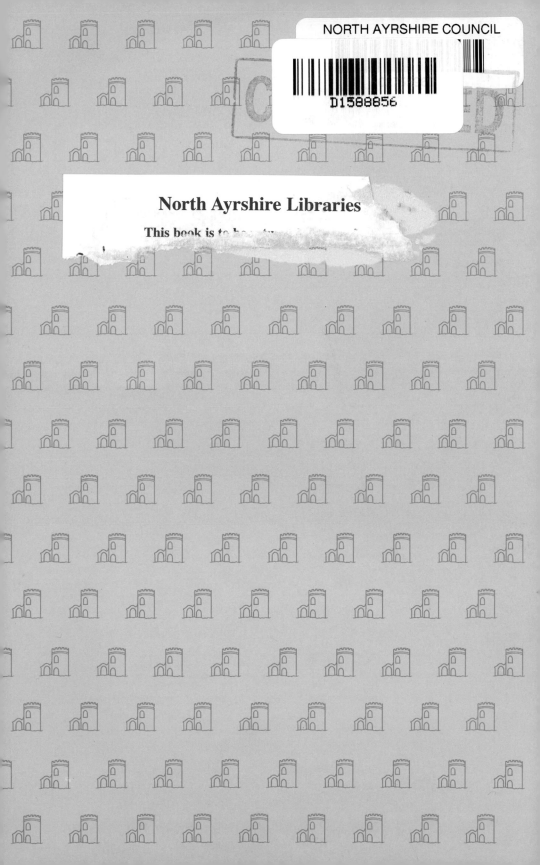

I've travelled the world twice over,
Met the famous: saints and sinners,
Poets and artists, kings and queens,
Old stars and hopeful beginners,
I've been where no-one's been before,
Learned secrets from writers and cooks
All with one library ticket
To the wonderful world of books.

© Janice James.

The wisdom of the ages
Is there for you and me,
The wisdom of the ages,
In your local library

There's large print books
And talking books,
For those who cannot see,
The wisdom of the ages,
It's fantastic, and it's free.

Written by Sam Wood, aged 92

CALL FOR FIRE

This is a first-hand account of fighting in the Falklands and the Gulf campaigns by the only British senior officer who commanded in both of these major wars. In 1982, Chris Craig was captain of the frigate HMS *Alacrity* — the only British surface ship to sink an Argentinian vessel. Nine years later, he was in command of the twenty-six British ships in the Gulf campaign. Craig's account gives a compelling view of the conduct of sea warfare and of the business of commanding warships in modern battle. It is also a moving portrait of the events that took place and of the ordinary sailors who, in extreme adversity, behaved with great courage.

CAPTAIN CHRIS CRAIG CB, DSC, RN

◆

CALL FOR FIRE

Sea Combat in the Falklands
and the Gulf War

Complete and Unabridged

CHARNWOOD
Leicester

First published in Great Britain in 1995 by
John Murray (Publishing) Limited
London

First Charnwood Edition
published 1997
by arrangement with
John Murray (Publishing) Limited
London

British Library CIP Data

Craig, Christopher
Call for fire.—Large print ed.—
Charnwood library series
1. Falklands Islands War, *1982*—Personal
narratives, British
2. Persian Gulf War, *1991*—Personal
narratives, British
3. Large type books
4. Great Britain—History, Naval—20th century
I. Title
359'.0092

ISBN 0–7089–8927–6

This book is dedicated to those who did not 'return in safety to enjoy the blessings of the land with the fruits of their labours'

Foreword

by General Sir Peter de la Billière
KCB, KBE, DSO, MC, MSC, DL

In recent British history our forces have been committed to two major conflicts: in 1982, the recovery of the Falkland Islands, and in 1991, the eviction of Saddam Hussein from Kuwait. In both campaigns the Royal Navy played a major role and, indeed, without their support the Falklands could never have been regained and the Gulf conflict would have developed in quite a different manner.

It is perhaps unique that in both these major campaigns the author played a key part: commanding the Type 21 frigate HMS *Alacrity* in the Falklands and going on to become the Task Group Commander of the twenty-six ships in the Gulf as a Commodore in his flagship HMS *London*. A measure of his success lies in the award of the Distinguished Service Cross for his role in the Falkland operation and his appointment as a Companion to the Loyal Order of the Bath in the Gulf War.

Call for Fire is Captain Craig's personal account of both these naval operations and it conveys vividly the tension and excitement of modern combat and the demands on a commander fighting a war at sea. He brings out with clarity the complexities of such operations which depend upon high technology and yet require sympathetic understanding and leadership of the intelligent and extensively trained men who control these modern weapon systems and complicated ships. The descriptions of fighting at sea are all set in the wider context of operations ashore and in the air.

Although the principles of war and of leadership are surprisingly consistent from one generation to another, the actual conduct of war itself changes considerably — not least at sea. In this book, the reader will find a valuable contemporary account of how these changes have affected maritime warfare.

It has always been my view that the Royal Navy has not received sufficient recognition of the role it played in both these wars and this book does much to put that deficiency right.

Preface

I am a Navy man. Since leaving school, I have known nothing else. Though my life has been full of interests and some massive enthusiasms, the Navy has had my soul and seagoing has had my heart. You might say I have been committed to the deep.

But it has been a good life; most particularly the heady, sapping, exhausting, exhilarating privilege that is sea command. To have carried that particular responsibility under the ultimate test of combat, in wars as necessary and contrasting as the Falklands and the Gulf, was both fascinating and inspiring.

For me, the Falklands was much the more straightforward campaign: a ship and a team that I knew well and came to love; an abundance of independent operations; and the constant drip-feed of adrenalin to sustain us. The Gulf was very different: a Task Group command which grew in size to nearly one quarter of our running Royal Navy and Royal Fleet Auxiliary strength; an improvised staff previously unknown to me; delicate stages of gathering tension *en route* to war; and much co-operation needed with other navies, littoral states and our sister Services ashore. Both of these experiences, nine years apart, were instructive, and each merits recounting.

But I have other reasons for writing this book. I have read enlightening first-hand accounts of sea-fighting, but have been disappointed that most of them describe events prior to 1945. Now, though there is much consistency in the principles of war and methods of command between one generation and another, there is a remarkable difference in the way the business is actually done. It deserves explaining.

I also hope to transport the reader — layman or expert — afloat, into the sophisticated killing machines that now conduct modern warfare at sea. In doing so, I hope to provide a reminder that some astonishing things were achieved by the mainly young people who fought at sea in support of the aims of this country in 1982 and 1991. Because their efforts were largely collective, it is easy to overlook the courage, character and efficiency involved.

The book might also serve to fill one or two gaps left by the Navy's steadfast reluctance to act as self-publicist. The very term 'Silent Service' is chronically outdated and I would like to see the title, and the habit, die. In a world of sophisticated communication and advertising, visibility is influence — and the meek do not inherit the earth.

Shortly after the Falklands War, when lecturing on the campaign, an allegedly intelligent questioner enquired of me: 'Surely the [Falklands] War was a disaster for the Royal Navy? The Royal Air Force shot down all the Argentinian aircraft, the Army crushed them on land — and the Navy just had its ships sunk.' I would like to think that this unenlightened man might read this book.

Not long after the Gulf War, Andrew Lambert, lecturer on war studies at King's College, London, and one-time lecturer at the Royal Military Academy, Sandhurst, wrote that the very poor publicizing of the naval war against Saddam Hussein was unfortunate 'as it emphasised the popular perception that the Gulf War was an Army and Air Force conflict only. In reality, the naval involvement was crucial.' I would like to think that those who read this book will agree.

Other than my disappointment over a lack of rightful publicity, I have tried to refrain from criticism of events which have merely arisen from the pressures of combat. War is an imprecise art, not an exact science, and hindsight makes everyone imperfect. Nevertheless, on occasions I have chosen to highlight mistakes that could have been avoided if I think the lesson needs to be learnt for the future. The handful of individuals concerned will doubtless have their own view of their alleged shortcomings.

In attempting to cover both campaigns within one volume, I am conscious that much has been lost, not least the ability to recount in detail the many achievements of those at sea. But this was never intended to be a comprehensive history, or even a thorough catalogue of all naval events. It is merely a personal — often highly personal — account of one commander's progress through two wars. Whatever the gaps, at least I can console myself with the knowledge that I have two advantages over the conscientious historian: as a determined diarist, I recorded events virtually as they occurred and I was there. On occasions within the book, I have recorded some of my more vivid memories as if they were actually happening — highlighted in the present tense — for that is how I still recall them.

And, from time to time, I have drawn an appropriate phrase from the few books that sustained me at sea; most particularly Shakespeare's *Henry V*, which so inspired me in boyhood and which still captures the heroic pulse of war in a timeless manner. The chapter epigraphs are drawn from the most relevant of these fragments which originally found their way into my diary.

Finally, in amongst the action, there is a good deal of my personal rumination — but war does make you think. The reader may conclude that the overall result is perhaps a somewhat haphazard combination of action and reflection. But what else is war?

* * *

There are only a very few occasions of great significance in most lifetimes: brief moments which can change that life for ever, despite not being recognized as significant at the time. Only later is it realized that a threshold has been crossed that can never be re-crossed. So it was with me on 2 April 1982 when I received my first call to arms. And that is probably the place to begin.

Acknowledgements

Many kind people have helped my research in writing this book. Though far too many to name, I am sure that they will not resent my singling out a few who have made particular efforts on my behalf: Sue Bonney, David Brown (and his fellow historians), Toby Elliott, Chris Esplin-Jones, Graham Mottram, Colin de Mowbray, Mike Shrives, Carolyn Stait, David Teer, Barbara Vowles, Peter Williams, and officers from HMS *Alacrity* in 1982 and my Task Group Staff in 1990 – 1.

My publisher, John Murray, and agent, Michael Shaw, deserve my deep thanks for bringing the book to life and focusing my aims at the outset. In particular, my editor, Gail Pirkis, merits immense gratitude for her great thoroughness and support in harnessing my efforts.

Above all, my wife Daphne has had to live with a demanding and competing 'mistress' for more than three years and has given countless hours and much patience as my assistant and adviser.

To all my helpers, I offer inadequate thanks — and hope that you derive some satisfaction from this book.

I should, of course, make it clear that the views contained within these pages are entirely my own and that they have no official standing or endorsement.

HMS
ALACRITY
TYPE 21 FRIGATE

WESTLAND LYNX

WARNING RADAR

NAVIGATION RADAR

GUNNERY RADAR

BRIDGE

EXOCET LAUNCHERS

GUN

CHAFF LAUNCHERS

SATELLITE COMMUNICATIONS

GEMINI BOAT

MISSILE RADAR

SEACAT LAUNCHER

TORPEDO DECOYS

QUARTERDECK

TWIN RUDDERS

CONTROLLABLE PITCH PROPELLERS

DINING HALL

STOREROOMS

MACHINERY SPACES

ACCOMMODATION

EXPLOSIVES MAGAZINE

ANCHOR

SONAR DOME

THE SOUTH ATLANTIC 1982

PARAGUAY

ASUNCION

BRAZIL

ARGENTINA

URUGUAY

VALPARAISO
SANTIAGO

BUENOS
AIRES

MONTEVIDEO

MILES
0
100
200
300
400
500

PUERTO BELGRANO

To ASCENSION I.
3,800 miles

TRELEW

COMODORO
RIVADAVIA

FALKLAND ISLANDS

To
S. GEORGIA
900
miles

RIO
GALLEGOS

RIO
GRANDE

BURDWOOD
BANK

200 mile total
exclusion zone
(TEZ)

60°W

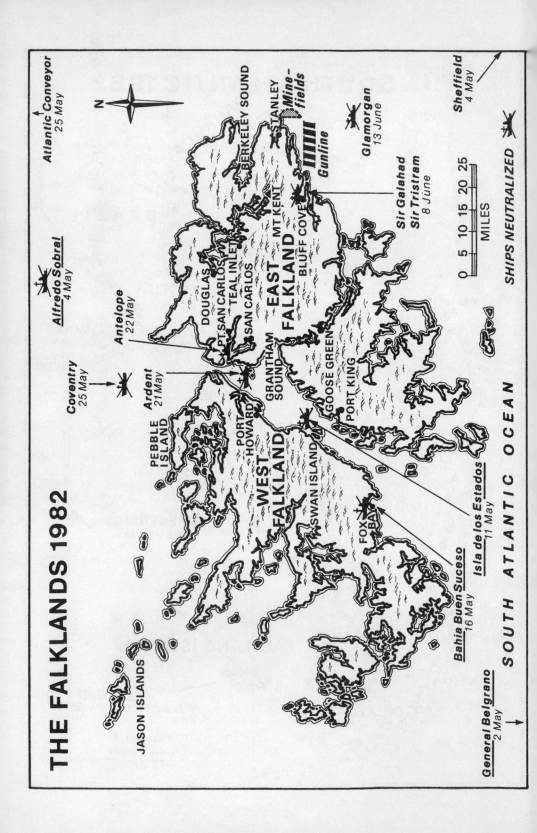

THE FALKLANDS 1982

N

Atlantic Conveyor
25 May

Alfredo Sobral
4 May

Coventry
25 May

Antelope
22 May

Ardent
21 May

JASON ISLANDS

PEBBLE
ISLAND

PORT
HOWARD

**WEST
FALKLAND**

SWAN ISLAND

FOX
BAY

General Belgrano
2 May

Bahia Buen Suceso
16 May

Isla de los Estados
11 May

BERKELEY SOUND

STANLEY

**Mine-
fields**

Gunline

Glamorgan
13 June

Sheffield
4 May

SHIPS NEUTRALIZED

DOUGLAS

PT. SAN CARLOS

TEAL INLET

SAN CARLOS

GRANTHAM
SOUND

MT KENT

**EAST
FALKLAND**

BLUFF COVE

**Sir Galahad
Sir Tristram**
8 June

GOOSE GREEN

PORT KING

0 5 10 15 20 25
MILES

SOUTH   ATLANTIC   OCEAN

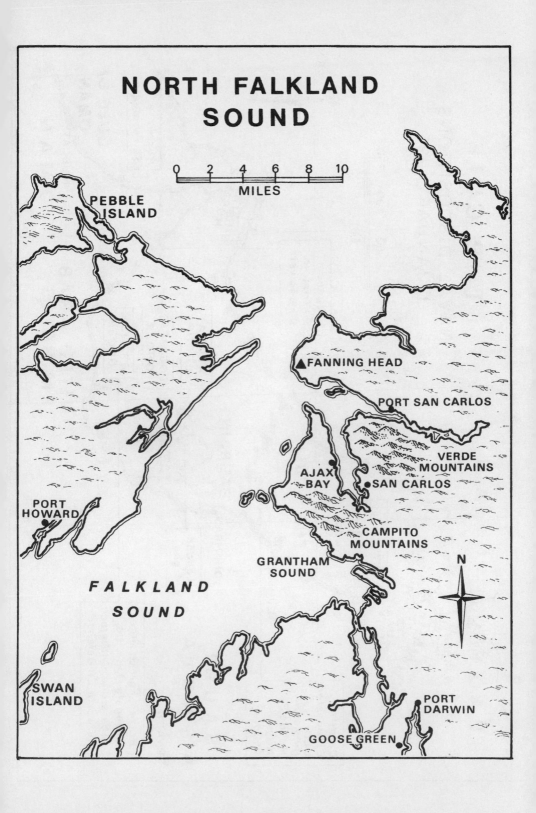

NORTH FALKLAND
SOUND

0 2 4 6 8 10
MILES

PEBBLE
ISLAND

▲ FANNING HEAD

PORT SAN CARLOS

VERDE
MOUNTAINS

AJAX
BAY

● SAN CARLOS

PORT
HOWARD

CAMPITO
MOUNTAINS

GRANTHAM
SOUND

N

FALKLAND
SOUND

SWAN
ISLAND

● PORT
DARWIN

GOOSE GREEN ●

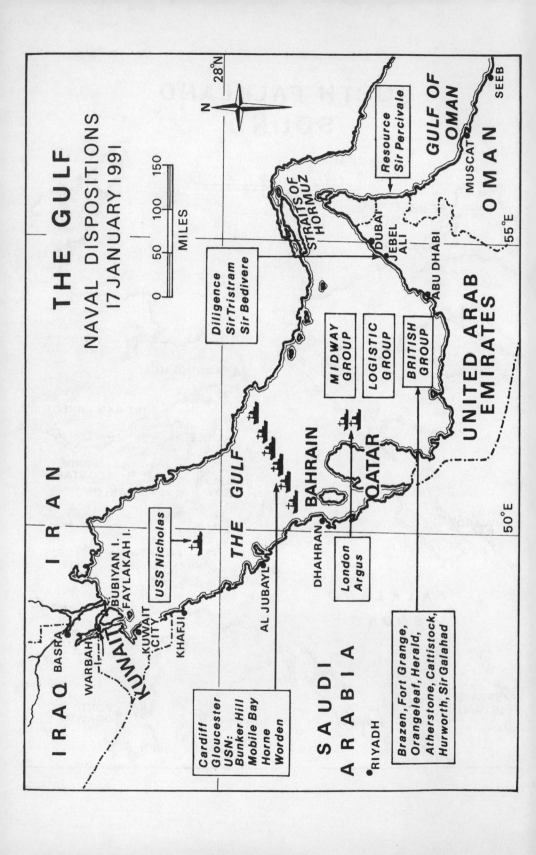

THE GULF

NAVAL DISPOSITIONS 17 JANUARY 1991

MILES
0   50   100   150

N   28°N

Resource
Sir Percivale

Diligence
Sir Tristram
Sir Bedivere

MIDWAY GROUP

LOGISTIC GROUP

BRITISH GROUP

USS Nicholas

London
Argus

Cardiff
Gloucester
USN:
Bunker Hill
Mobile Bay
Horne
Worden

Brazen, Fort Grange,
Orangeleaf, Herald,
Atherstone, Cattistock,
Hurworth, Sir Galahad

IRAQ   BASRA

IRAN

WARBAH

KUWAIT   BUBIYAN I.
FAYLAKAH I.

KUWAIT CITY

KHAFJI

AL JUBAYL

THE GULF

DHAHRAN

SAUDI
ARABIA

•RIYADH

BAHRAIN

QATAR

STRAITS OF
HORMUZ

GULF OF
OMAN

DUBAI
JEBEL
ALI

ABU DHABI

MUSCAT

OMAN

SEEB

UNITED ARAB
EMIRATES

50°E   55°E

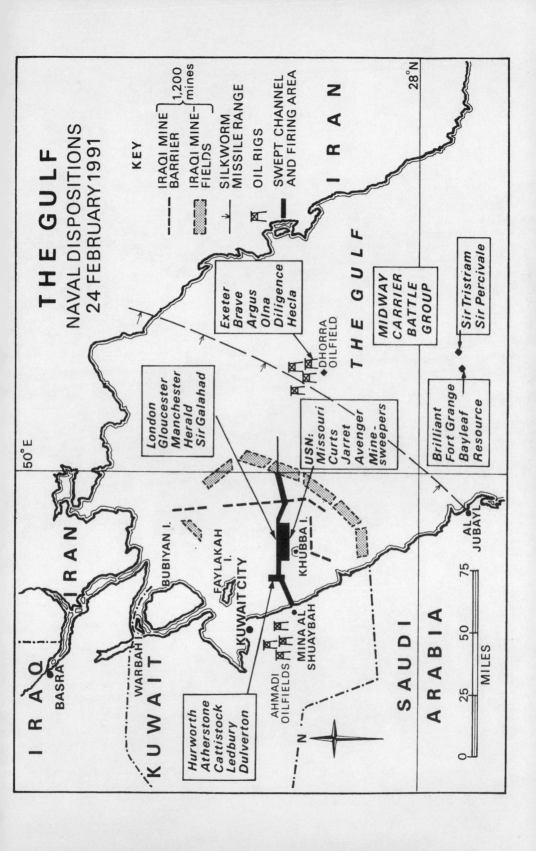

THE GULF
NAVAL DISPOSITIONS 24 FEBRUARY 1991

KEY

IRAQI MINE BARRIER
IRAQI MINE FIELDS ⎫ 1,200 mines
SILKWORM MISSILE RANGE
OIL RIGS
SWEPT CHANNEL AND FIRING AREA

IRAN

IRAN

IRAQ
BASRA

WARBAH

KUWAIT

BUBIYAN I.

FAYLAKAH I.

KUWAIT CITY

AHMADI OILFIELDS

MINA AL SHUAYBAH

KHŪBBA I.

50° E

London
Gloucester
Manchester
Herald
Sir Galahad

Hurworth
Atherstone
Cattistock
Ledbury
Dulverton

USN:
Missouri
Curts
Jarret
Avenger
Mine-
sweepers

Exeter
Brave
Argus
Olna
Diligence
Hecla

DHORRA OILFIELD

THE GULF

MIDWAY CARRIER BATTLE GROUP

Sir Tristram
Sir Percivale

Brilliant
Fort Grange
Bayleaf
Resource

AL JUBAYL

SAUDI ARABIA

28° N

N

0   25   50   75
MILES

BOOK ONE

The Falklands
1982

1

Go South

2 – 15 April

'Now thrive the armourers'

THE wet westerly wind funnelled up Channel, tore the surface of Lyme Bay into strips of white, swooped across the pebbled causeway down to Portland Harbour, and tried maliciously to saw the slender grey warship from her taut anchor cable. But the frigate had coped with far worse, and it was not the wind that was to give HMS *Alacrity* a night to remember.

I woke reluctantly; 0323 by my bedside clock. We had come to single anchor at midnight and I had climbed into my narrow bunk a little before 0100.

Sharp knocking was repeated. There was no escaping the reverberations within the tiny steel cocoon of my sleeping cabin. 'Yes?' I was short on sleep after three weeks of busy ship weapon-training and my voice reflected it. Tomorrow I would relinquish my command of eighteen months with immense regret, and the prospect did nothing to restore my goodwill.

The door opened. Boyish and apologetic, the duty signalman stood uncertainly in the glow

3

of the red night-lighting. 'Taff' Jones surveyed my recumbent form with undisguised curiosity, clearly contrasting it with the better-groomed, assertive and altogether more vertical image he was accustomed to viewing on the bridge. He too sounded tired.

'Sorry, sir. I have an Immediate Exclusive signal for you,' he sing-songed whilst waving the piece of paper alongside my ear. I flipped on the bedside light, thus destroying my night vision for at least twenty minutes, took the signal from him with a sigh, and started to read what was quite clearly a directive. I could feel the ship surging to her cable before the freshening wind as the slap of wavelets along the tethered steel hull became more pronounced: Portland was always so bloody exposed from the west, and had given me many a sleepless night over the years. *Alacrity* twanged again, like a cat stretching itself into life, as if sensing what was in my hands.

Recovering my humour, if not yet my full sleep-fuddled faculties, I grinned at Taff: 'If this is the Ops Officer's idea of a belated April Fool, then he and I are about to fall out!'After all, 1 April was but three hours past, and I was due to leave the ship the following day. Was this an audacious spoof by my team?

I thought back eighteen months to 1980, to my first two weeks in command. We had been ordered to sail in the middle of the night from Singapore to what was then known as the Persian Gulf, where an Arab dictator called Saddam Hussein had just invaded Iran. The

4

signal that night had the same flavour as the one I now held. Too slowly I came to the right conclusion: it was authentic. Our programme was about to change and, to judge from the other addressees, ours was but one of many. Somebody wanted us to steam 8,000 miles south to somewhere called the Falkland Islands. Where the bloody hell were they?

I reached for the microphone clipped to the steel bulkhead alongside my head and commenced the miserable task of rousing 200 men prematurely.

'Officer of the Watch?' I had kept the ship in seagoing watches due to the short night at anchor. Four dutymen were on the bridge, checking that the ship was not dragging her anchor, keeping their sleeping colleagues safe and ensuring that the 'Old Man' was shaken with any urgent signals. He had been.

'Tell the First Lieutenant and the Heads of Department I want to see them in my cabin. Fifteen minutes.' A right flurry of rumour that will start, I reflected. *Alacrity* was coming back to life and it was the morning of 2 April 1982. It had begun.

My only knowledge of the Falklands stemmed from some rather attractive stamps I had collected as a boy; and had there not been a bit of a battle with Admiral Graf von Spee in 1914? Their Lordships would have been disappointed by my ignorance but I could not help a certain sense of frivolity. The signal was pure comic opera: scrap-metal merchants raising the Argentinian flag over South Georgia indeed.

It sounded as if Britannia had merely to huff and puff to blow the whole lot away. What a disruptive bore.

We weighed anchor within the hour, courtesy of our quick-start gas turbine engines, and were secured alongside for storing at Q Pier as the watery spring dawn tried hopelessly to soften the stark limestone face of the Isle of Portland which reared above us. Given the uncertainties as to what was unfolding, and the security classification of our sailing instructions, the rumour grapevine excelled itself. *Alacrity* was going far south — and it seemed the whole world knew.

Throughout the morning, a succession of men, stores, provisions, protective clothing and goodwill messages all threatened to sink the ship long before the Argentinian Air Force was to try. The quantity of food alone was astonishing: frozen, dried, canned, fresh — we were not about to starve. Perhaps the Ministry of Defence had a three-year blockade in mind?

Most important to my sailors were the contents of the ship's canteen. They would die for Queen and Country, but not without 'Nutty' (sweets and chocolates) and certainly not without 'Goffas' (cans of unbearably sweet, fizzy drinks). My irrepressible Supply Officer, Anton Maguire, felt that we had not embarked enough — and how right he was — so he took his mini-van out around the streets of Weymouth and bought prodigious additional stocks. Once the rotgut was aboard, I was confident that we could cope with anything. Nelson probably felt

6

the same way about rum.

The most pressing question in my mind was answered when Admiral David Halifax, Chief of Staff to Commander-in-Chief Fleet at Northwood and unfailingly gracious, rang me by secure telephone from the bomb-proof cellars of his headquarters in Middlesex. It seemed Their Lordships felt it inappropriate to change the well-established captain of a ship about to go to war: thus Commander Christopher Craig, Royal Navy, would remain. My unfortunate relief, one Commander Andrew Ritchie, would have his appointment changed. I was elated; to have watched my treasured ship go to her greatest challenge without me would have broken my spirit for years to come. Selfishly, I gave damn-all thought to the disappointed Ritchie, already *en route* to a first command which he would never claim.

Nor did I consider my family who had just finished packing the car in Bournemouth ready to collect me for a long-awaited holiday. My wife Daphne was already conditioned to a marriage of innumerable compromises in the name of duty. Her years as an officer in the Women's Royal Naval Service were a considerable help, as was her durable nature. If she had known what turbulence lay ahead through two wars, she would have taken our booked holiday cottage and remained there for the next ten years. My two small sons, Matthew and Duncan, had little grasp of what was afoot, but change was exciting so they were happy, if confused. At that moment, their father was little the wiser.

Following my unwelcome and somewhat mysterious telephone call, Daphne simply unloaded the car and refilled it with the astonishing list of garments I had dictated to her. With a sinking heart she read the unmistakable message; her husband was going somewhere cold, he was going there fast, and he was going for some time. She reminds me that I also stated I would not have missed it for all the world.

And so I busied myself with ship preparations and admired the energy that Flag Officer Sea Training and his staff at Portland were generating on our behalf. Similar vitality was in evidence up and down the country in military establishments by the hundred. Admiral Sir Henry Leach, Chief of the Naval Staff, in his robust support for the dispatch of a great naval task force, had staked his professional reputation upon ships being ready to sail within five days: one did not make that sort of pledge lightly to the Prime Minister, Margaret Thatcher. He needed a little help. If not yet quite of Dunkirk proportions, the British people were starting to revel in their latest challenge.

We sailed through Portland Breakwater at sunset on 2 April, having taken just fourteen hours to tear up our programme and ready ourselves for war on the far side of the globe: I was to find out later that it was the fastest reaction time of any. Our sleek 3,400 tons by then held 500 tons of fuel and 50 tons of fresh water; soon it would also contain 500 high-explosive shells, 12 Seacat missiles, 12 homing torpedoes and 6 depth-charges. We were heavyweight disguised as welterweight and ready for a fight, as my signal stated: '*Alacrity* is stored and provisioned for war, being now *en route* to Devonport to take on war ammunition. Awaiting further orders.'

It had been a long day and we went down Channel fast, Olympus boost engines burning diesel fuel at more than 13 tons an hour. Having prepared myself never again to have *Alacrity* running beneath my feet, it was a glorious feeling. She thrust her long, graceful neck into the south-westerly swell which surged up Channel to meet us — and I was back where I belonged. The ship buzzed with the expectancy of some great combined endeavour; thus it seemed entirely appropriate to receive the signalled codename for sailing a British armada to recover the Falkland Islands — Operation Corporate.

On our arrival in Plymouth, the determined men of the Naval Armament Depot and the adrenalin running in my sailors combined to set a world record for ammunitioning. Sleek missiles, high-explosive shells, homing torpedoes, cannon bandoliers and thousands of lower-lethality bullets settled the ship several inches deeper into the murky waters of Devonport. Our sister ship *Antelope*, under similar orders, was taking on her fireworks further upstream.

Signal traffic was heavy as we conducted final preparations. The British tabloids were already in full swing, and all news resonated with the rattle of sabres. Metaphors were trite: the Spirit of Agincourt, of Trafalgar, of Dunkirk, of the Blitz, was allegedly dominating the nation. Uncertain as to whether I should be excited or nauseated, I settled for the former. In contrast to many Englishmen, I have always found enthusiasm comes more readily to me than cynicism.

Despite the pugnacious hype of the Press, caution was being voiced by politicians throughout the world, not least in Whitehall. In truth, British defence policy and foreign policy had become increasingly misaligned over the preceding twenty years. Defence had been preoccupied with the Soviet Union; diplomacy with the distant preservation of the status quo; and successive governments with keeping their options open, and seeking more 'bangs' for less 'bucks'. The mix was incompatible. I do not see politicians, diplomats and servicemen asking to share the same table in Heaven. A third of them won't be there anyway.

It was no great surprise when, over that first weekend, Lord Carrington accepted responsibility for 'the very great humiliation' that was the Argentinian invasion and resigned. During my previous two years working in Whitehall for the UK Chiefs of Staff, I had considered Britain to be ambivalent over the Falkland Islands even then: thus I was not surprised that Argentina had become confused. If we could have shed responsibility for the barren jumble of rocks through some low-cost compromise of ownership, then I believe we would have done so. Indeed, the emotional reportage of the nation's passion to save 1,800 Falklanders I found to be a little hypocritical.

Following a discordant past, shallow goodwill prevailed between Britain and Argentina throughout the 1970s and achieved a new framework of co-operation. It was only broken by some fresh Argentinian bellicosity in 1977 which prompted the British Labour Government to demonstrate resolve by dispatching a naval force comprising a submarine, two frigates and a tanker. The deterrent worked.

Then, in 1980, the Foreign Office Minister Nicholas Ridley proposed to the House of Commons a 'leaseback' of the islands to the Argentinians. Predictably, Governor Rex Hunt's Falklanders were implacably opposed, and thus Lord Carrington refused to lean further upon them. The emotive proposals were tucked away for another day.

The following winter, the Army commander General Leopoldo Galtieri became President of Argentina, ominously declaring that 1982 would be the 'Year of the Malvinas', their name for the Falklands. He had inherited an economy in tatters, annual inflation of 150 per cent and a revolution building against atrocities committed by the military during the repressive five-year 'Dirty War' of the early 1970s, which saw nearly 15,000 people simply 'disappear'. Accordingly, and as so often in history, a military ruler chose to risk external military action in the hope of unifying his people.

Triumphant visits to the United States late in 1981 fuelled his misconception that the right-wing Reagan Administration considered President Jimmy Carter's impassioned criticisms of Argentina's human rights record a thing of the past. Galtieri's new relationship with his powerful northern neighbour was nevertheless competing with the Anglo-American 'Special Relationship' — and a gathering personal affinity between Margaret Thatcher and Ronald Reagan. A wiser man would have guessed which way the Americans would jump if the issue became critical. In believing that they would remain on the fence, Galtieri made his first strategic error.

Not surprisingly, Argentina hardened its official claims to ownership of the Malvinas early in 1982; a demand dating from as long ago as 1833 when the British sent HMS *Clio* to land and declare sovereignty. As a former Spanish colony, the Argentinians saw it as their right to retain the offshore islands, just as had Ecuador with the Galapagos, and Brazil with the Trinidade Islands. Their claims were doubtless fuelled by the British Conservative Government having announced a large cut-back in conventional forces, including withdrawal of the patrol ship HMS *Endurance* from the South Atlantic. Galtieri saw a lack of resolve — and the wall of deterrence crumbled.

Actual rule over Argentina was by then in the hands of a military junta, consisting of Galtieri, the head of the Air Force, Brigadier Lami Dozo, and the much more influential and aggressive head of the Navy, Admiral Jorge Anaya. Anaya was in fact the real Svengali behind the plan to regain the islands by force, called Operation

12

Blue. Military history often reveals naval officers to be ready schemers — which doesn't entirely surprise me.

Desultory talks between Britain and Argentina finally foundered in February 1982, leaving the way clear for Argentinian military action against a Falkland garrison of just eighty Royal Marines and one patrol ship, *Endurance*, commanded by a farsighted and increasingly anxious Captain Nick Barker. He had detected and reported the early signs of likely aggression, but nobody wanted to hear.

The Argentinian invasion force embarked at Puerto Belgrano on Sunday, 28 March. The landing ship *Cabo San Antonio* and the icebreaker *Almirant Irizar* were accompanied by the destroyer flagship, *Santissima Trinidad*, her sister ship *Hercules*, the frigates *Drummond* and *Granville*, and the submarine *Santa Fe*. A naval transport accompanied them — the *Isla de los Estados*. The force was commanded by Rear Admiral Jorge Allara and was to be supported by another group of warships headed by the aircraft-carrier *25 de Mayo*, which was to hold to the north-west of the islands.

The invasion group had to endure a south-easterly passage of nearly 800 miles through fierce storms to reach their target. *Cabo San Antonio* was well beyond her carrying capacity, with nearly 900 seasick men below decks which were often rolling to over 40°. Ironically, the US Ambassador to the United Nations, Jeanne Kirkpatrick, was actually dining the Argentinian Ambassador on 1 April as his

13

assault ships were making their final approach to East Falkland, and as President Reagan was making an eleventh-hour telephone call to Galtieri, pleading for restraint. But, even as the call was being put through, the first men were slipping ashore. The Junta was convinced that the speed of the invasion would not provoke military action from an enfeebled Britain. They were committed.

By dawn on 2 April, as I was taking *Alacrity* alongside at Portland, nearly 8,000 miles to the south two Argentinian invasion groups were moving laboriously overland to mount attacks upon the capital, Stanley, and to take Government House. To the northeast of East Falkland, a beach recce party from the submarine *Santa Fe* completed their task and the first men of the marine assault force poured ashore through the bow doors of the *Cabo San Antonio*. By 1000 they had occupied the town of Stanley.

Though the Argentinians were under strict orders to minimize British casualties for fear of provoking a backlash from Margaret Thatcher, Major Mike Norman and his garrison of Royal Marines were under no such constraint: the Argentinians lost one man killed and two others wounded in brisk exchanges. Indeed, it was a profound relief to the invasion-force commander, Rear Admiral Muller, when Rex Hunt surrendered the islands to avoid further unnecessary slaughter. The initial occupying garrison under the command of Brigadier General Menendez numbered 630. Though its

14

officers and NCOs were regulars, their soldiers were on twelve months' conscription. Invasion had been a great deal easier than retention was to prove to be.

Meanwhile, much had been going on in Westminster and Whitehall. When Intelligence reported the invasion force approaching the Falklands on the evening of 31 March, Margaret Thatcher summoned key ministers to the first of many crisis meetings, this one taking place in the House of Commons. Her informal War Cabinet was to meet daily thereafter, usually mid-morning. Proceedings on 31 March were punctuated by the First Sea Lord, Admiral Sir Henry Leach, arriving to brief his defence minister, John Nott, only to find himself briefing the Prime Minister instead. His advice was unambiguous and courageous: the Royal Navy was quite capable of mounting a 'retrieval force' over nearly 8,000 miles of wide ocean, and could depart within a few days. However, a further three weeks would be needed to commence operations amongst the islands, thereby allowing plenty of time for diplomacy. The next day, 1 April, his advice prevailed over the counsel of the many prophets of doom and a great Task Force was readied.

On the following day, the UN Security Council approved Resolution 502, demanding immediate Argentinian withdrawal. The vote of the USSR was critical, but skilled diplomacy and some heart-searching amongst the Soviet bloc ensured that only Panama voted against. Britain had right on her side.

On 3 April, and far to the south, after a passage of 1,400 miles from Argentina, the frigate *Guerrico* and the tanker *Bahia Paraiso* took the frozen grandeur of South Georgia from the tiny reinforcement of twenty-two Royal Marines at Grytviken. Once again the Argentinians were given a foretaste of British pugnacity as the Marines fired a rocket projectile into *Guerrico* and shot down her Puma helicopter. The mission accomplished, the Junta was given no time to celebrate as they became aware of the much-publicized assembly of a British Task Force. Their alarm was profound and they commenced a frenzied reinforcement of the garrison; it was all going horribly wrong. By then, even I was coming to realize that the Falklands crisis was far from comic opera.

Over that last weekend, final orders were issued. UK-based ships would all sail on Monday, 5 April. *Alacrity* was to rendezvous with the aircraft-carriers *Hermes* (aviator Captain L. E. Middleton ADC) and *Invincible* (gunnery officer Captain J. J. Black MBE) off the Scilly Isles and escort them at their best speed to the south, to the interim staging-post of Ascension Island. Meanwhile, Commander Nick Tobin was to take *Antelope* as shepherdess to some lumbering logistical landing ships, which would comprise part of the amphibious force. Poor Nick, I liked my orders best.

The tankers *Olmeda* (Captain A. P. Overbury) and *Pearleaf* (Captain J. McCulloch) and the stores ship *Resource* (Captain B. A. Seymour)

16

would comprise the initial support: few people knew that the stores/ammunition and helicopter-carrying auxiliary *Fort Austin* (Commodore Sam Dunlop) had already sailed southward from Gibraltar as early as 29 March.

The balance of the ships that would make up the initial Task Group were those that had been engaged in Exercise Springtrain in the Mediterranean; they would intercept our intended track *en route* to Ascension Island, just south of the Equator. They included the guided-missile destroyers *Antrim* (aviator Captain Brian Young) and *Glamorgan* (gunnery officer Captain Mike Barrow); the antisubmarine frigates *Brilliant* (submariner Captain John Coward), *Broadsword* (navigator Captain Bill Canning), *Plymouth* (aviator Captain David Pentreath) and *Yarmouth* (aviator Commander Tony Morton); the air-defence destroyers *Coventry* (navigator Captain David Hart-Dyke), *Glasgow* (submariner Captain Paul Hoddinott) and *Sheffield* (submariner Captain Sam Salt); the general-purpose Type 21 frigate *Arrow* (aviator Commander Paul Bootherstone); and the tanker *Tidespring* (Captain S. Redmond).

I was surprised to note how many naval aviators and submariners destiny was about to place in command in the South Atlantic. There has always been rivalry between specializations of the Royal Navy, particularly when it comes to qualifying for the cherished privilege of sea command. But even in my most parochial moments, I would not generalize about the ability to command being dependent upon

17

a man's specialization. There are, however, aspects of aviation and submarine operations which must be beneficial to the business of war combat command. Command in war is all about high-intensity risk-management: aviation is the same. Serving in surface ships has risks aplenty, but few are as sustained or intense as those provided by life-and-death operations in the air. Aviators learn early to balance risk-taking against gain. Our nerves are hardened to it and the good ones love the adrenalin that it releases. Naval aviation thus provides an excellent preparation for the stress of battle.

I can sympathize with the ire of the surface navy man when he sees such a large proportion of sea commands going the way of these alleged 'amateurs'. But the fact remains that the man who climbs into an aircraft takes with him a code of the deepest professionalism. Of the COs about to fight in the South Atlantic, more than half wore wings on their sleeves. The redeeming feature of this debate is that such rivalry as exists is pretty benign. Most enlightened men simply admire experience that is not their own and count themselves blessed that the Navy is still wise enough to want to select from the widest cross-section for command appointments.

★ ★ ★

Back in Devonport, I was more focused than when complacently readying my ship for the prospect of meeting Saddam Hussein's navy two years earlier. We offloaded every unnecessary item with but one unfortunate exception: as previous holders of the Fleet Gunnery Trophy, we still had the silver cup for its new winner, HMS *Sheffield*. Having heard that she too was headed south, I made the poor decision to carry it to her.

A previous captain of the *Sheffield*, Rear Admiral Sandy Woodward, was to command the British Task Group. I knew him only by reputation as a very bright submariner. He was currently with the Springtrain group in the destroyer *Glamorgan* and would transfer to his eventual flagship, *Hermes*, as she headed south.

On 3 April, Parliament approved taking up ships from merchant service. Such vessels were known as Ships Taken Up From Trade — STUFT — which gave ribald sailors some potential for mirth. The STUFT included the P&O liner *Canberra* (Captain W. Scott-Masson), which was destined to carry the 3rd Battalion of the Parachute Regiment, together with 40 and 42 Commandos, Royal Marines. Nine British Petroleum commercial oilers became supertankers for topping up our own fleet auxiliaries, whilst numerous merchant ships and even North Sea ferries were chartered or requisitioned to transfer stores, equipment and men. Even our heavy warships had to effect less exotic transformations: the amphibious assault ship *Fearless* (Captain Jeremy Larken) replaced her bitterly disappointed young officer trainees with experienced men to conduct the real business that the departing fresh-faced midshipmen so coveted.

Our naval bases commenced miraculously fast merchant-ship conversions (Portsmouth alone was to complete twenty-five) in which most vessels received enhanced communications, satellite receivers, additional fuel tanks, fresh-water distilleries, extra accommodation, replenishment gear, helicopter-operating equipment and, often, a flight-deck. Semi-warships emerged virtually overnight.

More ominously to us, *Uganda* (Captain J. G. Clark) became a hospital ship, the Royal Navy survey ships *Hecla* (Captain G. L. Hope), *Herald* (Captain R. I. C. Halliday) and *Hydra* (Commander R. J. Campbell) were converted to 'sea ambulances', and four oceangoing tugs were readied in anticipation of ship damage. Ashore, an organization was being established to conduct the gloomy business of casualty reporting.

In Plymouth, Admiral Sir Bob Gerken and a large team of people, in and out of uniform, regular and volunteer, were already harnessing the vast infrastructure needed for war. Down in the naval base, *Alacrity* had an exhilarating expectation about her which was, by then, not without anxiety. We had little idea that we were shortly to become part of the greatest show on earth, not only for the firesides of Britain but also for many other countries.

On the Sunday afternoon — 4 April — preceding our day of departure, I took a run through the vast, sad, declining Devonport Dockyard. Walls of drizzle spewed out of Cornwall, shrouding weather-beaten stone jetties

20

and glistening buildings as I splashed across slick cobblestones. The one solitary modern refitting shed contrasted starkly with the faded grey and blue of many ancient dilapidated buildings linked by endless long-rusted pipes and rails.

In the year that I first joined the Fleet, 1962, the Royal Navy possessed 7 aircraft-carriers, 7 cruisers and 138 destroyers and frigates. As we prepared to fight Argentina, we had 4 carriers, no cruisers and well under half the number of escorts. Since the Denis Healey Defence White Paper of 1966, we had seen a steady reduction in size, worsened by the 1981 decision to axe a further 10,000 men and scrap our amphibious assault ships. Effectively, the cost of the Polaris/Trident submarine strategic nuclear deterrent was emaciating our conventional forces — leaving us with too many commitments and far too few resources. It was a gaunt Navy that our nation was once more turning to for help, and all of its decline seemed charted in the fading glory which surrounded me as I returned, soaked, to my ship.

On the night before departure, *Alacrity* was secured beneath a huge dockyard crane, its swinging jib overhanging us like a gallows. As if such symbolism was not enough, the crane was temporary home to hundreds of mewling seagulls who spent the night covering my immaculate ship with excrement. I reassured myself with the old wives' tale that to be so 'bombed' means good fortune.

Watery dawn saw a visit from our Squadron Captain, Hugo White, to wish us well. And then it was time for final departure. I took the conning microphone on the high exposed wing of the ship's bridge as our sailors moved stiffly about the damp upper deck in the half-light, making last preparations. I ordered all lines but one removed, leaving just a single long wire running forward from the jetty up to the very point of our bows. A nervous stoker also tried, inadvertently, to leave us still attached to the mainland by a thin steam line, which seemed to reflect our reluctance to face the unknown.

'Special Sea Dutymen closed up, sir. Ready for sea in all respects.' I caught the flash of a smile from my ever-buoyant First Lieutenant, Lieutenant Commander Colin de Mowbray, as he made his report in the gloom. Below my feet, watertight doors were checked clipped and dozens of men were nervously closed up at their positions: a hundred separate pieces of machinery were already running smoothly and awaiting my call. Time to set them to work.

'Starboard thirty-five. Slow ahead port — slow astern starboard.' I gave the orders with deliberately slow precision. Let's make this a nice calm departure.

I watched the full weight of *Alacrity* slowly tension up the wire as engine turned against engine and my obedient ship started swivelling on the spot, walking her trim little stern off the jetty. Our terse radio message reminded the hovering tug to keep clear. This was *Alacrity* and she needed no help: tug assistance was for wimps!

The flight-deck was swinging well clear of the

22

wharf now, 30 – 40° inclined, and leaving me free to move astern past the two vessels moored close behind us. Quivering lightly, the ship stood on her well-fendered nose, ready to answer the call. It was time for a little panache.

'Let go forespring. In fenders. Three short blasts, navigator. Half-astern both engines. Set lever five zero.'

Our sirens shattered the dawn with three shrieks of warning to passing craft; the wire snaked back inboard; the propellers bit; and white swirls of wake slid beneath as we shot out backwards into mid-stream. Free again.

I commenced a flashy turn on the spot, leaving little clearance to the shoals on either side; engine against engine at high power; thundering wash of mud and broken water all around. I ordered *Antelope* into station astern, slipped the brakes — and we were off past the harbour-front. Countless Royal Navy hulls had departed through these waters for conflicts over the centuries: Plymouth had been the bosom of our Navy for generations, during which time there had been eight previous ships bearing the name *Alacrity* — the first dating from 1806. Our ship motto was: 'I hasten to help.' Tell that to the Falklanders.

Tumult and acclaim surrounded the carriers *Hermes* and *Invincible* on 5 April when they sailed from Portsmouth. As the carriers passed down Channel, their aircraft embarked from the Naval Air Stations, Lee-on-Solent in Hampshire, Portland in Dorset, Yeovilton in Somerset, and Culdrose in Cornwall. More tellingly, three British nuclear submarines, *Spartan* (Commander Jim Taylor), *Splendid* (Commander Roger Lane-Nott) and *Conqueror* (Commander Chris Wreford-Brown), were already running southward, fast and deep, well ahead of us.

The ballyhoo for the Portsmouth departure of the carriers was not mirrored further west. As *Alacrity* led *Antelope* out of harbour at just after 0700 that same morning, not a head turned on the Torpoint Ferry as we passed. But at least there was a small knot of our loved ones, declared and undeclared, clustered on the overlooking Devil's Point as the two sleek frigates swung past Mount Edgcumbe, out through the narrows, and on past the shadow of Drake's Island. As we headed south for the open sea beyond the breakwater, the damp and doleful group of girls was soon swallowed up astern in the seeping mizzle. Signalling our final turn, the mournful blast of our sirens echoed flatly back up the dockyard and across the soaked hillside to stately Admiralty House. It said goodbye. Generations of naval tradition were going with us; national expectation was be our spur — or our burden.

Transit past the Eddystone Lighthouse and through the Channel revealed the need for even better lashing down of anything that could move, the deep swell seemingly breaking loose most of our new stores. And so all ships streamed south-west to their rendezvous, carried on the wave of energy that had been generated throughout the land by the prospect of war.

On arrival off the Scillies, 30 miles west of Land's End, we loitered in dense fog and watched on radar the dignified approach of the mighty carriers and the tanker *Olmeda*. The evil, moist vapour that surrounded us had strangled many more experienced mariners in these waters over the years. As collision with the flagship would certainly have grabbed a headline or two, and though I normally liked to join another force with some flourish, this was no time for glamour — prudence ruled. So we slid inconspicuously on a slowly converging course into our sector screen ahead of *Hermes*, finally reporting ourselves in station, 5,000 yards away from the glowing amber blob on our radar screens. That blob was in fact 28,000 tons, nearly 750 feet long and contained 1,400 men but we gained not a glimpse of the carrier until dawn the next morning, by which stage we were wallowing deep in rising seas south of Ushant. The heart of the Task Force was established and it was pulsing steadily southward.

Biscay was relatively benign, although the steep swell was enough to unsettle some new seagoers. But I was too busy to engage in sympathy. I still cringe at the unstructured nature of our preparations during that early passage south: war is too important a subject to be dealt with so haphazardly. Too many of our guidance publications were relics of Second World War philosophy and, though our training and equipment were excellent, ours was still a peacetime culture. No significant combat experience existed among the Task

Group and despite trying to think through the realities of war, we kept returning to the artificialities of peace, many years of which engender complacency.

Nevertheless, we were taking potent warships south. My own was one of eight rakish Type 21 frigates that had been a private venture, designed and built remarkably quickly by Vosper Thornycroft and Yarrow's Shipbuilders: *Alacrity* herself had been commissioned in 1977. Controversy attended the design from the outset: a 50 per cent saving in weight, which gave better speed and stability, was achieved by building the superstructure of aluminium. But aluminium has a much lower melting-point than steel, so there was risk in this elegant solution — namely meltdown in a serious fire — and some reduction in the strength of the structure. Yet nothing comes for nothing.

Strikingly elegant lines and astonishing acceleration gave Type 21s a reputation as the 'boy racers' of the Fleet, their commanding officers living up to the image with great zest. Harbourmaster complaints of excessive speed or wash were usually in evidence after Type 21 arrivals or departures at their ports. We dismissed much of this as mere pettiness. Self-christened 'The 21 Club', all ships were united in a deep camaraderie, much envied by other squadrons. Without exception, they were happy vessels which saw themselves as an élite.

The fighting heart of each ship was a computerized command and control network centred on the operations room below the bridge.

This system gave the air, surface and sub-surface picture for 100 miles around. Radars, electronic radar-detection sets, interrogators to identify friend or foe, sonars, a lightweight helicopter and the human eyeball all fed this system. Enemy contacts were automatically tracked and the resulting mass of data was refined and presented at high speed, to allow the efficient use of all weapon systems. In an arcade on Blackpool seafront, such high-tech wizardry could have earned a fortune.

When the operations room was in its darkened action state, fifty men were sandwiched together in the gloom, controlling what was, to the uninitiated, a bewildering, ghostly flickering of neon tracks, labels, velocity indicators, information totes and numerical readouts. Dozens of fingers punched unceasingly at orange keyboards. Hooded figures hunched, looped together by their headsets. Verbal exchanges in a good ops room were barely audible: in a bad one, it sounded like Question Time in the House of Commons — but arguably still got more done.

As we continued south, my conscientious young correspondence officer and would-be aviator, Sub Lieutenant Kevin King, came to enquire what he should do about the dozens of petty routine reports that we were normally required to render over the weeks ahead. My flamboyant hurling of the correspondence office key into the Atlantic was greeted with the widest smile I saw throughout the campaign. Whilst I did have a duplicate, the prospect of war certainly exposes irrelevancies.

Alacrity lived her insulated life largely informed by the objective tones of the BBC World Service, with whose bulletins on the crisis the signals from the Fleet Headquarters at Northwood could not compete. Even our youngest sailors abandoned the rhythmic delights of popular music for the news, which was broadcast throughout the ship. A great British tradition sustained us.

One evening, I listened to our local Plymouth MP, Dr David Owen, give a typically uncompromising radio interview. He had been a young, talented and somewhat unpopular Foreign Secretary two years earlier when I worked in Whitehall. Claiming that dispatch of the Task Force had less to do with liberating remote islanders and far more to do with the UK being seen to resist unacceptable aggression, he believed we were contributing to future stability in an inherently unstable world. I admired the underlying good sense of his words — which were, much later, to be in great demand as peacemaker and peacekeeper.

Whatever the true reasoning behind our dispatch, we ship-commanding officers certainly had no anguished conscience as we heaved our way down past Portugal. Let Opposition politicians Tony Benn and Tam Dalyell argue theirs; we would do our country's will without inner torment, though frankly, at that stage, 90 per cent of the Task Force believed their dispatch still to be mere posture. Whilst a grand adventure, it was all 'jaw, jaw' not 'war, war' — it would not come to arms.

General Alexander Haig, US Secretary of State, was by then committed to the role of peacemaker, single-mindedly shuttling diplomacy with the zeal of a latterday Henry Kissinger. He was a gifted and energetic individual, whom I had met and admired during his time as the NATO Supreme Allied Commander in Europe. His energy was to be sorely tried throughout April as there remained concern in the UK that the US might try to deflect British resolve in order to avoid damaging her Latin American policy. But thankfully the USA maintained her initial stance of even-handed non-alignment — and the Secretary of State amassed some extraordinary air miles.

Meanwhile, ships that had been engaged in Exercise Springtrain in the Mediterranean had dispersed, some heading south to rendezvous with us whilst the unfortunate *Battleaxe*, *Euryalus*, *Aurora*, *Dido*, *Engadine* and *Blue Rover* were stripped of every item that could be of benefit to the southgoers, and then sent home to watch the excitement of the following weeks on their television sets. They passed us heading forlornly north — hardly fire and brimstone — and I felt for them, knowing what my emotions would have been had positions been reversed.

And so we continued towards our staging-post of Ascension, resolve stiffening with each vivid sunset. Most pressingly, we needed information about our potential foes — and plenty of it. The price of nearly forty years spent preparing exhaustively to resist Soviet expansion was that we knew next to nothing about other possible opponents. A flood of highly classified intelligence information started to swamp our ships, and we went to work.

The key Argentinian advantage was closeness to home: they could deploy almost all their forces against whatever proportion of our Navy we chose to place off the Falklands. Such proximity granted them ready logistical support, whilst our lines of communication were twenty times as long as theirs. I hoped to God that somebody in the Ministry of Defence (MOD) was doing careful homework on how we were to be supplied with war stocks of fuel, ammunition and stores if battle commenced.

As the days grew longer and warmer, I started each one of them the same way by ordering the ritual of daily user checks, during which all on-watch personnel function every piece of ship equipment, all of it against the clock. Performance was compared with the target time and a succession of separate reports were received — guns, missiles, ammunition, torpedoes, systems, machinery, damage-control equipment, communication circuits, sensors, stores, medical state, helicopter. The endless feedback cascaded on to my on-watch warfare officer and then to me to note the results and direct the necessary action.

We were, quite simply, auditing our ship; and our very survival might hinge upon the results of strengths to be exploited and weaknesses overcome. Once completed, *Alacrity* and her captain were ready for the day, and I turned my attention to our external and internal exercise programme. At all times warship command in the Royal Navy is the very acme of accountability. Every happening within its hull, every action of its people, every function and malfunction of its equipment must be reported to the captain.

The sea-going Navy spends virtually all of its budget-limited time at sea in the tiringly persistent pursuit of excellence. Training is all, and the past indulgences of leisurely passages around the world have gone for ever. The most valuable conditioning of all comes from in-company time: when two or more ships are gathered together, combined exercises rule each day.

Sadly, the relatively high passage speed to Ascension gave us little time to manoeuvre away from the planned track for such training; any deviation necessitated many hours thereafter at full power to catch up with the force. Nevertheless, our computer systems allowed us to conduct many simulated exercises whilst maintaining course, and ingenuity achieved the rest.

The whole complex spectrum of naval warfare was being re-keened: gun and missile firings, evasive steering, and helicopter reporting procedures to allow simultaneous silent missile attack by ships depending upon their aircraft aloft to tell them where the enemy was without having to give away their own position on radar. By night, station-keeping exercises for the bridge crews involved patrolling sector screens

31

vigorously, sonar sets sweeping the greatest possible volume of water, and manoeuvring solely on orders relayed by tiny shrouded signal lanterns. We spent countless hours sharpening such battle-winning capabilities; and, all the time, I insisted that — in my ship — we would think only of war. My sympathy went out to Nick Tobin and *Antelope*, by then well astern, escorting their five logistical landing ships that were lucky if they ever exceeded 12 knots, whilst we raced around the ocean at 30 plus, playing our war games.

Training emphasis in the carriers was naturally upon their air groups. Resident Sea Harrier (SHAR) squadrons, No. 800 (Lieutenant Commander Andy Auld) in *Hermes* and No. 801 (Lieutenant Commander 'Sharkey' Ward) in *Invincible*, had been reinforced by aircraft from the training squadron at Yeovilton in Somerset. This gave us a total of just twenty Harriers. Anti-submarine Sea King helicopters, of No. 826 (Lieutenant Commander Doug Squier) in *Hermes* and No. 820 (Lieutenant Commander Ralph Wykes-Sneyd) in *Invincible*, hovered ahead of us with their detection equipment, sharpening screening skills to detect any threatening submarine within the sonic net cast by their dipping sonars. Assault Sea Kings of No. 846 Naval Commando Squadron (Lieutenant Commander Simon Thornewill) were redistributing stores between the ships with a regularity that was training in itself.

The frigates took turns to tow a splash target — a bobbing sledge — astern for it to be pulverized by the SHARs. Cluster bombs, 2-inch rocket projectiles and practice bombs burped from the slim shapes of the diving and wheeling aircraft to the evident delight of our sailors. Though interception of enemy aircraft would be the Harriers' primary task, they were clearly intended to undertake a little 'earthmoving' against Argentinian troop positions as well.

Excitement was injected into our preparations when Fleet Headquarters initiated Operation Paraquet, under the command of the destroyer *Antrim*, with the aim of regaining the island of South Georgia from the Argentinians as an early propaganda coup. The War Cabinet had decided on 7 April that it was worth dividing our relatively small force; there would be time for the ships to rejoin the Carrier Battle Group before any invasion of the Falklands could be mounted. *Antrim*, *Plymouth* and *Tidespring* were to sprint ahead to meet with Nick Barker's *Endurance* which had been shadowing the Argentinian ships off South Georgia: *Brilliant* was to join later. This small group of ships thus became a third element of the Task Force: the other two being our Carrier Battle Group and the still-building Amphibious Group whose separate elements were by then trickling south behind us. The carriers and the amphibs were all destined to meet up at Ascension to re-store and regroup before proceeding further south.

It was a pleasure to experience our first truly tropical weather but there was no chance to enjoy it. On 9 April we were off Madeira: on the following day, the Canaries, imagining the hedonistic pursuit of pleasure by holidaymakers undisturbed by the prospect of distant war whilst we lost ourselves in preparation. Aircraft were repainted in drab wartime livery and ship side numbers were obscured. Home comforts were stripped out: plastic panels that might be blasted into a thousand razor-sharp projectiles were taken down, and carpets and fabrics disappeared into storerooms. Damage-control drills readied everyone for the worst, whilst missile systems were tested endlessly and gun mountings were regreased. Spanish interpreters and special communications experts were on their way to join us, as were some brand-new Sea Skua missiles for our Lynx helicopters.

Signalled intelligence covered everything from Argentinian soldiers' boots to analysis of the Latin temperament. Our Hong Kong Chinese laundrycrews ('dhobi men') were offered the chance to get off at Ascension but our man elected to stay. Naafi managers and assistants also largely stayed, indeed several were to cover themselves with credit in the conflict which lay ahead.

The Force had swollen with the addition of *Broadsword* and *Yarmouth* from Gibraltar whilst *Invincible*, who had been struggling with gearing defects since her hurried departure, was dropping behind. Also well astern of us was the squat and ugly *Fearless*, the landing ship with aviator Commodore Mike Clapp embarked as Commodore Amphibious Warfare who would take charge of a landing operation. With him came Brigadier Julian Thompson, Royal

Marines, Commander of the 3rd Commando Brigade, as Commander Land Forces. Both men had well-established staffs. The two officers were to get on extremely well with each other during the campaign, a command harmony which was not always mirrored throughout the Force. Like Task Group Commander Admiral Woodward, Brigadier Thompson was a Cornishman, but there any close fellowship ended.

On board *Alacrity*, our sense of fellowship was being fostered with typical panache by my second-in-command, Colin de Mowbray, who had formed a 'Standing Action Morale Party' (STAMP). A clever gimmick, the team included two personable extroverts, Leading Regulator Cole and Leading Physical Training Instructor Davies, and was targeted against morose or anxious members of the crew. Early buoyancy of spirits had been declining as men started to think through the full implications of war, but the team's spirit was irresistible, and the move was shrewd and perceptive. By then, too, their spirits were being further brightened by mail drops from RAF Nimrods newly deployed to Ascension.

On 10 April, the European Community placed an embargo upon arms and military equipment intended for Argentina, and later banned Argentinian imports. Europe was not sitting on any fence. Perhaps it was to be war after all.

At 0400 on 12 April, the British Government declared a 200-mile Maritime Exclusion Zone (MEZ) around the Falklands — our three nuclear submarines had clearly arrived in position — to deter reinforcement and resupply of the islands by sea. Argentina promptly responded with an Exclusion Zone of their own, out to 200 miles from their coastline, which we subsequently ignored. Whilst it was highly unlikely that our opponents were prepared to ignore our zone and run the gauntlet of our submarines with their merchant ships, they knew it would be another fortnight before we could interfere with their air transport. Thus we guessed that they would merely increase the rate at which they flew supplies from their Comodoro Rivadavia resupply air base to Stanley, but at least it was going to take them a great deal longer that way.

During the second week in April, we acquired some travelling companions — low-flying Soviet Bear D recce aircraft from Luanda, West Africa. These huge-winged snoopers thought nothing of flying more than 5,000 miles from their bases, feeding the Soviet intelligence plot. Their vast forms seemed to hang motionless from their four large engines as they watched and waited like the rest of the world for this unlikely confrontation to take further shape. Impressed that *Alacrity* was now on screens in the Kremlin, I only wished that we had had time to paint ship before departure.

The Soviets had something to report on Friday, 14 April, when Sandy Woodward's flag was hoisted on the yardarm of *Hermes*, he having transferred with his staff from *Glamorgan* as the rest of the post-Springtrain ships melded with us. On the same day, I pulled FLASH precedence signal off the back roll of our teleprinter — an habitual means of eavesdropping upon signal traffic to other ships — and read that *Brilliant* was to form yet another group of ships, by taking *Coventry*, *Sheffield*, *Glasgow* and *Arrow* south as fast as possible, stopping only when their fuel reserves were down to 30 per cent, there to await the valiantly trailing slow tanker *Pearleaf*. Once they all hit the heavy seas of the deep southern oceans any fast progress was going to be uncomfortable and I did not envy them. But somebody wanted lots of chess pieces on board in case there was to be a change in the rules of the game.

Overnight on 14 April, *Alacrity* was ordered to simulate an Argentinian missile-firing ship. Opening from the main group at speed, we were soon out of radar range, allowing us to swing wide and come in from an unexpected direction just before dawn, using our Lynx helicopter radar to seduce force attention. Though simulated missile firings from ourselves and the defenders were inconclusive, both sides claimed victory. In a rare chance to exercise a little bravura, I obtained approval from *Hermes* to conclude my run from right ahead of her, leaving a mountainous wake and passing very close down her starboard side at a combined closing speed of more than 60 miles per hour. The grey giant stayed implacably indifferent to the Jack Russell terrier snarling past. Suitably deflated, I came back to heel in my new screening station.

In a somewhat forlorn attempt to mask

the composition of our force, we all rigged alternative navigation lights to simulate merchant shipping. Lieutenant Mark Scrivens, one of my officers of the watch,suggested I might like to improve the subterfuge and 'play like a passenger liner' by arranging all-night, upper-deck movies for the ship's company. I retaliated by saying that if I had another such suggestion I would lock him up and 'play like a convict ship'. When he responded that as long as we ended up in Australia like all good convict ships, he would have no complaint, I fell back on my dignity and terminated the conversation. Sometimes I felt my ship needed a little more discipline.

On a more serious level, our sense of interdependence grew daily. Men were keyed up but largely contented; as ever, most problems disappear from a close-knit community when it is really busy. My uncompromising determination that *Alacrity* should be ready for war gradually became accepted by all, and thus I encouraged more than I goaded. Everyone knew the price of failure and all possessed the best spur to achievement — personal and collective pride. In the clinical and often passionless business of naval warfare, leadership has many guises but, in my book, most of them involve imparting resolve — 'momentum'.

On the very few occasions that I did need to be abrasive, I recalled that I used to be a kind and relaxed CO — but that was before the night when I gave six hours' shore leave to a different ship's company, during a passage from the UK to Hong Kong. The decision was flawed. The ship was only in for ten hours to take on fuel and stores, and the port was Olongapo in the Philippines — then the sin city of the Far East. I finally found myself on my open bridge in a tropical downpour at two in the morning, attempting to sail the ship at the appointed time with only the Chinese laundryman and the ship's cat to help. Ever since that night, I find that I can be an unduly demanding man.

On a not too dissimilar theme, our first Task Group casualties owed nothing to Argentinian aggression. Two young sailors had been given a memento by a young lady (the same one) on their last night in Plymouth. When nearly 2,000 miles south, they found they had contracted venereal disease. Newly joined Surgeon Lieutenant Steven Shaw seemed almost embarrassed to tell me, and I fear that my response should perhaps have been more dignified and stern. 'Ne'er mind, Steve. Fix 'em quick. It may prove to be a blessing — put them off sex for life and make 'em more efficient sailors.'

There were other casualties of a hasty departure. Some poor souls checked the small print of their life-insurance policies and found war risks excluded. Others were in the midst of torrid domestic dispute, even divorce proceedings, leaving my officers spending many hours counselling and encouraging. Hundreds of miles out at sea there are no social services: we look after our own, albeit with the long-distance help of the Navy's excellent welfare service in base ports, backed by our informal network of

39

loyal wives providing each other with mutual support and information. I was not to know until after my return that Daphne had become fully involved with this effort, despite living well away from the Plymouth area. The wives of my engineers, David Dyter and Steve Roche, had, together with several others, both played a large part in this effort. My subsequent social contact with a number of the wives, and full discussions with my own, left me in no doubt that however fine the efforts of individuals and of the Naval Personal and Family Services, there was potential for more coherent organization of support once the shooting started.

Despite the few unhappinesses, spirits were high. Sailors can summon up character, humour and resolve like few others. Perhaps daily life afloat is the answer — a claustrophobic messdeck is the most interdependent community. In adversity, sailors bond together and suffer each other with massive forbearance. Such mutual goodwill allows them to endure tension and toil much better than most, and yet they have their own code — not tolerating the selfish, the unclean and the truly anti-social.

The younger men are yearly better qualified academically; several good GCSE results often being the norm and occasional fine A-level passes being by no means rare. Indeed, the average technical rating of the 1990s has a background of education and environment often little different from his junior officers who are no longer motivated predominantly by 'duty' and 'the Flag', as they were when I first entered the Service. I have less difficulty with this change than do many of my senior colleagues for it has brought with it several benefits. Most young officers are, by comparison with my day, brighter, more worldly, more sensitive, better able to relate to their men, and more technically minded. But the new culture costs the Treasury much more money — good conditions of service are now the expectation of all.

This character of our younger people has consistently inspired me, and I do not share national lamentations over the quality of our youth. Indeed, my few disappointments have tended to lie with older and better established men. Perhaps the 'more to lose' philosophy has something to do with it. Our society might do better looking at the failure of the older generation to provide suitable role models and leadership: when encouraged and well led, our youngsters can be superb. The average age of the sailors of *Alacrity* was less than 23.

And sailor humour is ever-present. It helps them cope with adversity and burst the bubble of pomposity — useful in a tradition-laden organization such as the Navy. Above all, sailors can always surprise you. Once, on a ship call to a South American port, my men had behaved so well as ambassadors that I signalled Fleet Headquarters in the UK as we sailed, extolling their astonishing virtues. My satisfaction abated somewhat when the First Lieutenant knocked upon my cabin door, entered and proudly showed me the front-page photograph of the local Catholic newspaper. The shot was of good quality, the eight faces pictured grinning broadly over their right shoulders being all instantly recognizable as part of my ship's rugby team. Less obviously recognizable were the eight naked, hairy bottoms which lay below the smiles, snapped by a grateful photographer in a local night-club as my men had 'mooned' to popular demand — doubtless inspired by the local brandy. Sadly, my signal had already been transmitted. Thankfully, most surprises provided by sailors are more pleasurable. I miss them still.

* * *

A flood of often emotional letters was by then pouring into all ships. Many of the writers merely knew *Alacrity* as a ship's name from the newspapers but there was no disguising their desire to stiffen our sinews as we sailed off to war. Letters were displayed on noticeboards and several sailors acquired pen pals as a result. Notwithstanding the customary young 'virgins' intent upon stiffening something other than their sinews, there were some inspiring wishes from which we derived much strength. There were many benefits in heading for a 'just' war, fully supported by the nation.

Amongst my air-mail letters, known as 'blueys', was one from a friend serving in Whitehall. He gave me a flavour of the in-fighting that had reigned before the Prime Minister had made the decision to deploy the Task Force. He claimed that the Defence

Secretary, John Nott, the Chief of the General Staff and the Chief of the Air Staff had apparently all been opposed to such an 'adventure'. Only the tenacity of Admiral Sir Henry Leach, supported by the Chief of the Defence Staff, Admiral Sir Terence Lewin, had turned the issue. Admiral Woodward was later to say that the MOD considered the operation 'far too risky'; the US Navy considered it a 'military impossibility'; the British Army thought it ill-advised because we 'did not outnumber the Argentinians sufficiently on land'; the RAF thought it would fail because the Navy 'could not survive in the face of a modern air force'; and John Nott was against the operation because success might prove that his decision to axe the assault ships and carriers in his 1981 Defence Review was wrong. Thus so nearly did the Junta come to winning its huge gamble. And thus, so nearly, did many people underestimate the continued effectiveness of British sea power. In 1982, it was still — thankfully — impressive.

On 9 April, the BBC had given extensive coverage of Al Haig's arrival in Buenos Aires to a nauseatingly well-orchestrated show of Argentinian patriotism. He was being targeted as a propaganda puppet and I hoped his talks were worth the price. To make matters worse, the programme had included a persuasive and articulate interview with the Argentinian Foreign Secretary, Dr Nicanor Costa Mendez, in which he challenged our claims to sovereignty. Grudgingly, I conceded that he had come across well: slick and dangerous.

The sovereignty issue was increasingly discussed on the BBC, and radically different interpretations were being made of the same historical events. Between the discovery of the islands in the early sixteenth century and the formation of a British community in 1833, only the most biased Anglophile could claim that Britain was consistent in establishing ownership. However, what is indisputable is that ever since 1833 a British community has maintained a steady presence. The present islanders are a stoic group, being about as Latin as roast beef and Yorkshire pudding, and their allegiance to the UK is passionate and unswerving. Thus constant occupancy of the islands over 150 years, the emphatic wish of their population, and Article 1 of the UN Charter attesting to the right of all peoples to self-determination, combined in my mind to resolve the sovereignty issue indisputably. The islands were part of the UK, not the property of Argentina.

Ironically, when later I visited South America in 1986, I was surprised by Latin cynicism over the Argentinian claim and by how often I heard unstinting admiration for 'Iron Lady' Thatcher. Most vividly, she was described to me one night in Chile by a very senior military figure as 'that lady with the balls!'

When just over half way to the Falklands I had an altercation with the Admiral's staff by signal — not a good tactic so early in the voyage. They had decided to shift round our helicopter aviators from the escorts, thereby spreading more evenly the limited experience of handling and using the brand-new Sea Skua missiles. But, by doing so, they would be totally disrupting the harmony of each ship's warfare team which took so long to build. I was furious at what I perceived to be an ill-conceived decision by big-ship staff who were unaware of the importance of cohesion to efficient small-ship teams. In the circumstances, my signal was restrained: 'Team unchanged for twelve months. Rapport now intuitive. Operations developed well beyond peacetime limits. Substitution risks gross impairment. May I keep them?'

Fortunately, my passion was persuasive and the decision was reversed, leaving my relieved Flight Commander and I to discuss even more effective co-operation between ship and Flight.

In the open ocean on 15 April, when still short of Ascension, Admiral Woodward decided it was time to inspire us. He ordered a massive firepower demonstration — for ourselves alone. Several ships streamed splash targets which the Harriers attempted to blow to pieces with rocket, cannon and practice bombs, whilst all gunships fired off combined broadsides of high-calibre ammunition. With the air full of cordite and ships bucking under the recoil, the Task Group came to life and the Atlantic reverberated with our vigour. It had been a clever piece of psychology by the Admiral and his staff, and it lit a fire in us all.

In fact, *Alacrity* had considerable firepower in her own right. Four Exocet surface-to-surface missile launchers clustered just below the bridge — a thrusting symbol of the ship's virility. Each

45

of the slender 17-foot-long missiles could deliver its 1,500 lb body into an enemy ship at a range of more than 20 miles. Further forward again sat the squat Vickers Mk 8 semi-automatic 4.5-inch gun mounting, weighing 25 tons. Its shells came up from the magazine in a hoist which resembled a bottling machine. Loading and firing were normally conducted remotely, with not a sweaty sailor to be seen: twenty-five shells per minute being fired at a velocity of nearly 3,000 feet/second for up to 12 miles. The versatility of the gun allowed it to fire — by radar or visually — high explosive, starshell illuminants and also radar confusers called Chaff.

Overlooking the flight-deck aft and situated on top of the hangar which housed the Lynx helicopter, crouched the Seacat missile-launcher. A venerable weapon system, it had been in service as long as I had and was frankly bearing up less well. Guidance was by television or by eye — this time *with* the help of a sweaty sailor. It threw a small missile a couple of miles at any aircraft stupid enough to fly straight at it, allowing impact or proximity fusing to complete the job. Aircraft who were not flying straight towards it were unlikely to be hit by Seacat, but as they would probably then be flying towards somebody else, I was quite relaxed about such inadequacy. Anyway, the theory of a combined force was that such fast, crossing targets would be engaged by those ships armed with the new supersonic, automatic Sea Wolf missile system. I wished I had one.

Our bridge wings housed two 20 mm Oerlikon guns which had been in service a good deal longer than both Seacat and Craig, with reliability generally better than both. Their high-explosive or incendiary shells emerged at 470 rounds per minute, travelled for about 1,000 yards, and at least provided an attacking aircraft with a distraction — becoming more pronounced if they hit him.

Our full weapon and sensor combination was bound together by long-range radio communications, satellite and HF, together with tactical UHF/VHF radio and data links. In sum, we offered the Admiral a highly capable killing machine, and we had enjoyed warming it through, whatever lay ahead. Most immediately, it was Ascension.

2

Combat Ready

16 – 30 April

'Tomorrow shall you bear our full intent'

ALTHOUGH there was to be no shore leave for any of us, Ascension was at least a contrast to the empty horizon. A carbuncle of a place lying on a latitude of 8° south, the red-brown volcanic ash rises 18,000 feet from the ocean floor, offering only its final 2,800 foot above sea-level. The result of an eruption from the now dormant mid-Atlantic ridge, the 34 square miles of rock and volcanic dust just 3,700 miles from Britain were to be our last landfall for nine weeks.

In an inspired appointment, military command of the island had been given to Captain Bob McQueen, RN, who I remembered flying Sea Vixen jets with icy cool from the deck of HMS *Eagle* years earlier. A get-things-done man, he was the scourge of all negative mentalities that arrived on 'his' island. Bob's tactful way of coping with an over-full garrison was merely to send home anybody he judged superfluous: some of his confrontations with RAF transport personnel moved into the realms of naval folklore. Much of the credit for the pivotal function played by the staging-post in ultimate victory can be placed at Bob's door.

The Carrier Group anchored in Clarence Bay to the north-west of the island at lunchtime on 16 April and, despite the fair weather, I put out seven shackles of anchor cable and kept the ship at one hour's notice for sea. Resupply had to take place by helicopter — a remarkable sight worthy of Francis Ford Coppola's epic Vietnam film, *Apocalypse Now*. For hour after hour, Sea Kings delivered their underslung loads whilst, high above the locust cloud, a continuous stream of fixed-wing aircraft landed and departed the main runway. C130 Hercules, RAF VC10s and various chartered aircraft allowed Wideawake Airfield on the south-west of the island to live up to its name, registering more than 300 separate flights in the day.

High-level visitors to the flagship included the Commander-in-Chief Fleet, Admiral John Fieldhouse, who had been given overall command of the operation from his underground headquarters at Northwood. As Commander of the Task Force, he was ultimately accountable to the Ministry of Defence, and would be providing strategic direction to the Task Group Commander, Admiral Woodward. The fact that both of them were submariners must have helped harmony. Helicoptered into *Hermes* for top-level planning, Fieldhouse was accompanied by the designate Land Force Commander, Major General Jeremy Moore, Royal Marines, who would eventually take over from Brigadier Julian Thompson. The master war plan was finalized that day, as was selection of the eventual Falkland landing location — though we escort COs were only made aware of the intended beachhead location one month later. 'Need to know' was the governing rule and, at that stage, *Alacrity* had no such need.

The Task Force was by then split into five groups: the carriers and escorts, the amphibious ships, the Paraquet force, *Brilliant*'s fast probe south, and the advance nuclear submarines. In the hope that South Georgia would shortly be regained, the remaining objectives for the Falkland Islands were first, to establish a sea blockade; second, to establish sea and air supremacy; and, finally, to gain possession. Meanwhile, diplomatic efforts were to continue unabated in pursuit of a peaceful solution, but were not to slow military preparations.

Whilst our high command finalized their plans, we were analysing the enemy, an exercise which dispelled the last of my earlier complacency. His surface, sub-surface and air threats were potent. A surprise attack, made by several of them simultaneously, would spell trouble: only advance warning could guarantee our survival. I thought back covetously to my days spent flying from our fixed-wing carriers in the 1960s, when we used to sneer at the lumbering, bulbous-bellied Gannet aircraft that carried their radar hundreds of miles ahead of the force. But they tracked everything that moved, and we could rarely be surprised. Sadly, those carriers and their early-warning aircraft were now no more — and we were about to miss them.

Obtaining the right equipment for our Navy from a thrifty Treasury had not been my battle, but I was to live, or die, by the force mix which had resulted. It is for just this reason that a fighting service should always keep a good proportion of operational, and preferably fighting, experience amongst its highest-level decision takers. Pure staff officers, of whatever quality, can lose touch with the realities of operating the equipment that they seek.

The Argentinian surface navy was headed by the aircraft-carrier *25 de Mayo*. Modernized and capable of 24 knots, she was as big as *Invincible* and carried squadrons of A4 Skyhawk attack aircraft. More importantly, she was believed to have the capacity to operate potent French-built Super Etendards with their air-launched Exocet missiles.

The *General Belgrano* was an old cruiser, with alleged Exocet-carrying potential, and would probably act as motherhen to an escort force which was far from insignificant. The Argentinians had started taking delivery of modern German-built MEKO 360 destroyers, each armed with eight Exocets and a fine gun, in addition to their Exocet-equipped MEKO 140 frigates. Intelligence upon the operational status of these modern ships was sparse, despite the fact that we had trained a large number of their naval officers. Somewhat harshly, I wondered about British military attachés who had been enjoying the social delights of Argentina in recent years. Had they ever left the bar? Or had some idle collator in British Defence Intelligence failed to analyse and distribute vital information? Either way, we needed better Intelligence, and more of it.

Ironically, the remaining enemy surface arsenal was headed by two British-built Type 42 destroyers, three British-owned versions of which were already *en route* to the Falklands. The two were *Santissima Trinidad* and *Hercules*, each carrying eight more infernal Exocets. The remainder of their destroyers and frigates were largely a sorry lot of World War vintage ex-American destroyers, but the three French-built A69 frigates (more damned Exocets) were an eye-catching distraction: I would certainly be looking out for them — *Drummond*, *Guerrico* and *Granville*. Uncompromising French defence sales only explained in part the remarkable popularity of the Exocet. It was simple, durable and cost-effective — and the Argentinians had lots of them.

Of the enemy aircraft, their five naval Super Etendards were the potential ship-killers. Though French Exocets had been delivered for these aircraft, we were still unsure of how many they had and how reliable the missiles were. Their remaining air assets were not to be ignored; nearly 100 Mirage, Dagger and Skyhawk jets were capable of carrying free-fall bombs, and we were all guilty of believing our own propaganda that the missile age had overtaken such primitive weapons. Nevertheless, it was becoming apparent that — if our limited numbers of Sea Harriers could be overwhelmed by enough attackers keeping low beneath our Sea Dart missile arcs — there were precious few Sea Wolf missiles to blow them apart. Most ships would be left to depend upon a gun of limited anti-air capability and a Seacat missile by then a generation misplaced.

Beneath the sea, we would be facing two small, silent modern German-built diesel-electric submarines called *San Luis* and *Salta*. Each displacing 1,200 tons, and capable of 22 knots when submerged, they were equipped with eight torpedo tubes firing 21-inch wire-guided torpedoes. They were supported by the older, bigger *Santa Fe*. A couple of torpedoes into *Hermes* or *Invincible*, putting half our Harrier force on the seabed, and we could all go home — the Falklands would stay Argentinian. I was unimpressed by the stupidity of one of my sailors who openly asked me on the bridge one day whether 'these dago plonkers know an Exocet from a bolas?' I later watched his face with interest as a pair of 1,000 lb bombs nearly disappeared down our funnel. Complacency has no place in preparations for war.

Meanwhile, far to the south, the Argentinian Army of Occupation was being reinforced at a significant rate. Cynicism over the motivation and effectiveness of their conscripts gave me little solace. The Navy's business was getting ashore and staying there: the subsequent battle on land was somebody else's problem.

★ ★ ★

An invaluable addition to *Alacrity* was fitted at Ascension. Satellite navigation (Satnav) equipment, costing little more than £1,000 a set, was already safeguarding many yachts around the world, but the Navy had been very late to catch on. Nevertheless, I was delighted to see its overdue arrival and it probably saved the ship's life several times over in rocky Falkland waters. An even more invaluable addition was supplied to *Hermes* at the same time: new American AIM 9L Sidewinder air-to-air missiles for the Harriers which homed on to the jet exhausts of their targets.

Ascension was also notable for *Alacrity*'s first mechanical breakdown when the starboard Tyne engine gearbox failed. My Marine Engineer Officer, David Dyter, wanted to wait at the island for spare parts in order to fit them swiftly and easily: I would brook no delay and refused. South was where we were needed. In the event, replacement bits were parachuted to us by Hercules, and two very dedicated engineers, CPO Pearce and PO Cochrane, spent ten sixteen-hour days working in impossibly hot and cramped conditions underway to effect a good repair. Our interdependence was already apparent.

The defect was not as debilitating for a Type 21 as it would have been for a number of other classes of ship. Adaptability had been cleverly built in to the machinery design. We had four gas turbine main engines — two Olympus (25,000 shaft horsepower) and two Tyne (5,000 shaft horsepower). On the two Olympus, I could

54

whip the 3,400 tons of *Alacrity* up to 30 knots from a standing start in little more than fifty seconds. Alternatively, on just one Tyne the ship could purr silently up to 5,000 miles at 14 knots before needing a filling station. Fed by so much power, our propellers could be slammed through from ahead to astern in seconds, giving exhilarating manoeuvrability. Float, move, fight; *Alacrity* was a clever, capable and cost-effective package.

The Amphibious Group started lumbering into Ascension anchorage on 17 April and clattering hordes of helicopters recommenced their swarming. We sailed next day in company with *Hermes*, *Broadsword*, *Glamorgan* and *Yarmouth*, and the auxiliaries *Resource* and *Olmeda*. There were 3,800 miles to go to reach our destination. *Invincible* followed later that evening, having only reached Ascension after we had sailed due to her gearing defects — she had but six hours of respite. Mike Clapp in *Fearless* remained behind to build his force and to allow his embarked military the chance to continue their physical conditioning. He also kept back half of the Commando Sea King helicopters from *Hermes* to assist with the endless distribution of stores.

Within twenty-four hours, jittery nerves were given an outlet. It started with a 'confident' sighting of a periscope by *Olmeda*. After that it became a farce of over-reaction, as several ships gained sonar contact and proceeded to hurtle around the ocean growling and snorting. Thankfully, the delicately poised international situation had caused the Task Group Commander to deny us the use of anti-submarine weapons, otherwise we would have had none left by the end of the day. Hour after hour it went on, with fleeting detection following fleeting detection, as we imagined an Argentinian submarine deployed forward to sink a British ship. It was midnight before we subsided wearily, reflecting upon our immoderate reactions to what was clearly an utterly bemused school of whales who had enjoyed gambolling amidst pinging sound waves and whirring propellers.

As for us, we had learnt the dangers of a fertile imagination. I vowed future restraint in the *Alacrity* ops room and had an implacable supporter in Lieutenant Commander Tom Tubb, my very efficient and experienced underwater warfare specialist and operations officer. After 'the great whale chase', Tom was a teasing, challenging flail to his underwater teams. Check and check again! Look for collateral evidence! The occurrence of false sonar contacts continued, but always culminated in the same final flat disclaimer from the flagship: 'NONSUB!' But it seldom happened to *Alacrity* after 18 April.

On 19 April, ship-commanding officers were at last summoned to the flagship. A flurry of helicopter transfers later and I met Admiral Woodward for the first time. Lean, laconic and self-effacing in manner, he was quietly imposing. As we all assembled in his stateroom on board *Hermes*, I was struck by what

56

a diverse team we COs were. Remarkable contrasts started at the top, with Captain Jeremy ('JJ') Black of *Invincible* and Captain Lin Middleton of *Hermes*. It was not necessary to hear whispers from the staff to know that these two ran utterly different ships. Gunnery officer 'JJ' was highly intelligent, laid-back and full of droll humour, being a confident delegator who unashamedly knew little about aeroplanes. Full of the humanities, he ran a relaxed regime, leaving his team largely free to exploit their own abilities. Aviator Lin was macho and massively assertive, being a punchy, lead from the front, grab 'em by the balls sort of man, with a combative manner and huge aviation experience. Both had many strengths but appeared to be less than bosom pals. Their differences were mirrored in their ship preparation: *Invincible* retained many creature comforts, whilst *Hermes* was bare-arse gutted for combat.

Our meeting was purposeful and I was impressed with an Admiral I knew only by reputation. He had been given a flaying by the media at home for an insensitive television interview and ill-chosen words, but was a very different man when readying his forces for battle; unemotional, clipped in his phrasing and brutally single-minded, he gave me great confidence which did not waver throughout the campaign. Instinctively I liked him and sensed that he was a straightforward person, devoid of bluster, who had only one yardstick — results. Trust and delegation would have to be earned, and any fools present could expect trouble.

57

Even today, I still consider him to have been underrated as a wartime leader simply because bravura and charm were lacking. He had all the other qualities in abundance.

He was pulling no punches. It would be war. If the Argentinian Air Force got amongst us, then we must expect to lose at least six ships. Our opponents must not be underestimated. Were there any questions? It was inspiring stuff — but the Admiral's bedside manner was less than reassuring.

Whilst aboard *Hermes*, I took the opportunity to talk with the Flag Staff. Staff Officer Operations was likeable, robust Commander Jeremy Sanders; whilst Staff Captains were Peter Woodhead and Andy Buchanan, intelligent aviator and submariner respectively. There were a lot of good men in the flagship and I was suitably heartened.

On my return to *Alacrity*, I broadcast a blunt and colourful message to the ship's company. War was inevitable; the Junta was an alliance of evil men, known by their appalling deeds; aggression was to be our strength; kill or be killed was the only approach to war; pugnacity was survival; the eyes of the nation were upon us. I relayed the hard-headed realism of Admiral Woodward, well laced with clichés, dramatic pauses and a hint of likely losses — a flavour of fear is a great motivator. All simplistic stuff, but about right for the moment. I needed them charged up and bloody-minded.

The guide ship, around which the force maintained its layered formation, was *Resource*.

It was a role she was to play for many of the days ahead as her course remained just west of south — 212° — and her speed a stolid 12 knots. *Alacrity* occupied a sector that was 25° wide and between 4 and 6 miles from her. We also started using complex zigzags as each ship settled into the time warp of defence watches with our clocks set forward two hours to Greenwich Mean Time (Zulu Time) to synchronize us with Northwood and Ascension, thereby avoiding confusion. Transmissions on HF radio and our more powerful radars which might be intercepted were denied; no information was to be offered to our foes or to those who might help them. There was a need to pace the training effort so that we did not enter the arena already exhausted, but the force was tightening up.

All beards were removed to ensure a good fit for the face-mask seals of our anti-gas respirators and many of my sailors grew young overnight. Drills by then included blindfolded escape routines, as even relatively small ships are infernally difficult to move through with surety when darkened or smoke-filled: sailors who have served in the same ship for years can be lost in seconds when deprived of visibility.

Daily, the Navigator had a large team of officers and senior ratings frowning gloomily over sextants as they attempted to check our satellite navigation position by taking sun-sights and star-sights. Even astro-navigation was being dusted off. The resultant neat little line of cross fixes picked its way down our charts, deep into the heart of the South Atlantic.

On 20 April, as Ascension was left far astern, Admiral Woodward sent us the following signal: 'Be prepared in all respects for war by 232000Z April.' Somehow I had never quite expected to see those words in print, despite having been in a fighting service for more than twenty years. On 23 April we would still be well short of the Falklands — and our leader was not about to be surprised.

As a further part of his personal preparations to anticipate the unexpected, the Admiral was attempting to win a more vigorous set of Rules of Engagement (ROE) from the MOD. ROE are a key part of modern high-tech, easy-communication warfare and I envied the fighting man of yesterday when communications were primitive and the killing power of his weapons was limited. Then his political masters had to grant him delegated freedom and real independence. Today, when secure satellite communications link governments to almost every one of their fighting men, there exists the expectation that precise political control must govern all military operations in tension. As a quid pro quo, politicians grant a series of criteria under which they will allow their military units to fire upon known or suspected enemy forces when their own survival is being threatened. Haggling ensues. Military commanders fight for freedom of action for their forces to guarantee their survival against surprise attack: politicians remain determined that their forces should not trigger unnecessary conflict. Inevitably, inherent tension reigns between the two sides.

Though the Admiral sought MOD clearance to attack suspicious unidentified submarines or aircraft approaching the force when little time might be available before attack, we were kept on a tight leash. Nevertheless, some freedoms *were* granted as we pressed further south, ROE amendments coming in almost daily. As each new set was approved, the Admiral would promulgate and implement the rules, using secure-speech radio to run impromptu quizzes, inviting COs to say what they would do in hypothetical circumstances. It kept us on our toes. ROE is a fascinating and, for all its flaws, a very necessary discipline which took on a new dimension with a sinister event which occurred on 21 April.

'Unknown aircraft. Extreme range to the south-east.' Too far out for Harrier interception. A ZIPPO response was called within the force — a set of planned countermeasures against possible aircraft or missile threat. The contact faded and the ZIPPO was cancelled. He had not been on a steady air traffic route and thus we had a new and potentially damaging presence with us. This unknown aircraft, who was so intent upon breaking into the security of our group, was given the codeword Burglar — and he would return.

The next day Burglar became cheekier, closing in to 140 miles and being identified by Sea Harrier as an Argentinian Boeing 707 — though we were still 2,000 miles away from the Falklands. Despite carrying warheaded Sidewinder missiles, the SHAR remained

61

forbidden to shoot down the intelligence-gatherer and shadower because of the strictures of our ROE. Was the intruder also acting as a tattletale, marshalling ships or submarines to an attack? Thankfully, we were still out of possible range of bomber attack, which gave us one threat less — for the moment. As Burglar came to his closest point, our helicopters laid great Chaff barriers in the sky, clouds of specially manufactured tinsel which send back confusing radar echoes of huge dimensions. The artificial snowstorm on the 707's radar screens must have given him a hell of a problem interpreting the number of ships and their formation which lay beneath. Clearly the enemy was desperate to know more about the advancing threat. They should have bought English newspapers.

Late the same evening, in response to an unknown surface radar contact to the south-west, *Alacrity* was detached to intercept it with *Glamorgan*. As we gathered speed and readied helicopter, gun and missiles for action, excitement rose through the ship, and I found myself swallowing altogether too frequently. Could this be the first moment of conflict? When the target was finally identified as an innocent merchantman, we turned back, almost disappointed.

Use of the Type 21 frigate against a surface ship threat in submarine-risk waters was a sound choice. Our eyes and ears were nearly as good as our teeth. Radars spread invisible tentacles of detection around the ship: the early warning set reached out to long ranges to detect aircraft and large ship contacts; the navigational set provided the accurate close picture that allowed the ship to control the helicopter to a precise torpedo drop point, as well as to pick its way through dangerous waters in nil visibility. To detect an underwater threat, our sonar listened in a vast dome of still water set beneath the keel. On a radar-like display any returning acoustic echoes were presented as blobs, supported by audible propeller hydrophone effect — if you were lucky. The sonar also allowed you to detect a running torpedo; one closing gives a distinct tone — and a large laundry bill!

Though becoming less regular, parachute drops of vital spares and mail from Ascension by Nimrod or Hercules long-range aircraft remained welcome. These aircraft were being refuelled in the air by Victor tankers, allowing them to transit almost 3,000 miles from Ascension to keep us supplied before retracing their steps. Accordingly, time-honoured baiting of the RAF was suspended — they were providing us with one of the three essential elements of morale at sea, mail. The other two are good food and being 'kept in the picture'. They too were working well.

But regular mail remains the most important factor in the claustrophobic lives of those far from home. My sailors relished the adventure of using our fast, rigid inflatable Gemini boats to recover the canisters of mail as they bobbed amidst increasingly large wave-caps, for we were by then approaching the Roaring Forties — the vicious ten degrees of latitude which so terrified mariners of old. Though modern warships are tough and capable, the sea can never be taken for granted and I was already wary of the stormy waters of the South Atlantic.

On 23 April, with the Group still 1,750 miles short of the islands, the British Government issued an unambiguous warning to those thinking of impeding our passage. 'Any approach by ship or aircraft which could amount to a threat . . . will encounter the appropriate response.' Although not yet backed by the necessary ROE to give us the clout to enforce it fully, decks were indeed being cleared for action.

Sadly, our first fatality in the Task Group was incurred that same evening, and well before we came to action. The transfer of stores between ships was being undertaken by the Sea Kings of 846, commanded by my good friend Simon Thornewill. Dark, talented and unflappable, Simon was a highly gifted aviator whose five aircraft were about to play a significant role in combat, much of it with their aircrew wearing new night-vision goggles. Indeed, it was the challenge of visibility and orientation whilst low over the sea which may have contributed to this first death. The pilot, an exchange officer from the RAF, had been transiting between ships with an aircrewman in the rear fuselage. As weather and visibility were poor, they were *en route* to *Hermes* for a much-needed second pilot when the large helicopter hit the sea, broke in two and sank, carrying with it the aircrewman, Petty Officer Kevin Casey.

The naval aviation accident rate had been admirably low over the previous ten years due to exhaustive training, precise attention to standards, and the introduction of twin-engined helicopter reliability. Nevertheless, pilot disorientation remains a prime cause of loss, with low-level night operations between ships being the highest risk area. Landing on a flight-deck means controlling an unstable aircraft by visual cues from a tiny, dimly lit, often lively, operating area. But forward flight without a visible horizon means a fast, constant and concentrated scan of several flight instruments to control the aircraft safely. Rely for too long upon either outside lights or instruments at the wrong moment and you can quickly become disorientated, plunging into superstructure or sea. Pilot stress rates at sea by night are thus extremely high.

Not content with such challenges, my aircrew had worked up new operating techniques wherein strict, safety-first peacetime restrictions were progressively eased. They were returning to the deck by night without any lights showing, with only the occasional narrow sweep of radar, and without the benefit of radio. Descent and then landing on a small, slippery, corkscrewing flight-deck under such handicaps was quite a trick. The process struck me as lethal, but it certainly offered no detection opportunity to an enemy and thus I endorsed their new procedures as helping to ensure our ship's survival, but I never stopped worrying for them. My Flight Commander, Bob Burrows, was the sort of officer I like: aggressive, determined and demanding — when he was around, things got done. I grew fond of the man and trusted his judgement. They stayed safe.

A logistical problem had by then arisen as a result of such flying practice. Ship consumption of diesel fuel for main engines is always high during busy periods, but the new flying rates of our aircraft were proportionally much higher still. We were all running out of aviation fuel whilst, behind us, the tankers *Olmeda* and *British Esk* (Captain G. Barber) were trying to catch us to top up our small tanks. Early lessons about wartime consumption rates were already being learnt: a similar shortcoming over ammunition would later bring us near to disaster.

On 25 April, firm sonar contacts by two ships in the force prompted clearance for the dropping of live homing torpedoes and depth-charges, all armed with high-explosive warheads — which probably resulted in desiccated whale. War can, like so many of man's endeavours, be a somewhat imprecise art.

We pressed on, always southward, as the days grew shorter and frost glittered by night upon the latticework mast arcing high above us. Although we still had more than 1,000 miles to run, I was almost ashamed to find that I was hungry for combat.

The prospect of war had other implications. I had to delegate more, not less. I could not remain in my operations room twenty-four hours a day and, although my sleeping cabin was only eight seconds away from bridge or ops room, there was no guarantee that I could rouse from a deep sleep to make a ship-survival decision in that time. Though there was much that I could hand to Colin as my second-in-command (who was invariably awake when I was asleep) the surface navy had not yet fully thought through the need for both to be interchangeable in war. Colin had other duties which clashed with replacing me in the operations room. Thus, my warfare officers had to be given freedom to fire weapons at a threat in certain circumstances if time did not permit consultation. Sadly, such delegation also had to be amended every time we received a different set of ROE — which was often. It was all a far cry from 'Shake me if it comes on to blow, No. 1.'

Outside the ship, command and control arrangements were less straightforward. *Invincible* had been given sole charge of air defence as the Anti-Air Warfare Co-ordinator. This was a massive responsibility needing clear delegation and little interference but it suffered constantly from two afflictions: never enough Harriers, and the Admiral's staff constantly wanting many of them for other tasks — air defence was so important that they often felt the need to intervene. A tricky and highly stressful arrangement, it was a remarkable tribute to the capabilities of all in the chain that it worked so well.

At this stage of our passage, I noted with delight that virtually the whole of the Type 21 Club was converging on the Falkland Islands:

Arrow from Springtrain and *Antelope* and *Alacrity* from Plymouth, whilst *Avenger*, *Ardent* and *Ambuscade* were being readied in the UK. A good lead was to come from the top: Captain Hugo White's *Avenger* would shortly transit the 8,000 miles south at an average speed of 28 knots through all weathers — a record for a warship that will probably never be broken.

As we battered our way south, I listened to debate on the BBC about the ethics of Britain's reaction to the invasion. The Government's position was morally simple but not devoid of controversy. It claimed to be acting under Article 51 of the UN Charter, prosecuting Argentina under the inherent right of self-defence against armed attack, namely the taking of the Falkland Islands. Diplomacy and demands for withdrawal having failed, our choice was stark — capitulate or use sufficient force to return the islands to British control.

Whilst we were moving our forces south, the 200-nautical-mile Maritime Exclusion Zone was buying us time by still forcing the Argentinians to use uneconomical airlift into Stanley airfield. But the 'keep-out' zone was also helping to simplify complex ROE, and doubtless to salve political consciences. It was saying, 'If you cross this threshold, I shall hit you.' Our submarines had free range within the zone.

Sadly, there was still nothing we could do to disrupt enemy air movements until we could get missile systems and interceptors within range. But, once we were within 200 miles of the Falklands, it was intended that the MEZ should become a TEZ — a Total Exclusion Zone. Any incursion by the enemy, above, on or beneath the surface, could then be dealt with. I noted from my chart that we should be in position to enforce it fully by 30 April.

Though President Reagan had described the disputed islands as nothing but 'a bunch of frozen rocks', it was increasingly clear that two nations were about to pay a very high price for their ownership and so I felt I needed a little more than the US President's eloquence to introduce me to what we were fighting for. Like many before me, I turned to the mariner's handbook, the *Admiralty Pilot*.

Comprising 200 separate islands, 120 miles across and 75 miles deep, the Falklands' surface area is scarcely more than that of the Isle of Wight. The two dominant islands of East and West Falkland are slashed apart by a 50-mile-long, narrow strip of water, known — unsurprisingly — as Falkland Sound. Sheep-farming settlements, linked by little more than radio, are scattered sparsely across a desolate land comprising peat, heather, ribbons of boulders, and open coarse grassland, called 'the camp', after the Spanish word for grass — *campaña*. The only town of size is the capital, Stanley, which is tucked at the extreme eastern end of East Falkland. Every three months, the Falkland Islands Company coaster *Monsoonen* called to reprovision and to collect the stocks of wool sheared from hardy Falkland sheep. Ominously, I read that the wind tends to blow for much of the year. It was wrong: it blows *throughout* the year — and damned hard!

I set the book aside, dwelling on the vision I had of some cross between rural New Zealand and the Western Isles of Scotland — both on a bad day and without the redeeming features of rugby football and malt whisky.

As we entered the last week of April, information that both the enemy cruiser *General Belgrano* and the carrier *25 de Mayo* were at sea gave our war preparations a cutting edge of urgency. Certainly Burglar became more arrogant and moved in closer still, clearly aware that we remained for the moment constrained from blowing him out of the sky. Nevertheless, our Harriers had by then shortened their deck-alert readiness state, hoping to be cleared to do just that.

It was on Sunday, 25 April, that our force was first lit by the fire of battle, albeit a remote one. In the afternoon, at 1500, I was called to the operations room to listen to astonishingly clear radio transmissions from our Paraquet forces. It was a vivid and emotional experience, relayed to us by freakish radio propagation over a thousand miles.

The stage was South Georgia, at a latitude of nearly 60° south, right on the edge of the Antarctic pack ice. The island is more than 100 miles long with spectacular mountains rising to 10,000 feet above 1,500 glittering, castellated square miles of ice and snow, set beneath an utterly savage climate.

The players were *Antrim*, *Brilliant*, *Plymouth*, *Endurance*, *Fort Austin* and *Tidespring*, together with their six helicopters and a force of Special Air Service (SAS) and Special Boat Service Royal Marines (SBS).

Having departed the Task Force on Easter Monday, 12 April, they had arrived off the islands at dawn on 21 April, *Brilliant* having diverted to join them on 22 April. The submarine *Conqueror* had landed an SBS recce party, whilst an ultra long-range flight of 6,500 miles by an RAF Victor tanker had yielded a radar search of the coast. Suitably reassured, warship commanders Brian Young (*Antrim*), John Coward (*Brilliant*), David Pentreath (*Plymouth*) and Nick Barker (*Endurance*) set about their business.

But the operation got off to a bad start. Placement of an SAS patrol on the exposed face of the Fortuna Glacier went terribly wrong as an icy 70-knot storm decimated their temporary camp. The subsequent rescue of this force by Lieutenant Commander Ian Stanley in his ancient, single-engined Wessex 3 helicopter, 'Humphrey', has rightly inspired innumerable naval aviators, and rarely has a Distinguished Service Order been better deserved. Heading his helicopter crew was a talented young observer of immense potential, Chris Parry, who would one day go on to command his own ship. Their efforts in appalling turbulence and driving snow squalls exceeded most safe operating parameters of their anti-submarine helicopter but saved the lives of twenty men.

After the Fortuna setback, reassessment took place. Intelligence reported that the enemy

71

submarine *Santa Fe* had just arrived in their area, but the 5,000-ton *Conqueror* was unable to get a detection upon the quiet 2,500-ton conventional submarine amongst the ice-laden waters. Further delay was unacceptable to Northwood and so, on Sunday, 25 April, *Alacrity* listened to the spectacular last act of Operation Paraquet — live!

Ian Stanley, clearly intent upon a Bar to his DSO, found the *Santa Fe* on the surface and attacked her with two depth-charges. Poor Captain Horatio Bicain then had his submarine assaulted again, by a homing torpedo from the *Brilliant* Lynx and then by missiles from the *Endurance* Wasp helicopter. It was a magnificent goading of the bull in a ring of ice by naval air power, and smiles were broad in my rapt and silent ops room. We admired and envied in equal measure the cool radio calls from the distant helicopters telling us that the *Santa Fe* was disabled, unable to submerge and escape.

Six helicopters then landed seventy SAS and SBS ashore, whilst *Antrim* and *Plymouth* fired more than 200 shells around Grytviken. The lonely station in the shadow of the mountains, hub of the entire whaling world earlier in the century and with all its buildings and equipment left in a frozen time-warp as they were abandoned when the whalers departed, must have resonated shockingly before the intimidating barrage. But it clearly proved persuasive: prompt surrender was quickly followed by a similar capitulation at Leith further down the coast. South Georgia was ours and the road to ultimate victory seemed shorter.

Brian Young sent an inspiring signal which was read out by Margaret Thatcher to a greedy media on the steps of 10 Downing Street: 'Be pleased to advise Her Majesty that the White Ensign flies alongside the Union Flag at Grytviken.' I assumed that the message was intended for the Queen.

In Argentina, a different signal was sent as the Junta reverted to type and scattered a series of courts martial amongst their unfortunate officers in South Georgia, starting with Bicain. They clearly believed in inspiring their labour-force.

Our spirits were further lifted by the arrival of *Sheffield*, who stiffened our anti-aircraft defences considerably. COs were then summoned once more for planning discussions aboard the flagship, this time to finalize attack plans. There was to be no delay: we were to close the islands directly from the north-east and attack at dawn on 1 May, immediately after the first of several attempts to burst the runway of Stanley airfield with a long-range bombing raid by an RAF Vulcan. In an ambitious piece of in-flight refuelling co-ordination, this aircraft would undertake a 7,000-mile round trip to and from Ascension with the aim of laying 10 tons of bombs across an airfield that we needed out of action. Resupply was annoying enough, but if Argentina deployed some of her high-performance aircraft to Stanley, then our air-defence problems would increase markedly.

The Sea Harriers were to follow up with 1,000 lb bombs and delayed action devices across the runway to disrupt Argentinian repair operations. Later in the day, a select group of gunships would carry out shore bombardment to keep things boiling: *Alacrity* was to be one of them.

Some verbal sparring took place between the two SHAR squadron COs, Lieutenant Commander 'Sharkey' Ward of 801 Naval Air Squadron from *Invincible* and Lieutenant Commander Andy Auld of 800 Naval Air Squadron from *Hermes*. Their differences concerned attack techniques upon the airfield — who was to conduct them, and when. Sharkey wanted to hit the airfield by night with his squadron, firing flares to identify their targets and minimizing the chances of Harrier losses under the shroud of night. Captain Lin Middleton of *Hermes* had been opposed, and anyway the need for a surprise Vulcan attack in darkness had finally trumped Sharkey's proposal. As this talented and extrovert pilot was not renowned for his self-restraint, the more phlegmatic temperament of Andy Auld seemed not to make for the greatest harmony between them. But fighter pilots are not paid to be easy-going.

Just as we ship captains were getting bored by the in-fighting and wondering if the jet jockeys were going to have any attention left to provide us with air defence, Lin re-entered the debate. The thrust of his interjection was unambiguous and left me with my main memory of the briefing.

'I know a bit about runway busting. Whatever

you think you're going to achieve, divide it by ten and don't cry if you fail even that!' How right he was. Keeping runways unavailable to the enemy is a hugely expensive and inefficient business. I returned to *Alacrity* hungry for action, and we pressed on — ever southward.

We were certainly not the only ones going south. Our trusty BBC advised us that the 2nd Battalion of the Parachute Regiment had sailed from the UK on 25 April, together with the other assault ship, *Intrepid* (Captain Peter Dingemans), the tanker *Bayleaf* (Captain A. E. T. Hunter), the ferries *Norland* (Captain M. Ellerby) and *Europic Ferry* (Captain C. J. C. Clark), and the *Atlantic Conveyor* (Captain I. North). *Conveyor* was a Cunard container ship and possessed two sizeable vehicle decks, a quickly constructed flight-deck and more invaluable Harriers. Indeed, a new naval squadron had been formed and deployed to reinforce our meagre interceptor group, and the Royal Air Force were sending their ground-attack version of the vertical take-off aircraft. We were scraping the barrel, for the prospect of impending winter in southern waters meant that a landing had to take place before late May if we were not to risk defeat by the elements. No long-war scenario could be tolerated.

Indeed, by then a whole succession of ships was strung out behind us for thousands of miles. Two dispatch vessels were to act as utility ships on the fringe of the main force: *Leeds Castle* (Lieutenant Commander Colin Hamilton — one day to end up with me in a

75

very different sort of war) and *Dumbarton Castle* (Lieutenant Commander Norman Wood). The mighty *Canberra* had arrived at Ascension on 20 April with her doubtless uneasy bedfellows of 40 and 42 Commando Royal Marines, and the 3rd Battalion of the Parachute Regiment embarked. The stores ship RFA *Regent* (Captain J. Logan) and the tanker *Plumleaf* (Captain R. W. M. Wallace), together with the forward repair ship *Stena Seaspread* (Captain N. Williams), were also *en route*. The newly painted white hospital ship *Uganda* was followed by the frigates *Argonaut* (Captain Kit Layman), *Ambuscade* (Commander Peter Mosse) and *Ardent* (Commander Alan West). I was particularly delighted to see Alan coming south: an effervescent charmer, full of natural gifts, he and I had shared a memorable preceding Christmas with our ships in Amsterdam.

For us, way to the south, the nights grew longer still. The Royal Navy now spends most of its time in the northern hemisphere and thus a different, southern, starry heaven was viewed by us all with rapt fascination. Task Group blackout had long ago become total and no other light could ever be seen; the pre-sunset ritual of darken ship had become exhaustive. And so, in a black ocean amidst black ships, we admired the glorious spangled sky — and all became amateur astronomers.

We had been gone from home for nearly a month and, although we had all had much longer periods of distant seatime, tension was seeping through to all ships. The lengthy passage gave me further opportunity to learn even more about the 200 sailors of my ship's company. Each adapted differently to the constant demands of defence watches, each assumed his own personal rhythm. There was less banter and high spirits, all being conscious of the need for off-watch shipmates to sleep undisturbed. Thus routine 'pipes' over the main broadcast loudspeakers were abandoned and *Alacrity* settled into the silent purposefulness of anticipating war. Ironically, some of our keep-fit fanatics were the first to suffer some reaction: deprivation of a narcissistic daily 'fix' of open-air training hurt. Indeed, I was suffering from the same complaint. Oh, the conceit of the young athlete — and the lapsed old one.

As if in intimation of dramatic events to come, our weather drew in on 26 April and savage gales gave us another pounding: the final 1,000 miles of our transit were going to be unpleasant. No Sea Harriers flew, but I was unclear as to whether this was because of the weather or because maintenance crews were merely completing the last servicing schedules to ready the jets for the intense usage of war.

In the foul weather, a particular concern to *Alacrity* was our gun mounting. If we kept it pointing straight ahead, then water leaked in around the base of the barrel: if we turned it through 180°, we had the psychological shock of coming on to the bridge and peering down our own gun barrel, whilst leaving the then forward-facing rear door vulnerable. We plumped for reversing it and, sure enough, within twelve hours of doing so, the huge sea burst in, leaving engineers and gunners to pump out the massive ingress of water and make repairs. Thereafter, in heavy weather we always directed the gun on the beam, offering one flat, waterproof side of the mounting to the pounding from ahead. Thankfully, it gave us no further problems, other than anxious faces on an adjacent tanker when we were refuelling from *that* side. Funnily enough, they always seemed to give *Alacrity* particularly good service.

The weather continued to worsen as massive head seas battered ships grown complacent from tranquil tropics. The same night that we flooded the gun, I was called with reports that a patrolling night watchman had heard the starboard anchor starting to smash back and forth in its hawsepipe: we had a problem. Several tons of anchor was meant to be tightly retained by a bottlescrew device that theoretically could not unwind; but it was doing so, and the back-up strops were in danger of parting. As the anchor was attached to several hundred feet of heavy cable, if it were to be released with a bang it would probably tear itself out by the roots and we would lose the lot. Embarrassing.

The walls of sea were still extremely large and coming from right ahead, which increased the challenge somewhat. Skilled seamen had to go out on the upper deck right forward, connect up the winch, haul taut the anchor cable, tighten the bottlescrew, and then re-secure all the strops. The only trouble was that the entire bow area forward of the gun was constantly under tons of seething black water. We readied a small team in oilskins and lifelines whilst I planned what we were going to do.

Running *with* the huge swell was the only answer, but turning across the face of such a large sea to do so would be unpleasant and had to be done fast if we were to avoid the risk of capsizing. Once we were down-sea, our speed in relation to that mountainous swell would be equally critical — too slow and we risked a massive sea bursting in through the helicopter hangar and hatches aft, severely damaging — and potentially even destabilizing — the ship. If we matched the speed of the sea, we could lose rudder effectiveness as we slid down the face of the swell, risking an out-of-control sheer and possible capsizing as thousands of tons of water rolled us over. Too fast, and we might risk the same fate by surfing out of control — and certainly sweeping away our exposed sailors. What we needed was a speed marginally slower than the water around us, leaving us precarious but stable as the worst of the killing wave-power merely slid, slowly and harmlessly, beneath us.

The evolution went well. My fast turn heeled the ship beyond 40° on the inclinometer — I had never before rolled that far in a Type 21 frigate — but it pulled us through the risk zone safely. It also woke every man abed and seemed to break free every item in our fully battened-down ship. Once on course, we achieved a safe speed and it took but thirty-five minutes of tension and toil for the three men working by torchlight in the howling wind and spray. They returned frozen but safe, and our anchors gave us no more problems. Greatly relieved myself, I celebrated by reawakening every man on board with the turn back to stem the swell.

Several other ships had sustained minor damage, and we all reported our frailty. The Admiral, in return, gave us a rap on the knuckles: 'The Can-Do attitude, while commendable in many respects, should not cause you to fail to tell me if I am breaking your ship by driving it too hard.'

If nothing else, it had been a salutary reminder that a large aircraft-carrier can be serene in sea states that shatter destroyers and frigates. Though I hoped the Admiral would remember the lesson, I still vowed moderation in the handling of my ship. Would that I could have seen then the brutalizing I was to give her in the weeks ahead.

The foul weather gave us several other useful reminders. Again I was struck by the strain on everyday life as men tried to do their jobs under constant physical bracing and tension. Despite the cooped-up existence, moving around a warship in constant high seas keeps one very fit as muscles engage in a constant isometrics schedule — tensing and relaxing several times a minute. I was particularly admiring of the cooks deftly at work in the galley, stabilizing pots and dishes through years of experience, and always producing good hot food — and motivation — for their tired shipmates. One of the ship's most muscular athletes — Leading Cook Parks — was a revelation as he braced and balanced heavy pots and platters in the confined space. Such skill was being reflected in almost every corner of the ship as separate specialists adapted to working in a virtual dodgem car.

Certainly, our swilled upper deck would have to remain out-of-bounds throughout the hours of darkness for all but the necessarily exposed lookouts, visual gun and missile aimers, and the ship's Flight. As we had proved that exposing our seamen on the forecastle forward for refuellings would often be impossible, we practised using an alternative replenishment point back near the flight-deck. By tucking the nose of the helicopter just inside the hangar, we could keep it ready to fly whilst our sailors could still fuel in relative shelter.

When men had to move down on to the tiny low quarterdeck, right aft, to deploy and recover the torpedo decoys, I was going to have to play the same variations of ship course and speed as I had for the anchor evolution. It was all a little daunting and I sent a cautionary signal on foul-weather ship-handling back to the Type 21s coming south behind us. It concluded: 'Not intended to be alarmist, they are fine seaboats — but things look different from down here.' Indeed they did.

Our Lynx helicopters were now repeatedly searching ahead of the force, carrying Sea Skua missiles for use, when approved, against enemy surface vessels. I was reminded that we simply could not exist without the benefits of the helicopter. Over many post-war years, the uninitiated had been slow to grasp the

81

potential of this ungainly flying machine in naval warfare. Fortunately, the experiences of Korea, Suez, Borneo and the Icelandic 'Cod War' had allowed the Navy to become the world leader in operating helicopters from escort ships by day and night in virtually all weathers. The arrival of the Westland Lynx offered each ship captain a great enhancement of his ship capabilities, and most of the Task Group escorts carried them. Having spent five years flying its primitive predecessor, the Wasp, I was particularly admiring of this aircraft.

Every Lynx mission, or alert spell, was exhaustively briefed by one of our two helicopter controllers. They were both very young sailors, but rose to the challenge, confidently coping with their captain's questions. Fuel margins, weapon loads, weather and sea states, all were dissected before I would authorize the flight. Aircrew were meant to rest for eight hours in any twenty-four, a source of much teasing from their seaman counterparts who were granted no such indulgence. Frequently tasked to fly three-hour sorties, with the overload fuel tank they could stretch this to nearly four hours. But nobody was keen to swap places with them when they were a hundred miles from 'Mother' on a pitch-black night with thousands of fathoms of icy Atlantic below them and when a total electrical failure or rotor snag could mean death.

The Flight Senior Maintenance Rating, bearded Chief Petty Officer Slater — dubbed 'Makarios' — and his Flight of seven maintainers, worked astonishingly long periods without a break.

Twenty-four hours continuously on watch was a frequent occurrence, their worst spell being thirty-one hours. How delicate maintenance tasks were undertaken safely through such a veil of fatigue and gloom I never really knew, but nothing fell off and everything that was meant to rotate certainly went on doing so.

The Flight had other tasks. Our torpedo decoy, a large, unwieldy yellow mini-submersible, had to be streamed and recovered at regular intervals as it could not remain astern of the ship whilst we were manoeuvring hard. Vast clusters of seaweed — kelp — were to be the hazard, and we had one decoy torn bodily from its cable by the sudden arrest, from 30 knots, of cloying weed. Highline refuelling, to top up hovering helicopters too large to land on our deck, allowed them to stay aloft for many hours when far from their own 'Mother'. Short-notice arrivals by force helicopters needed help with winch or underslung load. And appalling deck conditions meant that the Lynx Gem engines were eating far more salt than was proper, thereby necessitating compressor washes that had to take place with boring regularity. All in all, the Flight was overworked.

As we hovered on the brink of war, the attention of the international community was being fed by Task Group embarked media: sixteen reporters, two photographers, two radio commentators and three TV correspondents. All were keyed up, having endured days of boring confinement waiting for a real war, which was at last about to be theirs. When asked if I wished to host a visit from a media team, I unwisely declined, not wishing my ship to be distracted at such a time. I still had much to learn.

One night, my officers decided to distract themselves by making an exception and broaching the last bottle of decent wine with their evening meal. It was a Thursday, for which day the traditional toast was meant to be, 'A bloody war and a sickly season'. This rang a trifle gloomily for my spirited team. Wisely they amended the *Alacrity* Thursday toast ever after to, 'Here's to next Thursday!'

Such caution was timely. On 29 April, we entered the newly established TEZ, of the same 200-mile radius and location as the Maritime Exclusion Zone that had preceded it. We did not know it, but Argentinian aircraft had just completed their five-hundredth resupply flight into Stanley airfield, having been forced to transfer 10,700 men and 5,500 tons of cargo by air.

A different sort of shuttle, that of Al Haig, had just failed, partly because of two fatal flaws in the Argentinian leadership: the Junta lacked a clear command system with which to consult, and it was dominated by the obsessionally aggressive Admiral Anaya who refused to see the inevitable outcome of the ill-conceived adventure. So, the Americans promptly shed impartiality. The US Defense Secretary, Caspar Weinberger, having provided the latest Sidewinder missiles to the Harriers, offered to lease us a huge, fixed-wing aircraft-carrier. Sadly, the Royal Navy was unable to man it, arm it, embark an air group, modify all aircraft and appear ready for action. But, nevertheless, it was a nice thought and typical of the single-minded support afforded the British cause by Weinberger. The Special Relationship was alive and well. Indeed, for the leading democratic nation in the world to have done other than support the UK position would have been absurd.

But then, out at sea, there came the event we had all been waiting for — first contact with the enemy. On 30 April, a 1,000-ton Argentinian deep-sea trawler called *Narwhal* closed our ships from the south-west. It was obvious to us all that her fishing was restricted to 'catching' massive information about the Task Group and 'canning' it home. In a time of high tension, there is a fundamental naval tactic — get rid of the shadower. Sandy Woodward did not have to tolerate her presence, and it fell to my ship to remove her.

'Kindly go and scare off the snooper, *Alacrity*,' said the Admiral on secure speech. 'If she enters the TEZ, decrew her — and sink her.' I received my orders with glee: we were on our way. The night is still printed vividly on my memory.

★ ★ ★

I order two Olympus boost-engines engaged, and we commence an accelerating, sliding, slipping arc out from our screening station towards the snooper. At full rudder, the ship heels fiercely away from the turn, screws biting savagely for grip as we leave boiling white crescents behind us. *The ship's company need to know we are going hunting.*

It is approaching midnight; almost precisely four weeks since the invasion, and we are about to seek redress. I order Action Stations and gun and missile readiness whilst we thunder on towards our puny adversary. Colin proudly holds nine fingers aloft to show me how many minutes it has taken crew and equipment to be readied for the 'action state'. Not bad. The whole length of our sleek vessel squirms and bucks under the combined 50,000 shaft horsepower.

Two miles to go. All our lights are extinguished, only the navigation radar emitting. Darkness is complete. Narwhal has no idea who we are; just a large radar echo racing across a black screen — on an exact interception course. It must have grabbed his attention. If I am tense, he is much more so.

He starts calling us on the International Distress frequency, clearly alarmed at the intruder on his radar picture — he has not read our Rules of Engagement. His challenges become strident, initially in Spanish, then some English. Anton Maguire, my extrovert and sometime Spanish linguist, does a fair job of interpreting.

'Why do you close my vessel so fast? What is your business? You should keep clear of my vessel under Rule of the Road.' All predictable stuff. His outrage is almost convincing.

I take control of the ship from the bridge where only the faintest red glow emanates from the control console over which the quartermaster cranes to hold his course; illuminated radar display and chart table are completely shrouded behind thick hessian curtains. I look out ahead — absolutely nothing. The Navigator, Lieutenant Simon Thorp, is counting down the range as we close; cool as ever.

'Revert to two Tynes, Officer of the Watch.' The scream and vibration of the Olympus engines dies away and we slide on under the whisper of the cruise engines, still closing, by now only a few hundred yards away and being deafened by his strangled cries emitting from our VHF radio set.

As we close to tens of yards his voice moves from falsetto to castrato: the words brief, emphatic and in lurid English. Scared and impolite. My bridge team are adoring it all, probably understand more of the four-letter words than I do. I hold back from switching on the 20-inch searchlight until we are at point-blank range on his beam and dwarfing him.

'Hit the light, Colin,' I order quietly. Suddenly, every timber of Narwhal is lit as on the brightest day and, in a pre-planned manoeuvre, our gun mounting swings round slowly until the barrel points right down into his bridge windows. I ask my team to turn down the volume on the radio as the Latin yodeller is now beside himself. He is, quite reasonably, very scared. But then we need to be convincing: I do not want to deal with this complication twice. At last Anton is allowed to respond.

'Make your course to the north. Proceed at maximum speed. Do not alter further. You are *not to return. If you do not comply you will be blown out of the water.' It even sounds good in Spanish.*

My Supply Officer clearly should have persevered with his language studies: there is no hesitation from our prey — we feel the roll as Narwhal *turns away. Northward — and at high speed. I wonder if the inadequacies of Anton's 'O level' Spanish might not have produced an even more dramatic message than I had intended. Thank God he has not chastised their sisters, or else* Narwhal*'s bow might have swung the other way and war would have started seven hours earlier.*

It occurs to me that our snooper's nerve might shortly return if he feels he has been too readily intimidated. Clearly the Admiral has the same thought: 'Put starshell over the top of him as he departs. Make him think that Big Brother is still watching him.'

The single shell bursts high, parachute flare swinging as the half-million candlepower casts an incandescent halo over the poor scurrying trawler. She keeps going and would have been well advised to have continued; for she is doomed. I turn the bows back to the south and signal: 'Brightened his day. ALA rejoining — guns tight.'

Mission over, we tuck back into the Force as the first glimmer of dawn washes the eastern skies: skies that will bring us much more than mere light before the end of this day. It is Saturday, 1 May.

3

First Blood

1 – 9 May

'Disguise fair nature with
hard favoured rage'

OPERATION BLACK BUCK, codename
for the long-distance RAF bomber raid,
achieved its first aim: fifteen airborne
link-ups of the main and spare Vulcans with
a cavalcade of Victor tankers were completed
successfully. Ironically, it was the stand-by
Vulcan which finally arrived over the target,
and I listened with pleasure to the one
brief codeword message, 'Superfuze', as they
completed their bombing run at a little after
0300 local time.

It was a relative success. From a release height
of 10,000 feet at 2 miles range, they laid their
stick of twenty-one bombs at 30° to the east/west
axis of the runway. The inclination of the drop
was calculated to maximize the chance of placing
at least one or two of the 1,000 lb weapons on
target. In the event, one hit, with a further
eighteen erupting through dispersals and fuel
dumps. Though effective as a morale-breaking
demonstration of British efficiency and resolve,
the raid was only a very limited blow against

enemy fighting capability. Nevertheless, it was a beginning.

And then it was time for the Royal Navy to go back to war. At first light, from a position 100 miles east of the Falklands, the carriers launched. Twelve of Andy Auld's 800 Squadron, bombed up and briefed, went for Stanley, then Goose Green to the west. Sharkey Ward's 801 Squadron aircraft were already in their air-defence racetrack over East Falkland with two more poised at deck alert. No. 800 delivered their combination of cluster bombs and parachute-retarded high-explosive bombs in low-level profiles and precisely on time, creating some chaos but little long-lasting effect upon the runway. Meanwhile, the Goose Green raid destroyed a Pucara propeller-driven aircraft and killed seven military personnel. On their return to the flagship, Brian Hanrahan, reporting for BBC television, was able to record that he had counted all the Sea Harriers out and he had counted them all back. But a cannon hole in the tail of one aircraft gave a taste of what was to come.

Despite the fine planning and tenacity of the crews, Lin Middleton's scepticism over runway attacks was borne out: I could almost see the knowing shake of his powerful blond head. But it too was a good start. Then the first enemy fighters appeared over the islands and some early air combat took place between Mirages and our Sea Harriers. No score was achieved by either side as the pilots settled down.

Glamorgan, *Arrow* and *Alacrity* had been

ordered inshore overnight, ready for the first bombardment, doubtless selected for our combined six 4.5-inch guns and the accuracy of our computer-controlled shore bombardment system. As even such gunnery is only truly effective when corrected by a trained observer, Bob Burrows was to be taking his Lynx in to spot the fire — to act as our eyes. A gleaming new general-purpose machine-gun had just been fitted to the aircraft and our irrepressibly gung-ho Instructor Officer, Tom McCrimmon, was elected volunteer gunner after a short practice and much posturing. The full spotting crew by then included recently embarked Captain Chris Brown, Royal Artillery, who fitted in well with our pirates, having cut his teeth in the bombardment of South Georgia before being transferred to us. I noted that the aircraft was overloaded with both rank and bravura.

We had assessed various spotting locations that might allow the helicopter uninterrupted observation without being shot down by shore defences. Of all the 200 islands which comprise the Falklands, we chose the tiny promontory of Kidney Island just 4 miles to the north-east of Stanley. The choice was not very bright. If it looked ideal to us, then it looked equally ideal to the Argentinians: they already had an armed patrol boat in the tiny harbour, as Bob Burrows was to find out to his cost.

Admiral Woodward rightly held the carriers out 80 miles to the east, at extreme range from the Argentinian Air Force, whilst *Glamorgan*, *Arrow* and *Alacrity* approached Stanley from the

91

south. I wondered how the 1,500 residents had enjoyed the Harrier sunrise. We were about to follow it with an explosive high noon, memory of which remains indelible, even today.

* * *

We go in at speed to the gunline, huge battle ensigns snapping grandly in the cold air. Orders are clipped and deliberate; no time for apprehension over what might lie ahead. Solid smoke smudges the brown skyline; the SHARS have done their business well. We lay off our guns upon the airfield, now less than 7 miles distant. Computers blend trigonometry and ballistics, producing passionless solutions which are fed to gun mountings, whilst high-explosive shells at last fill the ammunition hoists. This time it is for real. All three ships report ready. Tense expectation fills us all as we approach our first moment of combat.

We open fire together, settling into a combined rate of nearly forty rounds (900 lbs) of explosive every minute. My command radar display shows a continuous stream of shells linking us to the arrowhead symbol on the target. The ops room reeks of cordite and I can clearly feel the reverberations of the other ships' guns up through my feet. We are truly at war.

Out to the north-east, over tiny Kidney Island, our Lynx pulls up from his low hover to direct our fire, only to find the enemy patrol craft appearing suddenly before him. A short burst of machine-gun fire from Tom

McCrimmon rakes the enemy vessel's decks, injuring a seaman, before the gun jams. On diving away for cover, they are promptly fired on by an armed fishing boat, the bullets shattering the helicopter's cockpit canopy and thudding into the fuselage all around the cabin. A low-level dash to the coast allows them to land briefly for a visual check of damage, which proves to be severe; fuel tanks are ruptured and the driveshaft to the tail rotor is partly severed. It is an easy choice: join the enemy for the duration of the war as prisoners, or risk a cataclysmic crash from the damage and run home. They lift from the heathered hillside and start back at low level towards Mother.

Mother is about to have problems of her own. The three ships have just finished firing 150 shells in less than ten minutes into an area about the size of Wembley football stadium. Though well aware that the Harriers and the Mirages have been mixing it over the islands, we have been so absorbed in completing the task that it seems merely an irritating distraction when the lookouts report unidentified aircraft approaching low and fast from the shoreline. There is no time for reasoning. Even the late cry that they are 'definitely not Harriers, more like enemy Mirages' fails to break the frozen tableau. Down the line of our formation they come, sleek crescents sliding through the funnel smoke and only just above the water, like huge black threatening ravens. And then they are on us. Two retarded 1,000 lb bombs explode close by in our wake, cascading water soaking the *flight-deck crew and lifting the stern with the underwater blasts as the rippling shock runs through the ship. Our two dutymen right aft in the rudder compartment cannot have overlooked that. Cannon fire rakes decks, drawing the first blood of the campaign in Arrow. Our only response is a few rounds of ill-directed light-calibre gunfire. Then the jets are past and through.*

'Wankers', breathes somebody reverently on the command open line intercom.

'All positions check for damage,' I order — slightly more constructively.

★ ★ ★

We had been lucky, damage was minimal. There had been four Mirages initially but one of them had been shot down by his own AA guns onshore: there was a deal of new learning going on for both sides. Our ships turned together and ran for the open sea as we recovered our shattered helicopter. It was an ignominious and nearly tragic conclusion to the elation of bombardment, and we were rueful — first blooding had so nearly been our last.

How had so much diligent training and preparation produced such a stutteringly inadequate reaction? Many days were to pass before we came to understand that our semi-paralysis was not unique and that most men respond thus when first faced with the savagery of battle. Virtually all who have fought recall the breathless freezing of existence that is the

94

initial moment of combat. It is almost the first reminder of the very fragility of life itself: slow-motion seconds that reveal the savagery of man intent upon killing his fellow man — you! Any war experience that follows one's first brush with the icy fingers of violent death is minor by comparison, however intense, however protracted. The days and nights ahead were to give us much more practice and we were to get so much better, but none of us would ever be the same again.

Our three ships returned to the Carrier Battle Group in formation, 3 miles apart, zigzagging at 26 knots. Whilst we had been taking our first blooding on the gunline, *Brilliant* and *Yarmouth*, together with three Sea Kings, had been engaged in a submarine hunt to the north-east of Stanley. The 209-class submarine *San Luis* was known to be at sea and she had to be killed or scared off early — the price of her torpedoes being unleashed amongst the carriers would be too high to contemplate. Captain John Coward, suitably warmed up by the South Georgia experience, was later to swear that he had held prolonged sonar contact with the Argentinian sub for several hours.

Early-morning excitement had drawn out a large number of Argentinian aircraft from the mainland but they had achieved little, other than battle-hardening three British warships. Fifty aircraft had been launched from their bases on 1 May but only twenty-five had arrived over the target area, and four of those had been lost. The agile SHAR had proved itself, shooting down two Mirages and a Canberra with Sidewinder. Both sides had only taken the temperature of combat; there was a great deal more to come.

Glamorgan, *Arrow* and *Alacrity* were back on the gunline that same night, more composed under the veil of darkness that was thereafter to be our normal operating environment. We three ships were to see a great deal of each other in the days ahead. *Glamorgan*'s Captain, Mike Barrow, was solid, nice-natured and dogged; he drove a happily efficient ship. The County-class destroyers were stately and graceful vessels, sections of upper deck being still constructed of teak — a time warp to a different era and a very different navy.

Arrow was driven by a fine friend and fellow aviator, Commander Paul Bootherstone. We had first met when we were both carrier pilots in the Far East in the 1960s and our career paths had remained entwined ever since. Though this gifted aviator had contrived without malice to break my nose in a social rugby scrum after a particularly riotous mess dinner some years before, we remained firm friends. One of life's thoroughly nice men, Paul was relaxedly unflappable.

The three of us were to become known as the 'Three Musketeers', due to the Flag Staff teaming us up on a number of exciting missions. We could only hope that such singling out was not due to any lack of friends in high places.

In the small hours which followed the initial day of war, darkened Sea Kings from 846 commenced their first covert landings of Special

Forces on to the sodden slopes of East Falkland — the capable men of the SAS and SBS were going about their clandestine business.

It had been a hell of a first twenty-four hours for us. Driving off *Narwhal*, shelling the airport, surviving air attack, escape, return to the gunline, and finally having to replenish with ammunition and fuel in a rising seaway, all made me hungry for sleep despite the sustaining surge of adrenalin which was still running through me. I had experienced quieter days.

On rejoining the force, as if we had not had enough, the Admiral gave us our first taste of a favourite discipline of his — post-event analysis. It entailed all command teams signalling the flagship with their impressions of significant events, and stating how they and their consorts had coped. The staff would then distill this information into an overall analysis of how we could all do better. Not a bad discipline for any organization; I have made use of the technique ever since.

Some lessons were very clear. Daylight shore bombardment with limited Harrier topcover was not worth the risk, and aerial spotting by helicopter was equally fraught. Similarly, co-ordination of our air defences inshore was inhibited by the blanking of radars from land returns, leaving the SHARs to revert to random visual dogfights which gave low-level attackers some chance of getting through.

Above all, Day 1 had taught us that — in the absence of airborne early warning — one element of our force was to be the key to

97

success or failure: our Sea Harriers would be critical. As a helicopter pilot and instructor, my fixed-wing experience had been twenty years earlier and limited to flying a delicate and occasionally headstrong little monoplane called the Chipmunk, and learning to land it on a grass strip alongside the Great North Road in Yorkshire. One Australian colleague found the siren call of the traffic irresistible, bouncing his way over the intervening hedgerow and joining the bustling vehicles. Somehow, we had all survived, but several were not so lucky in the future. Two exciting years in the Far East, flying from the fixed-wing carrier *Eagle*, left me much impressed with the courage and skill of the jet jockeys. As search and rescue plane-guard, I spent countless hours hovering alongside the 50,000-ton carrier, watching thundering fighters return to the plunging flight-deck by day and night. I winched up bedraggled pilots and recovered the broken bodies of the less fortunate as we lost a dozen aircraft over two years. With them, to the bottom of the murky South China Sea, went ten of their aircrew.

Such experience had allowed me to confront my own mortality more thoroughly than my young sailors in the South Atlantic. And it had also left me deeply admiring of our naval jet flyers as aviators; at their specialist game they were near to being the best in the world. Utterly professional and exceedingly brave, they were already tilting the scales our way. But, with only twenty Harriers in the force, we still lacked enough to win our war.

On board, we were determined, for our part, to do better. In particular, my Gunnery Officer drilled his team unmercifully. Graham Baxter was cast in the ideal officer mould. A strong-minded and self-assured natural leader, he had started his career on the lower deck as an artificer apprentice. He was a gem. As a bonus, he knew Type 21s from stem to stern, having previously been Navigator of *Ardent*.

His gun and missile director, the inimitable Chief Petty Officer Rhodes, was overheard haranguing a young man who had not opened fire with his 20 mm gun but who had, with some justification, pleaded that he had not known they were definitely the enemy. The Chief's cockney-toned response was to the point. 'Listen, son, you can tell the hostile ones 'cos they're the ones wot are spitting fuckin' death at you!' I no longer had any need to inspire savagery: all my people by then knew that somebody was intent upon killing them. The next time we had to kill first.

On 2 May, the UN Secretary General, Perez de Cuellar, urgently proposed a ceasefire and mutual demilitarization of the Falklands. It came to naught. On the same day I was approached by Bob Burrows with an equally implausible proposal. We needed to get our badly shot-up Lynx across to RFA *Fort Austin* to have it mended by her battle-damage engineers. I was being invited to take *Alacrity* within 800 yards and then Rob Sleeman would fly, low and slow, to the large stores ship. The reason why he wished to fly low and slow was to allow him to ditch without dying when the jubilee clip that had been bound around the partially severed tail rotor driveshaft disintegrated, as it surely would, from the stress of another flight. It was a mark of how thoroughly I had set aside my normally cautious peacetime aviation standards that I agreed. There was simply no other easy way of doing the transfer. The clip held, and with it my career. Our Lynx returned after three days, patched and battered but very much ours.

The build-up of the Intelligence picture was even more dramatic. Not only had the Argentinians proved their ability to mount air attacks 400 miles from home, their major surface ships were also known to be grouping, several to the north-west around the *25 de Mayo*, and more to the south-west around the *General Belgrano*. Admiral Woodward duly tucked his carriers just a little further to the east to stretch the opposition, and waited for the picture to clear. Three British nuclear submarines now ringed the Falkland Islands but sadly the one tracking the *25 de Mayo* had been hauled off its close escort task; the absence of information on the Argentinian carrier was a worrying disadvantage which was, ironically, to decide the fate of the *General Belgrano*.

The Admiral plumped for offensive defence as *Glamorgan* was ordered to take *Arrow* and *Alacrity* to the south-west at high speed as a surface action group against the *General Belgrano*. Though the enemy cruiser was on the far (western) side of the Burdwood Bank, a shoal covering an area some 200 miles by 60 miles, once she was over the shallows, our nuclear submarines would have an impossible task to track and attack. The water was often much less than 300 feet deep — a veritable pond to a 6,000-ton nuclear sub. But the threatening ship was about to be removed without our help, and we were soon recalled.

Notwithstanding the two threatening Argentinian groups, the ultimatum of 23 April, and the Argentinian Air Force trying to blow three of our ships to pieces that very morning, British ROE still precluded attack upon the Argentinian surface navy. Admiral Woodward was clearly disturbed by such inconsistency and sent a somewhat presumptuous signal inviting *Conqueror* to attack the *Belgrano*. It was intercepted at Northwood (as he intended that it should be) and inspired a rushed approach by Admirals Lewin and Fieldhouse to Margaret Thatcher seeking formal approval for such an attack. Once again, the Lady was not found wanting in resolve. Brief consultation with the War Cabinet produced clearance and, at 1601 on 2 May, Commander Chris Wreford-Brown in *Conqueror* unleashed three Mk 8 torpedoes at the *General Belgrano* from within 1,500 yards. He carried out a flawless attack, placing the torpedoes, of a vintage even older than their target, into the sturdy cruiser and she duly sank, whilst *Conqueror* evaded counter-attack from the Argentinian escorts.

As an emphatic response to a known threat, the attack had been effective enough. But as a deterrent to the entire Argentinian surface fleet, it was invaluable. The enemy never again appeared at sea in a position to play any part. Sadly, 321 out of 1,000 Argentinian sailors had had to lose their lives to ensure that a large number of British sailors did not do the same. Doubtless, some armchair idealists still believe a magic wand could have achieved the same result, thereby leaving their responsibility-free consciences intact. One hopes such dreamers will never be asked to safeguard their country's interests in war.

Indeed, I found it ironic when the war was over to listen to impassioned accusations of war-mongering against both the Government and the Royal Navy for the attack on the *Belgrano*, including claims that the ship and its escorts did not constitute a threat to the Task Force. This conclusion was based, it seems, upon the fact that Captain Hector Bonzo had the bows of the *Belgrano* turned to the west rather than to the north-east at the moment she was torpedoed by *Conqueror*. The claim was nonsense: the *Belgrano* was threat indeed. With her fifteen 6-inch and eight 5-inch guns, her position — only 35 miles outside the Total Exclusion Zone — was the important thing. She could have turned in a trice to close the Task Force at more than 20 knots with her helicopter guiding her. The suggestion that she should not have been attacked because she lay just outside the TEZ was also misguided. I found it astonishing that the Government did not remind critics more forcibly of the warning of 23 April that any vessels interfering with our recovery of the islands would be dealt with appropriately. In an illuminating interview by British television many months after the cessation of hostilities, the Argentinian maritime commander Admiral Allara was asked what he would have done if he had been in Admiral Woodward's position. Unhesitatingly he replied that he too would have sunk the *Belgrano*. 'After that message of 23 April, the entire South Atlantic was an operational theatre for both sides,' he had to remind even British viewers.

The sinking of the *Belgrano* produced reactions. Locally, a planned night bombardment for *Alacrity* was cancelled at the last minute. Internationally, the reverberations of such a large Argentinian death toll in one short action were deafening, testing the resolve of our supporters and inflaming the Latin bloc that backed Argentina. Few grasped that *Conqueror* had, with the help of her archaic torpedoes, bottled up the entire Argentinian surface navy. The scales of advantage had just tilted emphatically our way.

That same night, our helicopters proved a much newer weapon than the Mk 8 torpedo. An 826 Sea King obtained a surface radar detection and called up *Glasgow* and *Coventry* Lynx, who then attacked the unfortunate Argentinian naval tug, *Alfredo Sobral*, with their sea-skimming missiles. It was the first operational blooding for Sea Skua. Confusion over radar contacts meant that poor *Sobral* took two pairs of the deadly weapons, the British helicopters believing they were attacking two separate vessels. Although the 860-ton hull survived, eight men died and eight more were injured. Any capability of the *Sobral* was extinguished amidst the blast and flames of the warheads, though the stricken ship just made it back to land.

The next day, 3 May, was a time for more introspection but no action. I had no conscience over the death toll in the *Belgrano*: war is a dirty business.

Just before dawn on 4 May, a second Vulcan attack went in against Stanley airport and this time all twenty-one bombs were off target. Meanwhile, the Task Group had moved back to within 100 miles of Stanley, thus being more vulnerable to air attack. But, in the open ocean, with layered defences in place, the Royal Navy believed itself to be well capable of defending itself — with or without early warning. On that day, we were wrong.

Our preoccupation remained enemy Super Etendard missile-firing aircraft. Thankfully for us, planned provision and support for their Exocets had been curtailed by the French. Only five Exocets had been delivered and only five aircraft were capable of carrying them. At the outbreak of hostilities, each Etendard pilot had but an average of 100 hours flying time on his aircraft although, thanks to *Hercules* and *Santissima Trinidad*, they were all familiar with the radar-detection capabilities of our Type 42 destroyers. The five aircraft had redeployed southward in mainland Argentina, from Espora to the Rio Grande air base, in mid-April, thereby minimizing their transit to the 'Malvinas'. Day by day, the British Fleet were between 350 to 550 miles away, depending upon Admiral Woodward's need to close the islands with the carriers. On 4 May, he swung the force a little nearer, the range reduced, and he offered the enemy the chance that they craved: they took it.

A distant Argentinian Neptune recce aircraft had been building up a picture of our ship dispositions by assiduously plotting our few radar transmissions, then shifting his position and doing the same, over and over again. This had given him a position on his chart without needing to advertise his presence by transmitting on his radar or closing to within our Harrier or missile range. His patience was to be rewarded, but he had not realized that the main body of ships, including the aircraft-carriers, were actually silent on radar. Accordingly, what he was plotting and reporting so carefully was merely the forward air defence line of our Type 42 destroyers. Thus these were to become the Argentinian targets, in the erroneous belief that they were the aircraft-carriers.

The ships were no more than 380 miles from Rio Grande when, at 0945, two Super Etendards took off, climbed high, took fuel from their Hercules tanker, and then commenced a stepping-down approach towards the Task Force. With radars silent they descended below the first tentacles of our radar beams — on their way to avenge the *Belgrano*. The weather was good by South Atlantic standards, we could see

105

for miles below the medium-level cloud, and the sea was calm.

Our ships were in a classical air defence formation, with the destroyers *Coventry*, *Glasgow* and *Sheffield* arced forward astride the likely axis of threat. Stepped back by some miles came *Glamorgan*, *Yarmouth*, *Arrow* and *Alacrity*. RFAs *Fort Austin*, *Resource* and *Olmeda* were close in to the carriers, which had *Brilliant* and *Broadsword* as their Sea Wolf missile defenders. I was seated at my command display with Tom Tubb across from me, and Graham Baxter prowling behind his gun and missile displays. Tom and I were playing imaginary Exocet games on the perspex face of the display between us, exploring ideal ways in which to avoid an attack. The infernal sea-skimming missile preoccupied us. One radio call turned our theoretical game into vivid reality.

'Handbrake! Bearing 317°.' *Glasgow*'s transmission was clear and precise. No doubt or hesitation: he had detected Agave radar — Etendards! Though the events remain a jumble of frozen fragments in my memory, our actions were all cool and precise; we had been through something similar to this before. I ordered Action Stations and the responding rattle of boots on steel ladders was deafening, even through my earphones. But *Sheffield* seemed to lack the same clear picture of the incoming air threat.

Two Exocets were launched from a range of less than 20 miles. Although one failed to acquire a target and ditched, the other

106

ripped in through *Sheffield*'s starboard beam, and scooped 15 foot of steel from her hull *en route*. Thankfully, the warhead did not explode, but 364 lbs of steel travelling at 680 m.p.h. and injecting a large quantity of unburnt fuel is lethal enough. The charge of fuel ignited, sending a blast of flame and acrid smoke through the crippled destroyer. Her engines, all power and the firemain pressure were disastrously lost as the fire moved outwards through the ship towards bow and stern. Many were trapped in smoke-laden compartments and several acts of great courage were needed to rescue unconscious and injured men. All her communications were cut and many minutes passed before flagship and force were fully aware of her predicament.

Arrow and *Yarmouth* rendered assistance, as did Sea Kings which lifted in underslung portable water pumps to help fight the fires, but all was in vain. The inferno was completely out of control and though the men fought long and hard to save her, Captain Sam Salt decided to abandon ship as the flames licked at the Sea Dart magazine, just four hours since the missile had first struck home. *Arrow* touched on to the hot plates of the destroyer and lifted to safety 225 men, whilst several others were evacuated by *Yarmouth* and the Sea Kings. In all, twenty men had died and a further twenty-four were injured.

Task Group elation at eliminating the *Belgrano* had dispersed in the brief flight time of a single Exocet: without early warning, we faced defeat. Accordingly, two of our nuclear submarines were soon to play a part little less significant than that played earlier by *Conqueror*. They were ordered to proceed, totally covert, to within a few miles of the Argentinian coastline and just off their main attack airfields. Every bombing aircraft that took off was to be checked by periscope and electronic intercepts, before being reported to us by radio. Such notice would enable us to shorten our readiness at appropriate times and significantly reduce the potential for surprise attack, even though we had just lost one of our three air defence destroyers. The early warning that the submarines provided by watching the enemy's front doorstep saved the lives of many men. That the achievements of *Valiant* (Commander Tom le Marchand), *Splendid* (Commander Roger Lane-Knott) and others were not recognized more emphatically after the war, I found a travesty.

The still-blazing hulk of *Sheffield* was initially left afloat to act as bait to attract enemy submarines. She was later towed away by *Yarmouth* before she foundered and sank 135 miles east of the Falklands. On the same day, Lieutenant Nick Taylor was shot down and killed in his Sea Harrier whilst attacking Stanley, leaving us to mourn our first Harrier fatality along with *Sheffield*.

Though sea command always left me with inadequate time for reading, the few books I carried for distraction included a favourite — an anthology of Keats' poetry. That night the poet's preoccupation with mortality allowed me to read a fitting epitaph to the first death toll amongst the Task Group:

108

When I have fears that I may cease to be
Before my pen has glean'd my teeming
   brain . . .
                          Then on the shore
Of the wide world I stand alone, and
   think
Till love and fame to nothingness do sink.

The losses had shaken us all deeply: we were vulnerable, and our heads were down. Despite the importance of Chris Wreford-Brown's achievement, *Sheffield* was planted deep in the subconscious; and the invincibility of the Royal Navy had been too readily dispelled. As the Admiral had previously commanded the shattered destroyer, I felt I knew something of his emotions at the bitter loss of his old ship — and a key part of his current defences. We might all have felt brighter had we known that two Type 42s, *Exeter* off Belize, and *Cardiff* in the Mediterranean, were even then receiving diversion orders to come south.

Walls of opaque vapour which then enveloped the Force over the next few days were a suitable reflection of our spirits. Although I lacked knowledge of the strategic thinking which was by then driving the war plan, I felt that the Group remained passive amongst the fog-banks out to the east for altogether too long. Depression was fuelled by the mysterious loss of two Sea Harriers on 6 May. Though the weather was clear aloft, there was a low band of cloud which extended right to the sea, and it was this that killed the two highly experienced pilots, both of whom were instructors. Descending to check a surface radar contact, they entered cloud and were never seen again. Whilst highly unlikely that both hit the water by mistake, it is very possible that a chance in a million caused them to collide in the cloud. It was a salutary reminder of the very high work-rate of the single Harrier pilot, flying combat operations in dreadful weather without the help of an observer.

On 6 May, Britain responded to the UN ceasefire demand by calling for the implementation of Resolution 502 (Argentinian withdrawal) without delay but offering no compromise in return. The UN valiantly continued its mediation efforts throughout the month but we had no doubt that, having committed the Task Force over 8,000 miles, Margaret Thatcher was not to be deflected from her aim unless the Junta cracked. Although the Group was held largely quiet to the east, *Alacrity* was getting more experience — and I was not complaining.

On 8 May, whilst *Yarmouth* was towing the still-burning *Sheffield*, we were sent to the gunline once more. Orders were received mid-morning and in the late afternoon the ship detached from the main force as the light was fading and proceeded very fast inshore to the gunline, totally covert, with only the relayed Force data-link picture for early warning. Having just received much-needed Intelligence of a large minefield in the sea east of Stanley — due to its segment shape it became known as 'The Cheese' — we swung far south before closing the coast.

Nobody wanted to spring that particular trap. Finally, we picked our way slowly past the cloying kelp — some charted and some showing as the slimy morass broke surface — and then we were on the gunline.

Our gun could create carnage amongst small groups of troop positions when its fire was being corrected by a spotter; but such control is the key. Firing blindly at planned target co-ordinates without any correction adds up to mere deterrence unless you get lucky. Nevertheless, the 4.5-inch shell, being more destructive than the equivalent size in field artillery, can still be a morale-breaker when delivered with no warning.

The associated gun-control system was a complex blend of computers and human skill, with the injection sequence needing to be fast and precise. With the computers locked to a known and prominent point of land, the spotter (either ashore or aloft) reported what the target was, how much firepower should be applied, and how many shells were needed to neutralize it. In the operations room, the spotter's data was received as part of their 'Call for Fire' signal that initiates such Navy support to land forces ashore. Co-ordinates were then injected, together with the ship's position, course, speed, tidal stream, wind, pressure, height of intervening terrain, and a dozen other variables. So many factors risked small input errors compounding quickly to produce an embarrassingly large spread in the fall of shot.

As an example of the price of failure, a good

friend of mine, and CO of another ship, was once engaged in a practice firing against a target being towed by a tug. He realized that incorrect inputs had been applied just as the gun fired. He then had the agony of watching his shells traversing his radar display directly towards *tug* rather than *target*; he claimed his hair turned prematurely white in the thirty-two seconds of flight. Although it was a perfect straddle, thankfully neither of the two shells hit the tug. The stoic tug skipper's response on radio reaffirmed that he was indeed *pulling* the target, not *pushing* it.

Our force spotters came from 29 Commando Regiment, Royal Artillery. Trained specifically to control artillery by observation from the ground or from an aircraft — and for the tense business of staying alive behind enemy lines to do it — they lived and worked with the Royal Marines SBS at Poole in Dorset and the habits of that adventuring élite certainly rubbed off. We were to get to know these swashbucklers well.

Mission completed successfully in the small hours of 9 May, we sped east to top up fuel tanks and magazines before dawn. We had fired ninety shells accurately into the target area and were heartened by the reports of our spotter in the Lynx. Such fast transits seemed always to produce the same slamming progress through invariably large seas. They would send my Engineer Officer, David Dyter, scurrying aft to check the cracks which had for some time been slowly opening in the lower superstructure and which were now worsening under South

Atlantic duress. Opening and closing amidships, they screeched like tortured souls, and caused him to return to the bridge where he mournfully reported our fragility and sought more genteel progress. Invariably I refused, offering him the Argentinian Air Force as the alternative.

Of all our tense and tiring business, there was nothing so bad as night replenishment at sea when we were already exhausted after hours of bombardment on the gunline. Navy policy in operations is always to keep fighting ships near to fully topped up with fuel — you never know where you may have to go next. This meant that underway refuelling was a nightly ritual after the high consumption rates of a fast passage to and from the islands. The drain on our Royal Fleet Auxiliary tankers was made good from the chartered commercial oilers who would tie up alongside to put hundreds of tons of diesel oil into dry tanks — a process called 'pumpover'. Taking the stuff back out of our auxiliaries in the combat area was infinitely more demanding.

★ ★ ★

The first challenge is to find your floating garage. Tankers and supply ships plough unswervingly through mountainous seas, indifferent to us tiny escorts. I have just been signalled my tanker for tonight, its relative position, and the time the sublimely complacent Flag staff expects us to plug in for fuelling. No excuses for missing your slot time, Alacrity. We slide through congested wake-torn water, cursing the

113

darkness and yearning to be free to use radar. A final calculation, adjust course and speed, cut under the huge dark bows bearing down out of the night, and swing wide to settle 500 yards astern. Each ship is fully darkened, rolling heavily and zigzagging every few minutes. This is a special challenge.

Increase speed to 22 knots and start my approach to the tanker. Where the hell is she? Faint dark shape in the night. Hope to God we are stepped off far enough. Keep the speed and cut through the underwater pressure and suction waves fast, before they can affect us.

'Now, sir,' intones the Navigator, despite the fact I can hardly see the tanker. Chop engine power and match her ordered speed. Cumbersome in our foul-weather clothing, we move reluctantly out to the bridge wing, being instantly cut to the bone by the elements. The wind screams through rigging and aerials; eyes strain. Still just a vast darkened blur: the two tiny red lamps placed on her masts to help judge alignment are useless. Am getting much better alignment from the dim white wash of her waterline. A clear night with a good moon would be no problem. When did we last have one?

Now we are up against the towering bulk. Slide in to less than 150 feet, wait for the gunline to be fired across the foaming gap between the two ships. Aim is bad. The snaking line fails to counteract the driving wind and rain — it falls short. Hold position whilst the soaked men up on the bows try again. Eventually, success: the thin white cord curves out across their replenishment position. It's in hand. Ropes start running between us: telephone cable, illuminated distance indicator line and, finally, the replenishment gear itself. Tuck the ship in even closer and make their task easier. We seem to be almost rubbing against her.

It takes forever, until the phallic fuel probe starts inching out towards our waiting receiver. Then a sudden rogue wave slams the two ships closer together just as the probe mates with the receiver cup. An octopus of writhing hose tentacles surges around our replenishment point and men scurry from the danger. Eventual connection is greeted with almost orgasmic relief by us all. I recall a grizzled Chief Boatswain's Mate confessing to me that 'a good fast coupling in a heavy seaway beats anything you can get for a fiver in Union Street'. His reference to the red-light area of Plymouth was vivid, if not lyrical. We have been at sea for more than thirty days and nights; there is no man who does not crave a more fleshly mating — though anybody who can focus upon such delights in this freezing wind must have the libido of Casanova.

Check for security — the mating is secure — start pumping — we need an hour's worth. No time for respite; the next zigzag course change is due. Signal lamp chatters. His siren sounds and his vast bulk starts to swing: I try to match the slide with a string of tiny course corrections — and without colliding. Inside the shelter of the bridge, the quartermaster obeys my helm orders, eyes locked upon his compass repeater, soaked with sweat at the concentration

115

involved and the strain of dozens of control movements every minute. We settle to the new course with relief.

Out on the wing, we hunch frozen with our breath vapour clouding about our heads. Sleet and sea seek out every seam in our foul-weather clothing and the vicious wind pulls angrily at our lungs. We incline away from it, cursing.

The Navigator advises me constantly; speed, position, distance and unexpected emergencies or malfunctions. Tonight is bad. Already blowing Force 7 and the seas mounting up, broken and mean. I divide control of the ship with him, myself giving the wheel orders whilst he controls the engines. Total interdependence: total trust.

Heavy loops of fuel-laden hose sag and extend between the two corkscrewing vessels. How many hours have we by now spent exposed to the winter elements, the better to detect a sudden sheer between ships? We console ourselves by looking down upon huddled sailors, frozen to their ropes, lashed tight with lifelines, swept constantly by icy water, and cut by ever-present wind. They huddle immobile, staring up covetously at the relatively dry deck of the tanker. Swilled by torrents of icy water, they cannot make even one sudden move on the icy decks for fear of a terminal slide into the deep. Night after night now, I have watched their hunched forms etched against boiling phosphorescence and have marvelled at their stamina. A life on the ocean wave is, in the South Atlantic of May 1982, a thoroughly acquired taste.

After fuelling, we often had to repeat the entire sapping ritual and top up our ammunition from an equally hard-worked *Fort Austin*. Although we always had to go and get fuel, ammo could come much more easily by helicopter. My sailors yearned for the ship to be provided with a Sea King to do the transfer by underslung loads. That's modern warfare — never, ever, enough helicopters.

On 9 May, *Coventry*'s Sea Dart missiles shot down two Skyhawks and a Puma helicopter, but it was from *beneath* the sea that a tremor was felt throughout the force when several ships achieved a sonar detection on the same day. From its short-alert condition, our Lynx was quickly atop the good contact. It seemed a valid target, and Rob Sleeman selected a torpedo to drop. I listened with satisfaction to the cool exactitude of the radio exchanges between Rob and our controller.

'Half a mile to run: check height, check switches.'

'Checked.'

'Stand by for weapon release. Stand by. Now.'

'One Bloodhound loose. Orbiting.'

Alacrity had released her first warshot homing torpedo. We listened to the beast circling its target, sniffing for detection on its sonar, seeking lock-on and attack. But there was no explosion and, after the full running time of the torpedo motor, we heard no more. Subsequent search of

117

the area revealed a huge tangle of thick kelp, disappearing down deep into the black ocean. It looked as if we had tried to weed Neptune's garden the hard way. That night we were back south of Stanley with the Lynx airborne on a different task, spotting our gunfire — but he was unable to sight the enemy. It had been a frustrating day.

At least some aggression had been restored to the Force. *Coventry* and *Broadsword* formed a newly conceived Type 42/Type 22 combination (Combo) and were sent inshore on 10 May to a position off Stanley to shoot down enemy night resupply flights.

Also on the same day, the *Narwhal* had cause to regret that she had not heeded my earlier warning. Detected on radar, strafed and then bombed by Sea Harriers, she was boarded by Special Forces from 846 and 820 Sea Kings. Thankfully for her, the Harrier's 1,000 lb bomb did not explode. Nevertheless, one man was killed, eleven were wounded, and the *Narwhal* was taken as a prize with twenty-three prisoners. Meanwhile, *Glasgow* blooded her 4.5-inch gun, sending 222 shells into troop positions in and around Moody Brook whilst, further round the coast, *Coventry* shelled Stanley and claimed two Skyhawk kills with Sea Dart. Her boyish and likeable captain, David Hart-Dyke, must have been elated at his success, matching the earlier efforts of his Lynx against the Sobral.

But I remained desperate for real action, to dispel the shadows of Sheffield and to allay doubts from our first air attack. My frustration spilled over into private criticism of the Admiral. Why did he not detect the mood, generate some action, and restore spirits? I was guilty of missing the big picture. His pause was designed to allow the amphibious southcomers time to move further across the great chart of the Atlantic; to exert pressure upon the Menendez Garrison; and to conserve our ships and aircraft for the one event that really mattered — invasion. Had I but known that *Alacrity* would be the ship selected to re-grasp some initiative, I would have been less restive.

4

Night Hunting

10 – 19 May

'A night is but small breath
and little pause'

ON 10 May, we received special orders. *Alacrity* was directed to detach from the Task Group under cover of dense fog before proceeding far to the west, probing harbours and inlets along the southern coasts of East and West Falkland. As if that was not a risky enough venture, unescorted and without any equipment to detect enemy radar, we were then required to do more. Taking advantage of darkness, we were to enter the slim strip of water that divides the two islands, Falkland Sound, and complete the 50-mile transit to emerge ('or possibly not', remarked my Navigator when he read the signal) at the northern end. *Arrow* had been ordered to make separate passage to be off the northern exit to meet us in the small hours of the morning and to accompany us back to the Task Group ('or to salvage the pieces', continued my somewhat morbid Navigator). My ship's company were less than enthusiastic.

The Admiral clearly had a delicate decision to make: nothing ventured, nothing gained.

Putting an escort, even a relatively low-value one, between the islands was certainly risky; but he had to know more about Falkland Sound. Were the waters mined? Were shore lookouts and defences effective? Could he perhaps disrupt enemy resupply operations? Getting answers involved risk. My risk. But it was a good decision and would indeed provide gain.

So *Alacrity* was about to have the privilege of proceeding 100 miles further west, and closer to more of the enemy, than had any of our ships previously. We were to gather Intelligence and to locate, harass and destroy any Argentinian resupply shipping to deter future movements. My Rules of Engagement were thankfully robust and thus initiative was not curbed — but I felt far from blessed. Initial elation at being granted long-awaited action abated further when I looked at the chart. I had little desire to conduct even an unopposed night transit of the tricky rock and kelp-filled waters. Doing so between overhanging shores full of enemy troops, through narrow access channels doubtless well-mined, and with God knows how much artillery or aircraft ranged against us, left me feeling decidedly unloved. Tom Tubb summed up a good deal of the crew's feelings: 'Have we offended somebody?'

We departed the Task Group late on the morning of 10 May, grateful for the dense fog which again blanketed the TEZ, the two Olympus engines driving us at 26 knots wide of Stanley radar cover. I paid close attention to the data-link picture being relayed to us from the

121

force but fortunately the Argentinian Air Force seemed grounded. Once due south of Stanley, we launched the Lynx for his coastal probe.

Three hours later, having built up a good and uneventful picture of East Falkland, we continued on to explore the so far untouched coast of West Falkland. To say that we felt exposed was a gross understatement; never have I been so glad to proceed through fog. The Lynx again came up with no excitements and thus, as night had fallen, we could no longer stave off the moment. We reversed our course to enter the narrow neck of Falkland Sound. The ship was subdued.

Simon Thorp and I had spent a long while discussing the four-hour passage plan together. At one stage he tried to persuade me to take the tightest of the three optional routes through the southern choke-points. His sensible logic was that it would be less likely to be mined: my better logic was that it left us more likely to run aground before we had even started. It is axiomatic in risk-taking that you should always concentrate upon dealing with the threat you *know* to exist, rather than those you imagine. And so we took the safer navigational option after silencing our echo-sounder; the noise of its acoustic transmissions would certainly explode any listening mine on the bottom.

Before settling into the ops room, I went briefly to the wing of the bridge. Fog had lifted into low stratus cloud and the drizzle was continuous. After five weeks of open ocean, I heard again rollers breaking on a foreshore and smelt the rancid tang of seaweed. But the threats that lay ahead remained totally shrouded in darkness. I went below for our entry to what our sailors were cheerfully calling 'The Valley of Death'.

We entered the Sound at precisely 2300, more than 130 miles from meaningful British support. Progress through the southern narrows was uneventful, with Simon providing his usual precise commentary from the hooded radar display at the back of the bridge.

We were in the 'Ultra Quiet State', the minimum of machinery running, our speed but 5 knots through the narrows, thereby stirring only minimal cavitation around our propellers — thus acoustically activated mines would have to work for their kill. I had selected the time to enter the Sound with care as a little before high water, designed to give us the greatest depth between keel and muddy bottom, with the tidal stream carrying us quietly forward. Any magnetic mine would also have to work for its kill. We had half a dozen lookouts posted on the upper deck, eyes straining into impenetrable darkness. Any moored mines on the surface in our path would *not* have to work for their kill at all.

The ship was at full Action Stations, messdecks empty and silent: all men were dispersed in small groups throughout the hull — just a few eggs in each vulnerable compartment basket. We slid through the calm inland waters like a ghost. Like our own ghost.

Just after midnight, we launched the totally

darkened Lynx to go south to Fox Bay to provide a noisy and obvious diversion: from the bridge wing I saw nothing of the helicopter as it slid up into the blackness. I varied my position between the ops room and the bridge — not that I could see anything from the latter.

At half past midnight we were no more than one-third of our way through, and still in confined waters. As the minutes had ticked by, the mood of gloomy apprehension had eased a little. Indeed, I reasoned that a key part of our reconnaissance task was to assess the possibility of a warship achieving a totally covert passage of Falkland Sound. Perhaps we had invested our lonely task with too much drama. Other than stirring fearful images of our impending doom, the night had, so far, been uneventful. We all wished it to remain so.

★ ★ ★

'Radar contact, bearing 079°, range 5 miles. Moving north-east inside the channel. Speed 8 knots.' The sudden whisper comes from the surface-picture radar plotter. The time is 0035. We give the radar echo a track number of 0305 and its small trailer shows it moving the same way as ourselves at the same speed. It is large. Time to ready the gun.

'4.5s stand to.' I can imagine the stir throughout armament positions as men hear the broadcast. Damn! What is it? Whoever he is, he still has a few miles to run to enter the open waters just north of Swan Island. Once

there, where the Sound broadens from 2 miles wide to almost 10, I will have searoom to identify him. Our Lynx is by now far to the south.

'HCO. Invite the Lynx to come back from his gallivanting. He needs to earn his flying pay.' The helicopter control officer keys his transmit button and a laconic and utterly bored Sleeman responds from high in the murk — he is on his way.

'Increase speed by 3 knots, Officer of the Watch. I want to close the distance between us. Once north of Swan Island, if he still doesn't know we're here, we'll take a look at him.' I desperately want his identity.

Minutes pass.

'Range closing. Course 020°. Speed 9 knots. Large contact.'

We know that the enemy has some naval transports dispersed about the harbours. Night resupply by sea has to be going on between the garrisons. This surely must be one of them. But what, if anything, can I do to identify him? What is called for? Dash or discretion?

'Anything visible, lookouts?' I ask lamely.

'Black as hell, sir. Not a glimmer.' I always imagined hell had quite a glow . . .

An eternity passes before the radar plotter speaks again. 'Contact emerging from the channel, moving out into clear water. Range 4.8 miles.'

'I have him on the A Scope. He's a big feller.' Graham Baxter is giving me the reassurance that I need: the ship is held by our fire-control radar — we have a target. 'Watch him very carefully.

If he sees us and runs in around the corner, we'll never winkle him out from the foreshore,' I caution.

A pause. It is 0107 by the ops room clock. 'Track 0305 altering course to port, sir. Seems to be increasing speed.'

Damn! He must have detected us on his navigational radar. He's large: the Falklanders have nothing substantial. It's the middle of the night and he looks to be on track from Port King to Port Edgar. The weight of evidence is unmistakeable. This has to be an Argentinian resupply vessel. If I give him another five minutes he will be tucked under the radar shadow of the island and will continue with the war effort. If . . .

Bugger discretion. This is a rare opportunity going begging.

'Increase speed to 20 knots. Illuminate track 0305.' I crack the order. To his credit, Graham Baxter does not pause for a second. His buccaneer eyes glitter black; he is enjoying the hunt.

The blast of the gun is shattering: the whoosh of nearly 3,000 feet per second muzzle velocity as the shell leaves the barrel is very audible. For men not in the ops room and thus unaware that it is ourselves taking the initiative, it must be terrifying.

'Lookouts stand by, Officer of the Watch, on a bearing of 010. Stand by . . . '

'Mark' cracks Graham's voice as the stopwatch second-hand indicates the moment of starshell ignition. Up in the murk the shell explodes and

126

the parachute flare starts its spiralling descent.

'Nothing seen,' comes the report. Hell, what did I expect them to see at nearly 5 miles range on such a filthy night? I curse and give myself the indulgence of just five seconds on the loneliness of command. To me the choice is obvious, notwithstanding lack of positive identification. He has to be the enemy and I have to hit him.

'Take track 0305 with gun! Fuze VT low.' The time for hesitation has gone. Graham and the team snap straight into full firing routine. Challenge and reply crack back and forth. VT shell fuzes are set to explode less than 100 feet above the target, scattering shrapnel down across him, disabling radar antennae, weapon systems and resolve — slowing him to allow me final identification before I decide his destiny.

All checks are complete. The gun is ready. The ops room is now hushed. We are about to make our presence far from covert.

'Contact still heading west, sir.' Decided.

'Engage!' Firing in anger. The noise is deafening, cordite reeks. The rounds continue. Lookouts are reporting flashes on the bearing of our gunfire.

'I think we're getting hits,' breathes Graham over the command open line.

'Contact zigzagging, may have slowed.'

'Check. Check. Check,' I order. The silence is a stark contrast. Pause.

'Still moving steadily north-west, sir.' I have to finish the job.

'Fuze DA. Go on.' I speak exceedingly slowly,

127

as all death sentences should be delivered. I know my gunnery team. Their exercise firings in the Med in February were outstanding. We have to be hurting him badly. DA stands for direct action — contact — fuzes; each 55 lb shell will explode on impact, delivering mortal harm. If he is one of their heavy transports, he can take a large number of direct hits without great destructive effect. We fire five DA; five more DA; then five more VT air burst.

More reports of flashes through the rain. There seem to be some secondary explosions. Now the report that is chilling in its finality.

'Huge orange flash on the bearing, sir. Right up into the cloud.' But the cloud base is 200 foot!

'Radar contact fading on all displays, sir.'

'Cease firing.' A silent pause; our ears are still buzzing from the recoil.

'Faint noise on sonar, sir.' Underwater explosions? Graham, Tom and I exchange glances.

'We must get out of here. Officer of the Watch, increase to 18 knots. Once out into less confined water I shall be increasing to 24 knots.' I try not to think of the open sea — still a further 20 miles away to the north.

'Helicopter Controller, tell the Lynx to search the area and report before returning to us.' Our firework display has to be visible for miles around: I have no desire to be cut off inside such confined waters.

'Nice shooting, Gunnery Officer. Let me take you home.'

Some minutes later our helicopter reports flickering lights close inshore but nothing else. We have to leave any rescue work to the Argentinians and be gone.

'Recover the Lynx. Start the Olympus, please.' Any worries about the high shriek of the big gas turbines are irrelevant after the past few minutes. It is 0144 as the Lynx sinks back on to the flight-deck, by which time Alacrity is straining through the turgid waters, yearning for open ocean. There seems to be nothing to lose by increasing confusion, so I fire two starshells to float down through the cloud over Port Howard. With luck the garrison may think they are being invaded.

★ ★ ★

We came out of the northern exit just after 0230. 'Like a cork out of a bottle' was how Paul Bootherstone described it later. Poor *Arrow* had listened to the gunfire to the south and had imagined us lost. I ordered an anti-submarine formation, we streamed anti-torpedo decoys, increased to 22 knots, and zigzagged our way home.

As we closed the force, Admiral Woodward came on secure-speech radio for the verbal version of the signals I had sent during the action. I described events briefly and concluded: 'Whilst I am sure that Argentinian propaganda will tell you that I have just sunk an innocent ferry full of nuns, I assure you, Admiral, that we have just blown up an enemy supply ship

129

carrying a volatile cargo which will no longer help their war effort.' He was utterly calm and unquestioning, welcoming me safe home: I did so like our unflappable leader.

But there was more to the night than had been apparent. A year later, on a rainy grey afternoon at the Naval Tactical School in Hampshire, an Argentinian combat report arrived upon my desk. It was by the commanding officer of the Argentinian submarine *San Luis*. In his lucid record, Captain Azcaeta described being on patrol on the night of 10/11 May just off the northern entrance to Falkland Sound. He tracked *Arrow* as she made her approach and achieved a possible attack position as she and *Alacrity* formed up for the return. He claimed his fire-control computer was unserviceable, allowing only manual control of one wire-guided torpedo. At 0430, he fired from a range of 5,000 yards, aiming for the southerly escort — *Alacrity*. He reported that the guidance wire broke but that a faint explosion was later heard, which could have been the impact of the torpedo upon rocky shallows. Our speed was such that he could not achieve another firing.

I had no reason to doubt his word. His timing and position fitted our departure precisely. I had elected to return at our best speed, conducting evasive steering and towing our torpedo decoys astern. I had been well aware that our high speed precluded us detecting anything on sonar, but that was yet another balancing of risk: to have been still short of Task Force air cover at first light could have proved disastrous. It appeared that God smiled on *Alacrity* that night; but his frown had been terminal for our prey.

It was to be some time before we found out that our victim had been the naval transport *Isla de los Estados*, *en route* from Port King to Port Darwin. Newly commissioned into the Navy in 1980, she was 266 feet long and had a deadweight of 2,684 tons. She had been carrying military vehicles and a deck cargo of 325,000 litres of aviation fuel — which was her great misfortune. Twenty-one men died.

Much later still, I received word that the naval captain in charge of the *Estados* had survived and that he wished to hear from the captain of the British warship his version of events from the small hours of 11 May 1982. So Captain Payarola and I shared correspondence. His account was compelling.

Having transferred cargo from the *Rio Carcarana*, *Estados* weighed anchor and sailed from Port King on the evening of the 10th: an hour earlier and they would never have been seen on my radar and would have escaped. Their northward passage continued uneventfully until they were lit by my starshell, which came as a complete surprise. Thus the earlier alteration of course and speed that we detected must have been a routine track adjustment rather than evasion of their pursuer. He advised Port Howard by radio that he was under attack, believing it to be mistaken friendly fire.

Our very first rounds were on target, there being an interval of only twenty seconds before shells exploded above them. A succession of

131

shells then hit, igniting aviation fuel, starting fierce fires, then destroying the bridge. The ship was already listing 35° to starboard when he, the badly burnt Steward Sandoval, and Able Seaman Lopez launched a liferaft and abandoned the stricken ship. Having watched the *Estados* roll over and sink, they struggled to the shore; the rest of their shipmates drowned or died of their wounds, leaving only the three of them alive. Soon Sandoval was to die as well. The other two crawled to shelter on the foreshore where they huddled until 16 May before attracting the attention of the auxiliary vessel *Forrest*, which carried them to safety. The privation of those two brave men, willing themselves to survive in icy conditions, would make a story in its own right.

I reflected at length upon my destruction of the ship and her gallant crew. I had little difficulty in reconciling my duty to disrupt the Argentinian war effort with the death and destruction that my gun had unleashed. Nor, indeed, did I have any doubt that I was right in not hazarding my valuable ship by waiting around to attempt rescue of survivors: we were sure that the enemy lookout and communication system would grasp the situation, note the *Estados* as overdue, and conduct search and rescue. Nevertheless, when I held Captain Payarola's letter in my hand and transposed myself to his blazing bridge, or his lonely foreshore, I felt intensely humble that God, or the fates, had dealt me a kind hand — and him a severe one. How much can a man influence his own destiny? Does fortune really favour the thorough and the brave? Or is it all just a celestial lottery?

Nearly four years later I was to take another Type 21 — *Avenger* — to the Falkland Islands. On a calm still day I stopped her 25 metres above the wreck of the *Isla de los Estados* which lay in the slime of the Sound. The vessel showed up clearly on our bottom classification sonar, being on her starboard side with her back obviously broken. I reminded myself of the sacrifices of war, when men are prepared to die for country, cause, or dream. I said a very belated prayer and we went about our business.

★ ★ ★

On the following day, 12 May, amidst rough seas, there were brisk exchanges of action. Four Skyhawks bounced *Glasgow* and *Brilliant* just south of Stanley. It was not to be *Glasgow*'s day. First her Sea Dart failed and then her gun jammed, giving *Brilliant*'s Sea Wolf the opportunity to become a naval legend by achieving a hat-trick of aircraft kills in one attacking pass. Two missiles destroyed two aircraft, leaving their wingman so distracted that he cartwheeled into the sea.

Shortly afterwards the Argentinians levelled the score. Another four Skyhawks came in across the high wavecaps, jinking and sideslipping sufficiently to give the Sea Wolf computer a headache. Confused, the system baulked, allowing the Skyhawks to put a 1,000 lb bomb

133

into *Glasgow*'s midship section, just 3 feet above the waterline. Having entered through the steel hull, the bomb shot right through the auxiliary machinery room and out the other side of the destroyer. It carried away fuel tanks and high-pressure air lines but did no damage to personnel, other than catching the attention of the on-watch stoker. Captain Hoddinott had a major damage-control challenge on his hands.

Better news came from the UK: land forces were to be beefed up still further by the dispatch of 1st/7th Gurkhas, the prospect of which must have terrified Argentinian troops, together with the 1st Welsh Guards and 2nd Scots Guards, both drawn direct from ceremonial duties at Windsor Castle and Buckingham Palace. These forces sailed from home on 12 May aboard the liner *Queen Elizabeth II* (Captain Peter Jackson) to massive razzamatazz. They would increase the ground forces available to General Moore to 10,500 men. Whilst these last land forces were being delivered safely south, it was important that we warships continued to maintain the initiative, put pressure on the Argentinian garrison, and destroy as much of their resistance and morale as we could.

On 14 May, *Hermes* and *Glamorgan* further seized the initiative. Both ships steamed westward until just north of East Falkland before launching an SAS attack upon Pebble Island. The destruction of eleven aircraft, including six Pucara, and an ammunition dump made this a highly successful foray, achieved without loss. Once again our Special Forces proved second to none, delivered and supported with style by the Royal Navy.

We had spent 13 and 14 May detached to escort the damaged *Glasgow* whilst she fought to complete welding repairs to stem incoming water. Such hard work to make her seaworthy came to naught in a heavy gale on 15 May and she played no further part in hostilities: she would soon start limping home. Withdrawn to receive repairs from the newly arrived support ship *Stena Seaspread* (Captain N. Williams) and her engineers, headed by Captain Paul Badcock, *Glasgow* had to be fuelled before departure. The adaptable *Seaspread* secured herself at right angles across the point of the destroyer's bows and steamed sideways to keep the stricken ship stable whilst all the time giving her fuel.

Meanwhile, the unceasing low cloud and soaking drizzle impaired the success of bombing raids against Stanley airfield, Sapper Hill and Mount Kent on 15 May. That afternoon, *Alacrity* was rewarded for her sharp-shooting: the Admiral ordered us back to Falkland Sound. The prospect of returning to the scene of our fiery carnival was even more unwelcome to my bemused sailors than had been our first foray, so I teased them that the Admiral could clearly only trust one ship in his Task Group to do important business — I don't think I was too convincing. The Admiral's radio briefing to me was typically understated, he being the type of man who would describe the end of the world as a 'transitory setback'.

135

'As you appear to be part of the local Falkland Sound scenery, intend you insert advance patrol. Instructions follow.'

I had no heart for an obvious response, so I kept my peace. On secure-speech radio he amplified: 'Our Special Forces have a small job to do. Put them safe ashore inside the Sound, will you, there's a good fellow. Try and avoid a fireworks display this time . . .'

A little chastened by this postscript I thought I might add one of my own. 'Presumably you'd like me to enter through a different channel this time, sir?' I chanced drily. We both knew that an insertion in this area at such a stage meant that Falkland Sound was the intended landing site: if the main channel approaches were full of mines, then the invasion would perish. I wondered again if he only knew the name of one of his ships. Wouldn't one of my colleagues like a little excitement? In truth, I felt absurdly flattered that he was entrusting us again with so important a mission. Such is the bravura of youth.

Our insertion team was just what I had expected: SBS, SAS and 29 Commando. When they embarked, I was not surprised to see that these men — the élite — were far from being 10 foot tall: high competence often comes in innocuous packages. However, their boss really fitted the traditional preconception. Captain Willie McCracken, Royal Artillery, was cast in the heroic mould and loved it. A vigorous Irish action-man, he possessed a mane of hair and the wild eyes of a true adventurer. Captain

136

Chris Brown had been whisked off to another mission and now we were confronted by this scruffy man with a powerful presence; he was something special.

Willie and his team had undergone their blooding in South Georgia with *Antrim*, calling down the massive shelling of Grytviken. Then, between 1 and 15 May, they had been heli-lifted around a succession of ships, controlling bombardments from helicopters and sleeping on uninviting steel in dingy corners. In fact, we had been kind to Willie, as he shared a cabin with David Dyter. I suspect David was pleased to see him go: watching incessant stripping and reassembling of weapons was unsettling.

We received our detailed orders and I responded a little tersely: 'Milk run orders acknowledged. Assume you wish me to verify both east and west channels are mine free, thus intend enter west — exit east. Do you wish me to suss out anything else?'

Alacrity was to put Willie and his men safe on a rocky foreshore called Rookery Point in Grantham Sound on the eastern side of Falkland Sound. From there, he was to set up an elevated observation position and be prepared to live on a bare mountain for two weeks without detection. In the event, his patrol was to play a key part in preparing for the landings, despite being lifted out by helicopter after only one week in order to play an equally significant part supporting the later advance of our land forces. I was to hear his cool voice over the radio on several nights, calling down death from the skies, obliterating trenches, moving on, and repeating the whole process all over again. If ever a man deserved his Military Cross, it was McCracken. I was glad I was a sailor.

It was odd, really. We never understood why the Army wanted to sleep in wet trenches, in the freezing cold, waiting for somebody to stick a bayonet in them. They never understood why the Navy wanted to live in heaving sardine cans, hundreds of miles from land, waiting for somebody to squash them flat without warning. Certainly neither wanted to join the other. (As for the Royal Air Force, neither the Army nor the Navy ever understood them — and certainly never wanted to join them!)

I ceased reflection and concentrated on my task. All I had to do was to pass through the northern entrance, beneath the Argentinian observation point of Fanning Head, take my vessel and 200 men in amongst the rocks, put Willie and his team ashore undetected — and be home for breakfast. We pulled out our heavily pencilled chart and started planning. As we worked, more bombing attacks took place against Stanley airfield before the Harriers changed their targets, detecting and badly damaging two enemy resupply ships, the *Rio Carcarana* off Port King and the *Bahia Buen Suceso* off Fox Bay. The Argentinian resupply effort was getting a little thin.

Continued foul weather again veiled our approach to the islands, which we conducted at 25 knots. My poor battered ship pounded her way across a heavy, pendulous swell, pockmarked by explosions of sleet. Again we went silent on all emitters — I had no desire to be the only radar bleeping so far from the Task Group. Though uneventful by comparison with our first sortie into the Sound, the insertion was still exciting and entertaining enough. We had four hours available to us, this being the interval between high water at the entrance and moonrise at 0430. It would be tight.

Black and soundless, except for the hiss of water along the hull, we slid beneath the bulk of Fanning Head, all superfluous machinery stilled, Tynes running only at trickle power, and radar now sweeping. I had taken control up on the bridge as I wanted every visual and navigational cue available to me. In fact, the whole operation had only one flaw. We took too long.

Simon gave us blind direction from the radar, with myself hanging unnecessarily at his shoulder like an expectant father. He did a beautiful job but once into the mouth of Grantham Sound the radar returns from the rocky headland were a compellingly close distraction. The First Lieutenant and his team winched the two Gemini dinghies quietly down into the greasy blackness from where two of our more confident Leading Seamen, Walker and Hopkins, drove them the few hundred yards through forests of kelp to land their eight passengers.

The first boat returned at 0330 but it seemed forever before the second came back: I would find out why when we returned to the open sea. We started to depart at 0404, our silent turn being made with one shaft driving ahead, the other astern. Our bow sought the entrance and we were gratefully moving again, leaving the dark tomb of the *Isla de los Estados* away to port. Glances at the clock became more anxious. At 0420, the Lynx let go two flares as a planned diversion over Port Howard just as I swung the ship's head north to traverse the few miles to open sea. As I did so, a great pathway of silver snaked to meet us. Moonrise. I cursed one of the only cloudless nights of the South Atlantic winter.

'God!' intoned the Officer of the Watch. 'Lit up like the bloody fairy on the Christmas tree.'

'Lousy analogy,' I responded tersely, before needlessly telling Graham Baxter to increase gun and missile crew vigilance. Surely the opposition could not miss us this time? We sparkled from stem to stern as if lit by ceremonial floodlighting. What was it to be? Artillery? An intrepid nightflier? Or was the damned invisible mine to exact its revenge for Argentinian dead? Shoulders were hunched as for our first transit.

All we had to do was to follow our nice bright moon river to the sea. Resisting the urge to crank on to 30 knots, I reduced to a slow crawl — our wake was already an eye-catching slash across the shining waters. And so we picked our way, a glittering crystal cut-out, sliding below the Argentinian observation point of Fanning Head. And still they did not see us. When finally we slipped gratefully past Tide Rock into the South Atlantic, it was to a collective exhalation. I signalled: 'As instructed, made no waves. Argies idle.'

A postscript to the Grantham insertion was only made known to us much later. Having been placed safely ashore and having got halfway up the black hillside, Willie McCracken and his team stopped at the sound of approaching feet. Willie duly directed his men to group, ready for a defensive firefight, but then decided from the number of approaching footsteps that they were facing defeat. It was only giveaway noises from non-human throats that finally made them aware that they might have considered surrendering to many even more apprehensive penguins.

After her heavy night, *Alacrity* had her own distraction on 16 May. *Hermes* had a Sea King helicopter ditch with a major malfunction, but her crew were recovered safely. We were then invited to send the persistently floating hulk to the bottom — but there was a twist. As we approached the bobbing fuselage, we saw two live homing torpedoes still strapped to the inverted belly. Only in retrospect was the next hour hilarious, as I minced my ship gently back and forth from as far away as possible, carefully directing small-arms fire in an attempt to perforate the helicopter without exploding the warheads. And all the while, I could imagine the small talk in naval bars for years to come.

'Remember Craig? Silly bugger who blew up his ship with our own torpedoes. Should have been certified.'

As we finally watched the aircraft start its terminal slide, two hours after first ditching, my Flight Commander chuckled. 'If I'd been flying that thing, had to ditch in it, and then

141

get out of the back before it sank, 'twould have sunk like a bloody stone in seconds!'

That night, *Glamorgan* was inshore, pounding targets at Darwin, Fitzroy and Stanley. On her return, she reported the first counter-fire from 155 mm howitzers that the enemy had placed on the high points overlooking our bombardment positions.

Although the softening-up for invasion was achieving results, we were frustrated at still not being able to disrupt the overnight resupply flights into Stanley airfield. Their pilots made low approaches from the west, keeping engines running for scant minutes of unloading before taking off for their return. Such efforts made our attempts to shoot them down a little difficult.

On 17 May, I smiled wryly when I received a signal from the Landing Force Commander in the still distant *Fearless*, requesting precise details of our route and speed, and the depth of water, in Falkland Sound. I did not have to guess too hard at where the final landings might be taking place. I sent the same signal to both Admiral Woodward and Commodore Clapp: 'After three transits of north Falkland Sound, 11 and 16 May, have passed through all channels. No hint of mining activity.'

The same day, *Alacrity* received a flying visit from a travelling padre, earnestly trying to get round the parish of the force. Although one of my duties as captain was to conduct a church service on Sundays, we had not had the attendance of an ordained minister since leaving the UK. Having welcomed the chaplain,

142

I then invited him to move freely through the messdecks to talk with the sailors. An hour passed before my Master at Arms, the ship's disciplinarian, appeared quietly at my elbow and asked to speak. He was concerned that I would be unhappy with what was transpiring below decks. The padre was apparently preaching to my sailors that the enemy was no different from them, that we should be compassionate, that we should understand that they too were scared and vulnerable, and that we should constantly sympathize. My Master at Arms was quite correct; I was unhappy.

I invited the very sincere chaplain to join me in the privacy of the charthouse where, as I recall, I briskly gave him my views of command responsibilities in war. Men had to be hardened, made aggressive, de-sensitized. War was no time for moral confusion. I wanted arrogant, self-believing fighters. And I wanted them to kill the enemy as quickly as possible wherever they could find him.

I am far from certain that he understood my dilemma. But I am certain that he deplored the lack of Christian values shown by a commanding officer in Her Majesty's Royal Navy. Neither point worried me. Having invited him to come back when the war was over, to restore myself and my men to civilized values, I returned him to his ship. For those who must do the messy business, combat is not the stuff of ambiguity.

Ironically, Sunday Services were the only time during the war when I was emotionally vulnerable. In times of peace, my on-board congregation would comprise no more than a dozen men out of 200, and half of those would come from my officers. But, as weeks of war passed, numbers increased fourfold, despite many more people being needed at their duty stations or on watch. I invited attendees to contribute through readings and leading prayers but I always conducted the Service and led Nelson's Prayer and the Naval Hymn. Each time, I had a private fight for control as our words resonated hauntingly between the steel bulkheads of the dining hall.

Oh Trinity of Love and Power,
Our brethren shield in danger's hour,
From rock and tempest, fire and foe
Protect them where so e'er they go.
And ever let there rise to thee,
Glad hymns of praise from land and sea.

I often found it hard to breathe, my words choking in a throat suddenly gone dry with emotion and recall. The softness, tenderness and sensitivity that had all been tamped down deep within me threatened to burst out before the very men who were feeding off my strength: I just hoped the inner turmoil never showed. Once the service was over and I returned to the all-absorbing obsession called war, I was restored. Love, family, caring, all had once more been dismissed at a stroke. There was work to be done.

On 18 May, my birthday, I found out the reason for the delayed return of the second

Gemini boat in Grantham Sound. My ever-thoughtful First Lieutenant had decided that the ship was going to give its captain a birthday present — a piece of 'Falkland Rock'. A hint was dropped to our coxswains who, having landed the SAS, proceeded to search through the black shadows of the Grantham foreshore for a suitable piece. Stumbling and slithering in the shallows, one of them embarked a huge smooth boulder which rewarded his tenacity by nearly bursting through the bottom of the boat — it weighed over 80 lbs. Thus, on 18 May, I was presented with an exquisite birthday cake by the ship's cooks, together with my suitably painted present. It was, I believe, the first piece of the Falkland Islands to have been recovered and I treasure it still.

I had another birthday gift when the Carrier Battle Group, its supporting Underway Replenishment Group of tankers and stores ships and the Amphibious Group all combined into a thirty-two ship armada on the same day. We now had *Antrim* and *Plymouth*, fresh from South Georgia, the amphibious assault ships *Fearless* and *Intrepid*, and a further fifteen auxiliaries and STUFT. *Antelope* had arrived overnight, together with *Ambuscade*. The latter had run down to his critical level of fuel (10 per cent) *en route*, needing to take ballast to restore stability and contaminating fuel tanks with salt water in the process.

Amongst the auxiliaries, *Atlantic Conveyor* carried reinforcement Sea Harriers: the hastily formed 809 Naval Air Squadron (Lieutenant

Commander Tim Gedge) was equally hastily transferred to the carriers with the RAF Harriers of No. 1 Squadron. With due sense of occasion, the seas had abated and we were granted a rare glorious evening. Ship after ship streamed from over the northern horizon and my team were deeply moved, particularly by the spectacle of North Sea ferries so very far from home. At last we had the capability to do the job. There was no way that the Admiral would want to keep these fat and juicy targets floating around in the target zone — invasion had to be very close.

We took our assigned screening sector ahead of the ships with rekindled verve — verve that was sorely tested over the next twenty-four hours, as we acted as 'goalkeeper' for *Invincible* whilst the Seawolf-fitted escorts were out of the formation. Given that we lacked an effective missile system to defend anything, 'goalkeeper' was a misnomer. 'Sacrificial shield' would have been more appropriate.

As an aircraft-carrier's life involves a succession of fast alterations, one minute turning into the wind to launch aircraft, the next swinging back to make ground in the required direction of the force's advance, the goalkeeper's life is demanding and extremely wearing on nerves and machinery. We were rarely off full power, battering through seas that barely touched life on the carrier but which were, for a frigate at speed, shattering.

Scant seconds before our big companion intended to alter, she would give us brief notification of her new course. This meant that our calculation of the heading needed to stay with her, avoid collision, and always stay precisely up-threat had to be fast and accurate. And always we had to remain within 500 yards of this pulsating metal mountain that could cut us in half in a trice. The seas had been mounded high by 30-knot winds and must have measured 25 foot from crest to trough: the ship groaned at the sagging or thrusting impact of the hull through each wave. At the end of twenty-four hours, I and my bridge crews were exhausted and I looked at the Type 22 frigates, the regular goalkeepers, with new admiration. My personal view was that my ship was much more likely to damage the carrier mortally through collision than was any Exocet, but perhaps I was just tired. Either way, I never wanted to see a carrier again — ever!

Despite the weather, and the hard driving, all the different forms of war-fighting business went on as usual throughout my ship. On one night I felt I could stray from my command centre to view the Flight at work. I came unannounced and stood invisible in black shadows that wrapped the hangar. Above and around me hung the double-lashed impedimenta needed to support our £3 million aircraft that was by then bucking down through cloud and turbulence to be reunited with the only haven for miles around. The broadcast speaker blasted from just above my head.

'473 is cleared to land.' Masked green light etched the waiting figures curled like Olympic sprinters in the blocks, lashings in hand, willing their aircraft safe home. The white landing circle on the tilting flight-deck glistened with running seawater as the Lynx came sliding slowly over the deck, downwash battering even me in my remote viewing position. No lights at all. I could imagine the pilot's eyes straining for cues other than just the faint glow of the marshalling wands being wielded by the Flight Deck Officer. The crew's features were outlined against dim red-lit cockpit instruments.

I could see Bob Burrows maintaining his quiet commentary upon their positioning to his pilot. Together they typified interdependence: one man's mistake spelt total crew defeat — and salty death. The ship's stern was rising and falling up to 30 feet every few seconds, with a heavy corkscrew roll snapping the swilling landing area in an endless spiral. A final kick on rudder pedals, deck steadied for a second before another roller-coaster slide, and Rob Sleeman saw his moment. The 2-ton aircraft plunged on to the slippery deck. The harpoon fired from beneath the belly, engaging the steel lattice grid on the deck, whilst flight crew swarmed to snap home lashings around the aircraft: 473 had come safe home. I moved humbly back to the shelter of the operations room, leaving my flight crew to cope with the muscle-tearing task of stowing their charge within the hangar.

There was always a tension between bridge and flight-deck crews. Moving an inert aircraft across an icy, heeling surface was bad enough: inching progression by means of winch wires, lashings and physical strength was exhausting.

Superimpose the ship altering hard on to a new course whilst the move was in progress and you had a formula for likely disaster. The sarcastic tones of Anton Maguire were a fine antidote to any thoughtlessness by the bridge team. 'Nice one, Officer of the Watch. Don't worry . . . it is an *anti-submarine* helicopter after all. It should be able to kill them quicker — now it's down amongst them!'

Only once did things go wrong but even then the Flight minimized the consequences and we merely ended up changing two main rotor-blade tips. That the Task Group did not leave half a dozen Lynx on the floor of the Atlantic is the finest tribute to the men of naval aviation and the many non-specialist sailors who supported them.

A welcome batch of airmail British newspapers surprised us with front-page headlines of our Falkland Sound transit and the sinking of the *Isla de los Estados*. The bragging tone of several of the tabloids was less welcome, inaccurately presenting our transit as an overt defiance of the Argentinians, complete with amplified taunts to the opposition to 'come and get us'. One tabloid had three-inch type on the front page — 'SUNK!' followed by: 'Captain Chris sinks Argie tanker'. Sadly, alongside the report was a full-face close-up of a toothless saluting guardsman supporting another story. My new Leading Steward endeared himself to me by muttering sympathetically: 'Never mind, sir; they could have put a topless dolly bird there from page three. That would really have blown your reputation.'

Within the ship, normality remained suspended for all of us. Tired lives were punctuated only by watch on, watch off; and the nerve-jangling shrieks from the main broadcast alarm calling everyone to Action Stations. My men worked two watches of seven hours, followed by two of five hours, before starting all over again. Seven hours spent staring at a radar screen was the longest period in which reasonable vigilance could be maintained by even the most diligent — or scared. But it did at least afford those off watch the sustained rest that was so necessary once they had eaten, washed and stilled raw nerves. Following sleep, it was time to eat again and take in a hundred pieces of information before being entrusted with the watch.

Ablutions were a performance, shower and toilet time kept brutally short. No man wanted to go to the bottom of the sea with his own bottom ringed by porcelain; so many remained constipated from a combination of tension and all too brief visits. In all toilet cubicles, Colin de Mowbray had diligently placed instruction pamphlets upon our survival drills, and they too were no inducement to linger. Dining hall and galley were the only social gathering points, with the upper deck cut off by clamped, watertight hatches. Sailors queued along the aluminium servery, collected vast portions and mixed freely at the few tables. The senior ratings had their own semi-privacy next door, whilst the officers ate in the wardroom one deck above. As is traditional, I ate alone in my cabin. I remember

150

the food not at all, despite the excellence of our chefs; all meals were snatched and thus unenjoyable. No relaxation, just all-consuming work — or sleep. Between the two, there remained only food or ablutions. Undoubtedly, this Jack was becoming a very dull boy.

But life was pretty dull for all. Despite imaginative efforts to vary jobs undertaken by men on watch, most were deep specialists who could rarely be separated from their key equipment. One slip from one sailor and we could all die. Each individual knew it. This was true male bonding — the highest expectation of each other. Hang together we surely would.

After *Sheffield*, many men slept in their flame-proof action coveralls but I laid down no compulsory regime. Indeed, in my short periods of true rest, I donned pyjamas in the belief that my insincere nonchalance would somehow impart confidence, if only to me. At least I felt that Noël Coward would surely have done the same.

At Action Stations the ship looked like a jumble sale. Bedecked with our personal survival equipment, we were cynical of our chance of achieving a successful escape up narrow ladders in an emergency. I remember goading the engineers about the sepulchral coldness of the ship which seemed little above the near-freezing temperatures outside the hull, and asking what was wrong with our steam heating. David Dyter's logic was impeccable: if we were to be plunged into the South Atlantic, we had best be appropriately dressed to minimize the change in temperature. I conceded the point but his good sense did not lessen my discomfort as I froze, immobile, at the command display.

At our hips hung respirator bags from which most people had long ago discarded their gas masks, replacing them with extra socks, gloves, nutty bars and even paperbacks for the quieter moments. As for myself, I had a particular weakness: Stonewall Jackson may have spent much of the American Civil War sucking on lemons from his saddlebags to keep awake, but for me it was extra-strength mints that nestled in my respirator haversack.

Despite air-conditioning, the atmosphere always seemed sweaty and stale. Ship aromas of oil, plastics and polish were joined by a hint of collective anxiety. Though Colin maintained an excellent daily broadcast of general events to the ship's company, I also chose to make my own fairly frequent transmissions to reassure them upon the more major events. One well-established senior rating always made a point of coming to me nightly in the operations room and quietly asking if it was safe for him to turn in. It was rather touching, as if somehow the 'Old Man' had divine notice of impending attack. Clearly, nerves were fraying.

I learned to recognize the men who thrived on stretching themselves to the limit — and the very few who revelled in self-pity. Above all, I admired the unexcitable: those who steady events merely by their presence and who do not need the reassurance of their decisions being constantly endorsed. I was reminded yet again that a leader is useless unless he can communicate: he must be able to control, to inspire, to influence. Most of all, combat calls for the brutal 'prioritizer', who eliminates the fanciful, ignores the unachievable, and swiftly identifies the possible.

The tempo of life varied greatly between individuals, depending upon their job. Stokers might spend most of their on-watch time touring machinery spaces checking temperatures, pressures, revolutions and readings, thereby becoming the fittest men in the ship. Damage-control parties gathered in small groups at their assigned positions waiting for the unthinkable to happen. Drills for fire-fighting, shoring buckled hatches, evacuating blind and desperate men were all conducted until ingrained, and the potential distractions of darkness, of smoke and gore, had been theoretically minimized.

In contrast, there were several remote watchkeepers entombed deep in the hull who were required to stay lonely and brooding with only fear and imagination for company. A tiny claustrophobic switchboard or the darkly clattering steering gear compartment were at the heart of loneliness. These men were the truly brave, for solitude unrelieved by the presence of others is the greatest test. In war, it should be minimized whenever possible. But there was no solitude in the operations room. Glowing radar screens were scoured and re-scoured for the faintest paint that might be a 400-knot aircraft or a 600-knot missile. Ship positions were plotted and checked. Equipment was tuned to the optimum: just one frequency misaligned could mean a lost contact — and a lost ship. Many men — one sense of purpose.

Through all this striving, the captain is virtually sustained by expectation, eyes follow him everywhere. In war, as in peace, he is still the hub of activity, but in war his people watch him constantly, not only to draw confidence, but also to glean clues to future events. If he weakens, they will chart his fall with anxiety, watching his every reaction. If he stays strong, they feed off his spirit and his resilience. Every trait of his character remains in stark focus, being magnified many times over. Though it can be draining, it is a fundamental source of his strength and resolve.

Just occasionally the good commanding officer plays up to it. And it is important to do so. I can be (some say often am) idiosyncratic, and certainly believe that the colourful phrase communicates rather better than dull brevity. A vivid cliché or a little dramatization does no harm; indeed it often holds the attention and inspires. Dry understatement has little place in inspiring and encouraging young men in the face of adversity. Hence my directive to my Weapons Engineer, Mel Purvis, to paint our Exocet launcher rails with huge black letters which spelled the names of our targets — the primary Argentinian warships.

All-absorbing command thankfully leaves no room for self-pity, for fear, for self-doubt, or for fatigue. Set the standards, set the pace: a probing question here; praise there; a mild rebuke to this man; much-needed encouragement to that. Always meagre 'carrot' and cushioned 'stick'. There is no need to drive people in war, they need playing like an orchestra.

Each ship is but an extension of its captain. When not planning, delivering and refining orders, he is pushing his mind to outmanoeuvre the enemy. Mental activity is constant, sleep rare, motivation immense, performance hugely enhanced. War makes weak men weaker; strong men stronger. Such uplift is usually overlooked by those preparing for combat, who often dwell too long upon self-doubt and the likely effects of fear and fatigue. Indeed, constant activity is the perfect antidote to fear — hence my admiration for those who stood alone in semi-darkness with no relieving distraction. All too rarely did I walk the silent steel decks in the quiet hours, stopping to ease the tension of weary watchkeepers. I was remiss.

The man in command in the Royal Navy is well supported by a structure built on tradition, sustained by habit, and stiffened by the strict Naval Discipline Act. These things lie on the air like a stabilizing cloud, holding everything together within the framework of community. But he himself is well trained for it: sea command in peace is nearly as demanding as that in war. Coping with fatigue night after night, having been called from inadequate sleep by a nervous or uncertain Officer of the Watch, demands fast and accurate decisions despite tiredness. And the captain's accountability remains absolute: the 'buck' for everything that happens in the ship starts and stops with him — the reflected glory of his people's achievement and the total responsibility for every failure alike.

As I reflected on such things, the conclusion was always the same. No life would be lost by any omission or oversight by me, nor would my ship let any opportunity go begging to contribute to swift victory. And, with the help of God, I would one day bring all my people safe home.

5

War of Attrition

19 – 31 May

'Now all the youth of England
are on fire'

WEDNESDAY, 19 May, saw the last reshuffle of men and equipment prior to invasion, during which we suffered more fatalities when an 846 Sea King carrying SAS troops crashed, killing twenty-two men. Attributed to a large bird striking the transmission, the loss of such deep specialists was dire as well as tragic.

Just after lunch on 20 May, the amphibious ships detached to the west for San Carlos, their advance restricted to a lowly 12 knots by the transports. Operation Sutton, re-invasion of the Falkland Islands, was about to commence. Meanwhile, the carriers and escorts continued south-west at speed, keeping our key leviathans from harm, with poor *Alacrity* still tearing around dementedly as aspiring goalkeeper. That night *Glamorgan* acted as a diversion south-west of Stanley, designed to convince the enemy that she was the precursor to invasion; nearly 200 shells aided her performance. By then, our fourteen gunships had fired more than 1,500 shells: a total of 7,291 would be expended before the end of the war. But there was to be a pause of four days in gunline activity: all escorts were needed for other things.

At last we were allowed to share the command's confidence. The Carrier Battle Group, including *Alacrity*, was to remain intact out to the north-east, whilst the invasion was to take place through San Carlos Water on the night of 20/21 May. Willie McCracken and his boys had done their business well. The Landing Force Commander, Brigadier Julian Thompson, with his headquarters staff would control the main military assault force from *Fearless*. The amphibious ships accompanying him were *Intrepid*, *Stromness* (Captain Barrie Dickinson), *Sir Galahad* (Captain Peter Roberts), *Sir Geraint* (Captain David Lawrence), *Sir Tristram* (Captain G. R. Green) and *Sir Percivale* (Captain A. F. Pitt), together with the merchant ships *Canberra*, *Norland* (Captain M. Ellerby) and *Europic Ferry* (Captain C. J. C. Clark). Their fighting escorts were *Antrim*, *Broadsword*, *Brilliant*, *Plymouth*, *Yarmouth*, *Argonaut* and *Ardent*. Screened by *Fort Austin*'s anti-submarine helicopters, these ships were sailing into the consciousness of millions of people around the world as they set course for their appointment with the Argentinian Air Force.

It must have been tricky for the Admiral to decide which fighting ships should enter the inevitable cauldron of the beach head. Was it best to maintain the established team who had escorted the invasion ships south? Or to take warships from the Carrier Group, battle-hardened by three weeks of combat? Several COs felt he got it wrong, but hindsight is easy. Personally, I would have put the hardened escorts into San Carlos: warships need to be combat-forged in the high temperatures of war to be fully effective. There is, of course, no certainty that any of the established escorts would have done any better than did those newcomers, but three weeks of high-intensity combat is a long time. I shall always feel a particular sympathy for those ships that had to do their conditioning under tenacious attack in what was to become known as 'Bomb Alley'. I told my ship's company of the planned invasion but most of them already knew: secrets do not flourish in a ship at sea.

Earlier storms had abated and the skies had cleared apart from faint hooked fingers of high cirrus cloud. The west was suffused with purple, then lilac, and then deep pink. It was a rare and glorious sunset and foretold the unwelcome clarity of the following dawn.

Later that night, under still clear but moonless heavens, the invasion ships slid silently into Falkland Sound. Alan West led the way in *Ardent* at 2000, followed two hours later by the 12,000-ton bulk of *Fearless* and then *Intrepid*. The two stubby assault ships, each with a complement of 600 men swollen by their military passengers, were tense and expectant after weeks of waiting. They entered at 2245 and were already docking down by 2330, allowing their landing craft to float out for the assault.

Thereafter, ships entered in succession, *Brilliant* bringing up the rear at midnight, with her greedy Sea Wolf sniffing for more prey in the dark skies. But everyone knew it would be the onset of dawn that would bring intruders from the west.

The Argentinian lookouts up on Fanning Head paid dearly for their continued inattention: an SBS Group was lifted ashore by two helicopters, one of which was piloted by Ian Stanley. They hit the observation point immediately after the fall of 268 shells from *Plymouth* to find twelve enemy dead and nine wounded. Below the shattered position, the majestic bulk of *Canberra* was just filling the night skyline.

The landing force divided into two groups: 3 Para and 42 Commando went ashore at Port San Carlos, whilst the men of 40 and 45 Commando landed at San Carlos itself. Landings commenced at 0400 and, by 0530, the squat little logistical landing ships that *Antelope* had escorted south were also entering the Sound. The waters off San Carlos were becoming congested, with *Norland*, *Stromness* and *Canberra* anchored in a line, and *Fort Austin* tucked in close to the shore. *Ardent* proceeded into Grantham Sound, ready to bombard Goose Green from first light.

At dawn, Simon Thornewill's Sea Kings started what was to become an almost endless resupply operation, lifting weapons, stores and men to establish the beachhead. Seven Sea King 4s were to carry 520 men and 288 underslung loads in one day. Artillery and air

160

defence went first, followed by the infantry, with work continuing at a frenzied pace as motorized rafts — Mexeflotes — were offloading munitions, rations, vehicles and fuel. Over the next five days, a total of 10,000 tons of ammunition and equipment was to come ashore, as Ajax Bay became the main supply dump and 500-bed military hospital. The landings had gone better than anyone had dared hope.

Out with the carriers, I followed signals, listened avidly to radio nets, and wished we were there. Though I felt we had become bit players, had I but known it there was plenty of action left for us too. Despite the Exocet threat being as real as ever, San Carlos was the new fulcrum. If the Argentinian Air Force could knock it aside they could still win. But enemy aircraft would have to fight through several layers of defence to reach their targets: first the Sea Harriers holding constant overhead patrols; then the encircling batteries of Rapier missiles being established on the grassy hillsides around the amphibious operating area; and finally the close-range missiles, guns and small-arms fire of all the assembled ships.

Compounding the attacker's difficulties — as it was always intended that they should — were the surrounding contours of the land. The 500-foot ridge of Campito and the Verde Mountains flanked the beachhead to the north and south. Thus low-level, high-speed bombers would have to approach from the north-west through a wave of fire from the warships. Failing this, they would have to swing wide before coming in from the south-east.

At dawn on 21 May, skies were bright and clear as the first Harrier defenders arrived over the anchorage at 0700. They held just west of San Carlos, remaining inhibited by a shortage of fuel, being nearly 200 miles from the carriers.

And then, with the first strong rays of morning, there came the Argentinian Air Force. Thereafter, *Alacrity* followed the action throughout the day from fragments of radio calls and signal intercepts, as if tortuously putting together bits of a complicated jigsaw. Sometimes there were sufficient pieces to give a clear view of the puzzle, sometimes not. The very tempo itself denied us much of the picture.

* * *

0840. Enemy propeller-driven aircraft — Pucara and some trainers — half-hearted attacks on Argonaut *and* Ardent *— no results. First SHAR in amongst the Pucaras; Sharkey Ward kills one. Early morning probe overland by our Royal Marines Gazelle helos — two downed by enemy ground fire.*

0930. First enemy jets — six Daggers from an early launch at Rio Grande; one explodes but Broadsword *is strafed — a 1,000 lb unexploded bomb punches into* Antrim *— finishes amongst toilet bowls of the after heads — none occupied.*

1000. More Daggers — one hit by Broadsword *Sea Wolf but* Antrim *cannon-raked in return.* Brilliant *now controlling Harriers. Dispassionate calls of 'Judy' (visual fighter contact with* enemy aircraft) overhead as SHARs snap into impossibly tight slow-speed turns, swivelling jet nozzles to decelerate — tuck in behind their prey — centre evading targets in head-up displays — wait for the growl of Sidewinder missile seeker head locking on as it detects jet exhausts — punch away Sidewinders. Skyhawk attacks on Ardent — Harriers intervene — Lieutenant Neil Thomas hacks his third kill. And it's not yet noon.

A pause, 42 Commando are steadily disembarking from Canberra as hundreds of pairs of eyes continue to search the west.

0115. Six more Skyhawks ultra-low level over West Falkland — they bounce the anchorage — two 1,000 lb bombs rip Argonaut — deep damage includes ship controls — she's nearly aground beneath Fanning Head. Now a gaggle of Daggers — great mix-up in progress — hail of ship small-arms fire — more Sea Wolf from Broadsword — now Seacat from Fearless — both miss. Brilliant is raked by 30 mm cannon — wonderfully cool fighter controlling — Graham tells me it's Lieutenant Commander Lee Hulme — only later do I find out he's working through the pain of wounds. Ardent has plugged 150 shells into Goose Green from 10 miles out — hope she's OK.

0144. She no longer is . . . our distant emotion becomes intense as our sister ship is raped.

In come the Skyhawks. One clips Ardent's masthead — leaves radar aslant — clears Seacat — now she's naked. Two bombs explode deep

163

in her hull — two more in the hangar — another unexploded in the machinery spaces. Curse bloody commentators safe at home prattling on about mistakes in attack profiles and bomb-fusing.

Lynx destroyed — Seacat finally blown skywards — the ship has lost all power — that means no gun either — she really is naked. Now heading for rocks at 18 knots — Alan stops her the only way he can — he lets go his anchor. Ardent is a dead ship.

* * *

As I listened to the radio nets, I imagined *Ardent's* final destruction superimposed upon the familiarity about me. A succession of explosions, steel ripping like paper, tossing men with horrific impact against equipment as valves and hatch clips jam solid with the blast. Blazing fires sucking greedily at everything in their path, resisting every effort to quench them with hose, extinguisher or foam. And always acrid, choking black smoke bellying through burst steel, as torrents of salt water from the ruptured firemain pour destabilizing tons high into the ship. Blinded, shocked and burnt men; all catapulted into chaos when seconds before there had only been order — normality. Now there is only carnage.

Damage-control reports relayed to Alan from the shattered stern led him to believe that the entire after end had been blown away and that a massive explosion of the torpedo magazine would shortly take her 200 men straight to the bottom. On the information available to him, he rightly ordered his people to abandon ship, he being the last to leave at 1500. His decision was fully justified by the Board of Enquiry after the war. Twenty-two men died and thirty-seven were wounded, nearly a third of their total strength.

Perhaps typical of the spirit of the ship was the canteen manager, John Leake. On declaration of active service he had effectively re-enrolled as a Petty Officer in order to man machine guns on the upper deck and to stay with his ship. His unflagging courage throughout the attack was rightly to earn him, amongst *Ardent*'s several awards, the Distinguished Service Medal.

As ever, our rescue Sea Kings were on the spot to help and, in a typical 'action man' performance, Surgeon Commander Rick Jolly — a dynamic surgeon from Ajax Bay hospital — was winched down to rescue badly injured men from the water. Tony Morton in *Yarmouth* gallantly touched alongside the battered Type 21 and lifted 142 shocked men to safety. At 0200 the next morning, the stricken *Ardent* sank to the weed-filled bottom of the Sound; her motto was 'Through Fire and Water'.

I remembered Amsterdam the previous Christmas; snowball fights and the cheery banter were more than half a world away. *Ardent* had been hit by seventeen bombs and missiles; not since the Second World War had any warship been the subject of such unremitting attack.

165

Thankfully, at 1430 came the last air raid of the day, an uneventful attack by five Skyhawks. Events had proved our worst misgivings about the tenacity and efficiency of the enemy air force. Five of our seven escorts were damaged, only *Yarmouth* and *Plymouth* were unscathed. *Ardent* was lost. Nevertheless, the enemy's preoccupation with warships, virtually ignoring the vulnerable amphibious and heavy transport ships, was astonishing. The beachhead was unscathed and land forces safely poised for advance. Furthermore, the Argentinians had lost 20 per cent of their attacking force — seventeen aircraft — and many more had been damaged. Neither side could sustain the attrition rate of that first day. Though the SHAR had again been our strength, ancient 20 mm Oerlikons and 40 mm Bofors had proved their usefulness — and no estimate was available for the thousands of 7.62 machine-gun bullets that arced into the skies over San Carlos that day. But how we needed more Harriers.

Overnight, *Broadsword*, *Coventry*, *Antrim*, *Brilliant*, *Canberra*, *Norland* and *Europic Ferry* all limped out from San Carlos: the first two to form their Combo off Pebble Island to improve warning and to eliminate some attackers before they reached the anchorage. As off Stanley airfield some days earlier, the principle of their joint positioning was the same — to exploit the effectiveness of the medium-range Sea Dart missile of *Coventry* without the distraction of land; and to protect her against low-level jets or missiles with the Sea Wolf, which

166

was capable of destroying supersonic targets. However, manoeuvring the two big ships close together was going to be a challenge.

On 22 May — Day 2 — Harrier interceptor effort was increased to sixty sorties, six more than Day 1: with the carriers rightly maintaining position 200 miles east of the islands, the SHARs were limited to less than half an hour over the Sound. The day before, they had been courageously running down their fuel stocks to maximize their time defending the ships, and then living on their nerves until they landed with tiny amounts of fuel remaining. Men and *matériel* transfers also increased, as the Rapier air-defence batteries were being dug in all around San Carlos. Those of us offshore remained preoccupied with the vulnerability of our comrades locked into the Sound. When Colin tried to get our Chief Electrician to stop carrying shells from the flight-deck to the magazine, he received an unanswerable response. 'Sir, my son is in San Carlos — on board *Fearless*.' The distracted father continued his labours.

Though clearly acting as the cork in the bottle of San Carlos, deterring and destroying, our ships were horribly exposed. Notice of enemy take-offs from our nuclear submarines off the Argentinian coast was being nullified by the fact that the aircraft launches were almost constant through the daylight hours. Attackers could make their landfall over West Falkland at ultra low level, hugging the undulating rock-face before bursting out upon the ships with only scant seconds of warning.

It was not a concept of operations for which our ships had been designed. Deep blue water operations in the north-east Atlantic with all the warning and defensive layers of a balanced NATO force was our business and had governed our ship, weapon and sensor designs. Given the circumstances, I was later surprised to hear criticisms of ship sinkings and damage. To me, the only surprise was that our losses were so few. For the entire invasion force to be placed ashore and screened without significant loss to themselves, and for the Argentinian Air Force to be neutralized by those ships and their aircraft, was a triumphant achievement. 'Nil-cost conflict' is a flawed concept voiced by the ignorant.

Further out with the carriers, more mundane business continued as we followed the inshore drama and awaited our next Exocet attack. As events ashore and the impressive performance of the Harriers made it all the more likely that the enemy would come again for the carriers, we were doubly delighted to see the arrival of another air-defence destroyer — *Exeter* (Captain Hugh Balfour).

All around the carriers, the air activity seemed constant: Lynx from the escorts; Sea Kings from the RFAs; and SHARs from *Hermes* and *Invincible*. Watching the carrier deck operations was always pleasurable. Launch was a tumult; helmeted pilots with visors down punched in co-ordinates to their navigation systems and gestured away the chocks; a green light

168

flashed up in flight control, the sweeping wand of the Flight Deck Officer cut away, and Harriers swooped upon the ski-jump before surging skywards. Glowing jet nozzles, retracting undercarriage; nose thrusting high — and they were on their way to 20,000 feet. On return, they would slide sideways into a high hover, perched delicately on four thrust columns gouting from the Pegasus engine nozzles, before subsiding wearily on to the rolling deck. It was hypnotic stuff.

Whilst *Alacrity* was recovering a stores air drop from a C130 Hercules on 22 May, more newcomers arrived. First *Antelope* appeared, accompanied by *Ambuscade*. An uglier new shape, *Elk* (Captain J. P. Morton), also showed over the northern horizon. Taken up from trade as an improvised ammunition carrier, she started calling us by signal lantern as soon as she was close enough for the morse to be read. A few moments passed before a very embarrassed Communications Yeoman Geere shuffled to my shoulder, holding his signal pad as though it were tainted.

'Do you know anybody on *Elk* by any chance, sir?' he enquired cautiously. The signal, from the Senior Naval Officer for me personally, was both funny and extremely rude. I ran my finger down the list of our expected STUFT until I reached *Elk* — all was made clear. Her Senior Naval Officer was none other than Commander Andrew Ritchie, who had been due to become the commanding officer of *Alacrity* on 2 April 1982. No wonder the signal was rude. Instead of racing around the ocean in a sleek warship, he was condemned to sitting on a slow powder-keg containing 2,500 tons of ammunition. My response was gentler and more compassionate — but also rude.

The relatively quiet day inshore prompted the Combo to split, leaving *Broadsword* to re-enter the Sound as *Brilliant*, *Yarmouth* and *Plymouth* slipped out to other missions: *Brilliant* and *Yarmouth* were going south through the Sound, the first Royal Naval ships to do so since our passage of 11 May.

The 23rd dawned with good visibility beneath fully overcast skies, prompting curses throughout the Force. It was *Antelope* who went straight in to San Carlos before dawn, escorting the first resupply convoy; four hours later her luck ran out as fast and as surely as had *Ardent*'s forty-eight hours before.

Her Lynx, having re-attacked *Rio Carcarana* in the approaches to Port King, was overtaken by enemy Skyhawks *en route* to attack *Antelope* herself. The shouted radio warning of the pilot was of little avail to his Mother. In quick succession, a 1,000 lb bomb ripped into her starboard side and another punched in below the bridge to port. Both weapons this time remained unarmed and nestled deep in the vitals of the stricken Type 21. With the attack beaten off, Nick Tobin took his ship to anchor in Ajax Bay where he embarked two Royal Engineer bomb-disposal men, Warrant Officer Phillips and Staff Sergeant Prescott. Whilst attempting to disarm the weapons, a massive explosion

170

started fierce fires, killed Prescott and maimed Phillips, and pushed the blaze towards the ship's 500 high-explosive shells. Nick's reluctant order to abandon ship was made just in time: the magazine went up within minutes of the last man leaving. Though she stayed afloat, *Antelope* flamed fiercely for much of the night before blowing up with a tremendous explosion in the small hours. Her back broken by the blast, she sank instantly: had she been manned, the death toll would have been nearly 200 men.

Her final moment was photographed and described later as the 'definitive image of the Falkland War'. That still photograph leaves me bemused at the public relations love-affair with television and the moving picture. The truly timeless images of symbolic significance that are burnt into the memory are those of the still photograph, not the mere transitory flickering fascination of television pictures.

My spirits were very low. It was little consolation that Lieutenant Martin Hale in his Harrier had destroyed another Dagger; or that the enemy Dagger force seemed to be losing about one-third of all their aircraft arriving at the anchorage. A second Type 21 had gone. To crown it all, *Alacrity* had just lost the use of one of her Tyne engines and, although I had ample flexibility using a permutation of the remaining three, I felt my ship was declining.

That night *Broadsword* went hunting for submarines with some Sea Kings; *Plymouth* brought out *Sir Percivale* from the anchorage; and we escorted in a convoy comprising *Sir*

Bedivere (Captain P. J. McCarthy), *Tidepool* (Captain J. W. Gaffrey) and *Resource*, taking fuel and essential stores into the amphibious area. *Arrow* was my fellow escort and I was in tactical command of the force. We formed up, placed the Lynx at fifteen minutes' notice for the air, and started our long and very pedestrian 14-knot passage. A short and vicious sea was running but I was frankly relieved that, having delivered our charges, we would at least return to open waters and the carriers. By then, none of my sailors was attracted to the Type 21 graveyard called San Carlos Water.

I became concerned that *Arrow* was slipping back in her sector screen, leaving a gap in our sonar coverage. Any loitering submarine attack would come in from ahead, and I wanted her to block it. Great chums though we were, I donned my headphones and called Paul on secure-speech radio with a simple message: 'Keep up or we risk a ship loss.' His response surprised and depressed me: his ship's hull cracking was by then so severe that it restricted him to but 12 knots, even in such a calm sea — his gallant efforts grinding alongside *Sheffield* to rescue her sailors had been costly. I felt embarrassed and admiring as I reduced the speed of the guide. For most of the Type 21s, aluminium fatigue cracking in the superstructure was creeping down to the upper areas of the steel hull, but *Arrow* was the worst, leaving Paul watching Atlantic forecasts with increasing anxiety in a far from seaworthy ship. I promptly forgot my few problems and biased *Alacrity*'s

172

patrol sector to cover some of his.

We delivered our convoy safely and retraced weary steps eastward. It had been a hell of a day which had left a second Type 21 on the bottom and expectation of plenty more fighting to come. When I heard that Lieutenant Gordon Batt had just been lost in his SHAR, I think I first became aware that I was tired. The intensity of twenty-six days and nights was just beginning to show. Paul was to stay in the calmer waters of the enclosed Sound. Later his ship was fitted with strengthening beams by the *Stena Seaspread* maintenance team, brought up from their maintenance haven in the east which was known as the TRALA (Tug, Repair and Logistics Area).

Ironically, that night I heard on the World Service that Iran had regained all her territory lost to Iraq since the outbreak of that war — a war that had dragged me from Singapore with *Alacrity* two years earlier. More than 100,000 lives and nearly £1 billion each month had been squandered to no effect. But I was destined to see further examples of the sins of Saddam Hussein.

Fifty enemy aircraft had so far entered San Carlos but none had attacked the stores and amphibious vessels. It was a fundamental mistake. They should have hit the more vulnerable ships early on Day 1 whilst their valuable cargoes were still unloading, and when the ring of Rapier missile batteries had still to be established. Perhaps they should also have tried harder to reduce our tiny force of Sea Harriers,

173

despite the SHAR's close-combat superiority. Either course, if tenaciously pursued, might just have turned the war their way. Although there was no masking the tenacity and gallantry of the Argentinian pilots themselves, post-war interviews were revealing. Their pilots felt it was their duty to go for the warships, to leave the way clear for follow-on attackers; and all of them had deep respect for the killing power of the Sea Harrier. Significantly, Argentinian radio was calling the Harrier '*La Muerte Negra*' — 'The Black Death'. Our land forces had been given just the breathing space they needed: establishing their base areas, setting up Rapier batteries, sorting stores, conducting final planning, regrouping — and preparing for the long-awaited move to the east.

On 24 May, at dawn, our SHARs placed a succession of lofted, retarded and airburst bombs into Stanley airport whilst San Carlos unloadings continued apace. The Combo was back off Pebble Island when the first attack arrived just before 1000, but this time it came in overland from the south — the enemy was about to change his tactics. Five Skyhawks put bombs into *Sir Lancelot*, *Sir Galahad* and *Sir Bedivere*; a second wave strafed *Fearless* and *Sir Galahad*, hitting poor *Sir Lancelot* with yet another bomb: whilst near misses went in all around *Fort Austin*, *Stromness* and the North Sea ferry *Norland*. The ferry was drawing praise for her pugnacity under fire, doubtless due in part to her spirited Senior Naval Officer, Commander Chris Esplin-Jones.

174

Though ship gunfire damaged eight attacking aircraft, it fell to the SHARs to level scores. Out of an incoming force of four Daggers, three were 'splashed' — Andy Auld taking a pair — and with them the Argentinian Dagger loss rate moved to more than 40 per cent.

As light faded the weather deteriorated, leaving the men of the Fleet Clearance Diving Teams free to move into the bowels of broken ships to disable unexploded bombs — the loneliest bravery in the world. That night *Plymouth* emerged from San Carlos, bringing with her *Tidepool*, *Norland*, *Sir Tristram* and *Sir Bedivere*.

Out at sea, in between the construction of our San Carlos jigsaw, we were all thinking about Tuesday, 25 May, Argentina's Independence Day. That the enemy would use the occasion to mount a morale-boosting effort was inevitable: we re-doubled drills, increased vigilance and waited for them to come out against us. We did not know that they had attempted an Exocet attack with two Super Etendards on the 23rd which had been unable to find us.

Sadly, the 25th again dawned bright and clear as Sandy Woodward took a balanced risk by bringing his carriers in to 80 miles to facilitate more SHAR time in the air. In 'Bomb Alley', early raids achieved no ship damage but *Yarmouth* destroyed a Skyhawk with Seacat, the pilot surviving to be taken prisoner on board *Fearless*. Better still, the *Broadsword* and *Coventry* Combo shot down two more aircraft off Pebble Island with Sea Dart

175

missiles and controlled three SHAR interceptions to successful kills. From their position, the two ships were achieving what had been so lacking — good fighter control unimpeded by land returns on radar. The concept, originally suggested by Captain Bill Canning, was working. But, at a little after 1400, they paid the price for such success.

If the combination was to work well it was always dependent upon two complex warships working in harmony under high stress, and such an arrangement was always open to failure. Some incoming Skyhawks were spared death-by-Sidewinder missiles when *Coventry* directed the Harriers to haul off their tail-chase in order to let the ship have a clear Sea Dart shot. A mix-up then occurred. The fast and low pairs of jets were not acquired by Sea Dart radar and then the Sea Wolf on board *Broadsword* became confused, denying that ship the chance of releasing her automatic missile. In the confusion, the ships manoeuvred across each other's line of fire, thereby letting the tenacious Skyhawks in for their kill.

The first attacking run sent one bomb ricocheting up through *Broadsword*'s side, destroying her Lynx; but the second attack was far more serious. Three bombs entered *Coventry*, all exploding deep within machinery spaces. Wide open to the sea down her port side, she was already listing as the Skyhawks departed.

As with *Sheffield*, smoke was intense. Within five minutes she was heeling heavily and within twenty minutes she had capsized: another nineteen men had died. Captain David Hart-Dyke escaped, albeit with nasty burns, and was the final man to leave — by the simple expedient of walking down the half-inverted side of his ship and stepping into the icy Atlantic. Sea Kings produced an exceptional series of winch rescues, lifting the survivors to safety. The City of Coventry had lost her affiliated ship but, less than seven months later, the ornamental medieval cross presented by the Cathedral to the ship and sunk with her was salvaged and returned to the United Kingdom to reside once more in Coventry Cathedral.

Later that same day, the Argentinian aircraft came again — this time for the carriers, which were by then even closer, having provided extra SHAR over the site of stricken *Coventry*. We were less than 80 miles east of East Falkland, well within the range of Etendard, which were now so adept at stretching their attack radius by air-to-air refuelling. Success against the carriers would win all.

Alacrity was in the advance carrier screen, patrolling our sector whilst seesawing back and forth in the deep, black South Atlantic swell. Air-warning radars were sweeping greedily for the morsel we all savoured — first detection of the enemy. Argentina's biggest celebration of the year was not about to become a carnival at our expense.

'Handbrake! Bearing 340°,' cracked the simultaneous reports from *Exeter* and *Ambuscade*. Every man in the Task Group now knew that the codeword 'Handbrake' was the Etendard radar — and that meant Exocet. Electronic warfare helicopters hurried to get out on to the correct bearing to jam the enemy radars; other helicopters dropped Chaff. *Invincible* was providing commentary upon the incoming Etendards. The time was 1537.

Exeter was our only picket, 20 miles upthreat of us and 25 miles ahead of the carrier. We piped Action Stations, men moved quietly to their positions, and we fired a radar echoing shell with our gun to confuse the enemy pilots. For the enemy radar transmissions to be detectable, they had to be within 100 miles, and closing at 400 m.p.h. It was undoubtedly another missile attack.

Out on our starboard bow, to the north-west, was *Ambuscade*. Right astern was *Hermes*. If she were to be sunk then the entire recapture of the Falkland Islands would die with her. No wonder the Argentinian pilots pressed on across the heaving cold ocean. Looming on our starboard quarter was *Atlantic Conveyor*, heavily laden with reinforcement helicopters, kerosene and cluster bombs. I thought of the four Exocets in their launchers on our own bows, of the 400 high-explosive shells left in the magazine, and the gleaming racks of homing torpedoes packed down aft. We would blow apart as readily as *Atlantic Conveyor* if we took a hit. My mouth was dry as we waited for missile launch.

I imagined myself in the cockpit of one of the incoming jets. Depart Rio Grande, aircraft heavy with fuel and Exocet, briefed on the latest enemy position. Medium-level transit 400 miles east, rendezvous with the airborne tanker, suck fuel, turn south towards the Malvinas. Fast descent with 200 miles to go — no radar on. First faint interception of British radar signals, hard descent again, right to the wave-caps, tucked in beneath the enemy radar beams. Keep boring in on a timed run, until within 50 miles. Zoom to several hundred feet and a quick transmission on radar. Relief at being above the sea spray and the buffeting turbulence below. Target selection: big echo must be *Hermes* or *Invincible*. Sharp descent again to avoid giving a single paint on British radar screens. Pop up for the final time. At last; let go the damned missile. Aircraft bucks with relief. Bank away and start the long, long run for home. Think fuel.

They had done their job well. It was 1538.

'Missile head radar! Exocet! Bearing 338°.' The cry came from *Ambuscade* and was repeated by two other ships almost simultaneously. Somebody's name was on this one. It had been a copybook attack so far. I altered course as we fired our Chaff rockets to distract the missile, turning flat-out. Swing the stern to him and check the relative wind. It needed to be exact if we were to stay within the decoy pattern. Let Exocet lock on to the decoys, not on to expensive and necessary warships. I could see the other ship radar contacts suddenly surrounded by their own fast-blooming Chaff echoes — sheltering under an umbrella of tinsel, ridiculous but effective. We waited, guns and missiles seeking a target; but we would be lucky to detect the slim incoming

Exocet in its final approach. We seemed to have been doing this forever. Where was the bloody missile? Who was he going for? Let it not be the carrier. Why so charitable? Let it not be *Alacrity*!

'Fast moving contact,' reports our radar spotter. '350° bearing, moving right.' The missiles were not coming for us. 'Contacts faded.' They were Exocet.

Then a pause.

'*Conveyor*'s hit; heavy black smoke aft,' reported the Officer of the Watch to my darkened command centre beneath his feet. Confirmation by radio and then by my Yeoman. '*Atlantic Conveyor* reports she has been hit by a missile on her port quarter, sir. She is assessing damage and will advise,' he explained pedantically. Assessing damage indeed; with cluster bombs and kerosene in her vast cargo holds she was in big trouble.

'Close *Conveyor* at best speed, Officer of the Watch,' I ordered. We were one of the closest: 'Hasten to help'. I was not worried about more Exocets; the Argies would not try to get through an alerted Task Group a second time.

Only long afterwards did we find out that the initial radar echo had been two Etendards in formation, very close together. Worst of all, they had actually fired two missiles, both now exploded deep in the big ship's entrails. Later reconstruction revealed that *Ambuscade* Chaff had seduced the Exocets, which had then flown on through it, acquired the huge radar-reflecting area of *Conveyor*, and mindlessly

180

taken their new target. As my Yeoman put it, with succinctness: 'Why didn't the bloody thing keep going and hit that water carrier, *Fort Toronto*? One bloody great hiss and nobody would have been hurt.' Though an exaggeration, it would indeed have been much much better for Admiral Woodward's Task Group if poor *Fort Toronto* (Captain R. I. Kinnier) had been the eventual bull's-eye.

To travel 3 miles took us nearly ten minutes: the Exocets would have taken less than half a minute. I swung wide, coming in on the quarter of the stricken giant, having moved to the bridge and taken control of *Alacrity* myself. The damaged ship was huge as we approached. Black smoke belched away in the wind on her port side: there was no way I could come in close there, we would all suffocate blindly. But to starboard, we would be exposed to the wind and surging swell that would grind us to paste against her thick steel hull. There was no real choice; starboard it was. Hoses and firefighters were made ready.

'Making our approach close up on to her starboard quarter.' I changed position to the port bridge wing so that nothing impaired my view.

★ ★ ★

The open air is unnervingly quiet after the cacophony of speakers, radios and orders inside. Momentarily, I seem entirely alone on the grey and desolate ocean — apart from the black funeral pyre that awaits me. We creep in slowly,

181

until the great black upperworks loom over the top of the bridge roof. Despite the low sea state Conveyor is rolling sickeningly.

VHF radio crackles into life. 'Alacrity — message from Flag.' Lord, what a time for the Admiral to get in touch. 'From Flag. You are not to endanger your ship in providing assistance.' The only occasion I can recall of Sandy Woodward backseat driving. It is a superfluous message. Nothing is more dominant in my mind than how we can help without taking mortal damage.

'Try and pass our headrope up to her. See if we can tuck up alongside.' I nudge the bows in under her side. Our gunline arches up over her deck edge and the rope is gathered in. Using one engine against the other, I slowly ease Alacrity up against the 18,000-ton mass of swaying steel. We hit with a grinding clang that shakes our entire length. Much more of this and we'll be a lot shorter. Firefighting is going on high above us on her stern.

Our hoses start to produce water, but cannot generate sufficient pressure, other than to cool a small portion of the hull that is starting to glow brightly around the steel plates. Paint starts rolling off in front of my eyes — the whole interior of the stern is ablaze. There is nothing to be gained by putting a firefighting team on board. Other ships are asking the flagship's permission to assist. Why on earth ask?

The bridge clock shows 1600; missile launch was only twenty minutes ago. Both ships swing together once more; the curve of her hull crunches our guardrails within 3 feet of my Exocet launchers. 'You are not to endanger your ship,' the Admiral has said. I know just what is on his mind. He cannot afford to lose the use of another escort; Arrow performed brilliantly assisting mortally wounded Sheffield but she opened up cracks that are now badly handicapping her. Yarmouth fared better alongside Ardent but she is sturdier and had been operating inside sheltered waters. Another resonating crash decides me. We cannot remain.

'Let go headrope! We'll lie off a few feet.'

We consult briefly with the now doomed ship on radio. They have just abandoned machinery spaces, smoke and flames being intolerable: 75 tons of cluster bombs are now encircled by flame. There is no way we can help contain the fire: it is already out of control. Smoke is coming off the steel abreast of us in angry streamers and explosions are thumping deep within the hold — cluster bombs starting to cook off. Their captain decides to abandon ship. Not a moment too soon.

Two jumping ladders snake down the ship side and the first figures in rubberized survival suits start laboriously climbing down across hot plates. I manoeuvre Alacrity off to 30 feet, having no desire to crush survivors between the two ships. Liferafts are plummeting into oily waves. Men tumble from the ladder end and swim, bloated with the air in their suits, to the six inflated rafts which await them: dayglow orange men and their matching dinghies surge and plunge in a whirlpool of icy water all around the leviathan's stern. One helpless figure slowly inverts and starts to drift away, his survival suit over-buoyant with unreleased air. We put our on-watch swimmer into the water, cutting through broken seas to the forlorn and sprawled balloon that is a man, before the embracing figures are drawn gently back to us by the lifeline.

'We can fire ropes across the rafts. Link 'em together. Tow the entire group back out of trouble, sir.' The shouted proposal comes from the First Lieutenant. Good boy! The quickest way we can save them all. But for God's sake, can they not come down that bloody ladder quicker: the entire hold is about to blow.

Liferafts slowly fill as we tower above the pitiful little group of mariners before plunging into the next trough. I work the engines constantly to keep us stepped off and yet offering them shelter from the elements. The last few are now clambering stiffly down the ladder whilst one of our Sea Kings is beating forward over the bows, slowly winching up those men who have been cut off forward. Brilliant and Sir Percivale are approaching to offer more help.

An increasing roar of high-intensity flames and explosions comes from inside the hull, obliterating the sound of our gunline firing its snaking cord across the liferafts. Pale faces look up forlornly and grateful hands gather in the cordage, securing it to the loops which ring the rafts. Take us away from this tragedy.

184

'All secured. No more survivors apparent sir.'
Colin gives me the assurance we are all waiting
for. The explosions are deafening. If our Exocets
cook off, there will be nothing left of us — or
Conveyor.

'Slow astern port.' I give the engine order
very deliberately. The bite of the single propeller
gently eases the pitiful cluster of liferafts back
from the plunging stern and carries our bow
away from them. I feel the breath leave my
body with involuntary relief as we are freed
from the time-bomb of Conveyor. I ease my
ship gently away until we are 200 yards astern.
One liferaft breaks from its securing line, drifting
under our bow. We call Brilliant *in to intercept*
him. I slow Alacrity *to a stop. Now we have to*
get the shocked men out of the water. It takes
another eternity to help the weakening figures
up the scrambling nets hanging over our port
side, by which time the light has almost gone
— except for the firework display that is Atlantic
Conveyor.

* * *

Logically, we were allocated as watchdog to
the flaming ship to search the surrounding
waters and report upon her blazing fate, whilst
Sandy Woodward quite rightly took his other
vessels away to avoid possible re-attack. We
had recovered seventy-seven men and several
more were lifted out by helicopter. Twelve
had died, including their gallant captain. We
also recovered three bodies. Their Senior Naval

Officer was Captain Mike Layard, one-time jet pilot and destined to become Second Sea Lord eleven years later. Admirable in adversity, he remained steady and cool despite the shocking ordeal and the loss of his close friend Captain Ian North. We signalled away the best information we had on the survivors, thinking of those at home who would shortly be grieving.

We too had been scarred. Caring for the survivors, we tried not to imagine ourselves one day being in their position. After all, we were immortal: for I had told them so.

Alacrity stood by the blazing, dying *Conveyor* whilst the South Atlantic darkness deepened. A Chinook helicopter parked on the flight-deck had long since burnt out: the still-glowing silhouette would not crumble but continued to stand, etched against the night sky like a photographic negative that flames and lingers before it shrivels. We zigzagged back and forth for fear of submarines and watched the ship's death throes. In spite of myself, I went on deck in the small hours and stood for too long unprotected against the cold. The once proud ship was melting before my eyes: a vast flap of her side simply fell away in an incandescent slab, as if she had just been disembowelled. I could watch no longer. I vowed it would never happen to my ship but I knew that, however prepared and however efficient we were, some great force beyond man would finally decide our fate. When later I slept, I was restless: *Alacrity* had glimpsed the ultimate reality of war.

We buried the dead at sea with full military

honours the following day. Our impressive young Midshipman, Johnstone-Burt, had grown up overnight, helping to sew the bodies within the ensign shrouds. I chose to conduct the burial service myself, feeling it to be my place — and easier on Mike Layard. The words were a blur and each slapping wave on our stationary hull was like a graveside volley. *Alacrity* writhed and bucked upon the deep swell, as if anguished by the tragedy and the losses.

So many survivors spread throughout *Alacrity*, *Brilliant* and the carriers posed problems in correlating casualty lists of dead and wounded men. Cross-checking was difficult and we were all conscious that back in the UK hundreds of anxious loved ones were yearning for news after the two tragic losses of the day. In Portsmouth, my cousin had heard an erroneous report of a nameless Type 21 frigate sunk the night before and had instantly driven to my home to be ready to console my wife in case it had been *Alacrity*. On her arrival, she was just in time to be reassured herself by my wife: news of the loss of *Coventry* had been announced — my cousin was married to Surgeon Lieutenant Oliver Howard, serving in the Type 42 destroyer. Mercifully, he survived the sinking. The timely and accurate flow of information to next-of-kin in war is essential.

Survivors' morale swung markedly to and fro. High on rescue; low on hearing of the loss of their captain. High after some beers; desperate after the burial of their shipmates. In conscience, it was important to say farewell to our new companions as soon as possible. There was work to be done and, in spite of ourselves, we had been sorely distracted and our morale hit.

On 27 May, all 133 survivors were to be reunited on board *British Tay* (Captain P. T. Morris) for the long journey home. Our laundryman, Mr Chang, who had bravely elected to stay with the ship, reconsidered his decision and left us as well. Who could blame him? He had just seen another of his countrymen buried at sea from *Atlantic Conveyor*, and it was not their war. The short operational life of *Conveyor* caused her to be known by her crew as the '30-day Wonder'.

Her loss was grievous in other ways. The Force had lost three Chinooks and six Wessex helicopters, together with four complete tented villages intended to shelter our advancing troops. The helos were to have flown equipment that would now have to be carried by men. Thus our land forces also had cause to mourn.

The events of 25 May had spurred the highest daily Sea Harrier sortie rate to date from the carriers — sixty-three by twenty-four aircraft. The Argentinians had been taking fearful losses and had far less bite than five days earlier. Nevertheless, given the example of one Capitan Pablo Carballo, there was some highly effective snapping to come: so far he had near-missed *Ardent*, had hit *Antelope* and had successfully bombed *Coventry*.

That night — the 25th — *Glamorgan* scattered bitter gunfire amongst the enemy outside Stanley, whilst *Plymouth* ensured that the Fox Bay garrison on West Falkland paid for our grief. Below decks in *Argonaut*, Fleet Clearance Divers were still fighting to get at the 1,000 lb bomb in her missile magazine. *Arrow* emerged from San Carlos, escorting *Fort Austin*, *Stromness*, *Resource*, *Tidepool* and *Sir Percivale*. We could tell that the land forces were about to move off. Not much sleep was being achieved anywhere.

★ ★ ★

My time of rising was dictated by the time I had turned in. A night convoy or a spell on the gunline, always followed by replenishment, saw *Alacrity* tuck back into her screening station just before dawn, and her captain tuck himself in at about the same time. Colin would spell me and I would sleep like the dead for four or five hours — if I was not called sooner by an air-raid warning.

Once roused, the day began fast: a brief shower, a fresh set of combat uniform, a bolted breakfast, a scan of the signal clipboard, and then into the dark world of the ops room. The on-watch warfare officer would take me swiftly through the radar picture, identify contacts, discuss the narrative of events, and brief me upon the ship's orders for the day, including the latest threat assessment. Up one ladder and I was on the bridge. A careful check of the chart, visual identification of each radar contact, a moment in my sprung chair as an antidote to the ship's movement, a check on the

189

vigilance of the on-watch staff, an assessment of the elements — visibility, sea state, cloud base — and then a return to my twilight world below. I was ready for the day.

The intensity of the period also allowed me to look carefully at myself to avoid frailty. In my hard-worked profession, I was then turned to for 120 hours each week and was on call for 168. Fatigue was my fear, I had no difficulty with the decision-taking or the isolation. Having grown up as an only child, with no father around and with a full-time working mother, I had grown fiercely independent and was a natural loner. Fortunately, I had never recognized the phrase 'the loneliness of command'. Exhaustion was the trap.

True fatigue takes you in two ways; the good CO learns to recognize the incipient stages and corrects them. First comes: 'I really can't be bothered, ' manifesting itself in an unaccustomed reluctance to challenge, to probe, to question. If uncorrected, this leads straight into the 'distorted judgement' phase, which can kill people. Dwelling too much upon one factor or another and staying wedded to a random preconception without logical reason; both lead to flawed decisions. I candidly invited Colin to advise me if he saw any sign of such trends: the absence of any feedback leads me to conclude that I paced myself adequately — or he was remarkably loyal.

With the tempo of fighting at its height, some men were living on their nerves. For many, the prospect of death was a preoccupation.

And for some, anxiety was surfacing in many forms: irritability, impatience, intolerance — even indigestion — grumbled away. Shipboard claustrophobia, normally not a problem for mariners, abraded the nerves of the vulnerable. I watched my people carefully, intent upon spotting the first potential sign of weakness that could turn into calamity. Again I valued Colin de Mowbray's counsel. He encouraged confidences and acted as an excellent conduit between a very busy and distracted captain and his edgy ship's company.

It was not just people who were fraying at the edges. *Alacrity* was carrying several important defects. Continued absence of one Tyne engine and a defective hull and fire pump both restricted us and made us vulnerable to severe flooding or fire. I was sorely disappointed. As an aviator with a considerable awareness of the importance of equipment maintenance, I had tried hard to grant every request of David Dyter and Mel Purvis to take their equipment down for routine servicing. Indeed, David reassured me later that his planned maintenance was in better shape after the war than before it. Nevertheless, we were suffering from many months of hard running.

Most important of all was the impending loss of my main armament. Our gun barrel was by then close to the end of its life due to extensive firings during my time in command, peaking in heavy exercise use in the Mediterranean late in the winter. An overzealous but correct bureaucrat had just signalled to remind me of the approaching limit and to ask for my intentions. As I was of the opinion that not firing the gun could prove much more dangerous than firing it, my response had been frivolous and unhelpful.

'Propose to continue until it falls off' was not quite what was needed. I was sent a stern reminder that a disintegrating gun barrel might kill as many as an Argentinian bomb, and that I was not to exceed the programmed life. In answer to my follow-up query, I was advised that, exceptionally, a gun barrel could be changed at sea, but only in a totally calm anchorage. I tried pleading with the Admiral's staff by signal. They rightly asked where I was going to find calm water in the open waters of a South Atlantic winter. I fumed — and counted each shell fired.

Then at last it was time for our land forces to start moving east, which they did on 26 May, five days having been necessary to establish themselves. Though it had cost the Navy dear, the invasion force was still virtually unscathed, only the loss of *Conveyor* having been badly disruptive. Brigadier Julian Thompson's original brief had been to remain at the beachhead until 5 Brigade and General Jeremy Moore reinforced him, but ship losses and restlessness in the UK prompted an earlier initiative. Plans to airlift 3 Brigade by helicopter straight to high ground overlooking Stanley had perished with *Conveyor*; it was to be a much more laborious advance with each man carrying over 100 lbs on his back across appalling country. So, whilst

42 Commando held the beachheads, and 40 Commando remained poised in reserve, 45 Commando and 3 Para would swing north-east towards Teal Inlet and 2 Para would advance first to the south-east — against Darwin and Goose Green.

Thereafter, news of future progress ashore would be vague and fragmented. Indeed the BBC was once again about to become our best source of information — as it probably also was to the enemy. The night before the raid, a radio announcement was made that an attack was about to take place against Goose Green. Ye Gods!

The gallant and successful assault cost 2 Para the lives of sixteen soldiers including their CO, Colonel 'H' Jones, but despite the Argentinian defenders being well dug in and outnumbering the Paras by more than two to one, their losses were much more grievous — 1,200 men surrendered, 140 were wounded and 50 died. It had been an emphatic military triumph which was to set the tone for the next three weeks.

Out at sea, there was the timely arrival of more ships to replace those lost the day before. Headed by the large destroyer *Bristol* (Captain Alan Grose), they included *Cardiff* (Captain Mike Harris), *Andromeda* (Captain Jim Weatherall), *Minerva* (Commander Steve Johnston), *Penelope* (Commander Pete Rickard) and our fellow Type 21s, *Avenger* and *Active* (Commander Paul Canter). The conventional submarine *Onyx* (Lieutenant Commander A. P. Johnson) was also by then in the area, sniffing silently for the *San Luis* on our behalf. An even more welcome arrival was a dense shroud of fog. But, ironically, by then San Carlos was almost empty.

That night, *Alacrity* was back on the gunline alone, the first time since the invasion, distributing 100 shells without a hitch. My bright and energetic Weapons Engineer, Lieutenant Commander Mel Purvis, was present for every firing, poised like a motherhen as 'his' gun did her business. Nurturing the system with loving care, he was always at my elbow with coolly reasoned advice; an ideal example of a good engineer and outstanding officer who could have excelled in any specialization. Given to leaping out on the exposed forecastle and up into the gun mounting to deal with rare misfires, he broke speed records in these capers.

On this occasion his progress was checked by the soft West Country lilt of Able Seaman Gage who called down to him from the lookout's position: 'Going wrong bloody way if I may say so, sir. The last one was awfully close to the bows.' It was only through this relayed cryptic comment that those of us in the ops room became aware that we were under our first artillery fire from the shore. Neither bridge nor visual lookouts had wished to 'distract' us in the middle of such a successful shoot. We had come a long way in less than a month from the ship that had frozen under first fire. Thereafter, at my direction, Anton Maguire maintained an excellent low-voiced commentary from the flight-deck upon the proximity of exploding shells as we picked our way in amongst the kelp banks: I was perfectly happy to be so 'distracted'. Luckily, without radar control for their 155 mm howitzers up on Harriet Ridge, the Argentinians' chances of hitting us were about the same as were mine of backing the winners of the Derby and the St Leger in the same season. I felt quite safe.

Meanwhile our third musketeer was being pressed into service; Paul Bootherstone and *Arrow* were putting 157 shells into Darwin in support of 2 Para's advance. But even their efforts were dwarfed by *Yarmouth* who discharged the largest one-night total of the war, 300 rounds.

On the following night, 27/28 May, we combined with *Glamorgan* and *Avenger* for a mighty shore bombardment to the west of Stanley, totalling 209 rounds, of which we contributed 111 carefully placed shells over three hours against troop positions up on Wireless Ridge, Mount Harriet and Tumbledown Mountain. All ships came under return fire from ashore.

By then we had the regular benefit of our own spotters on the ground, directing our guns with clinical precision. As we slid into our allocated position on the gunline, the gun controller reported: 'Call for Fire coming in, sir' — and the cycle of well-rehearsed orders and responses between Army ashore and Navy afloat began. I reached above my head and turned up the volume on my speaker, only to hear — with great pleasure — the unmistakable gentle brogue of Willie McCracken telling *Alacrity* where to place her shells. Out on his bare mountain, he had to speak softly to avoid being overheard by the opposition in adjacent trenches.

Once starshell had provided the spotters with the necessary illumination to see the enemy trenches, our rounds were highly effective and allowed us to neutralize many targets. I had long since given up reflecting upon the bloody carnage that was encapsulated by the word 'neutralize' — *Sheffield*, *Ardent*, *Antelope*, *Coventry* and *Conveyor* had dulled my sensitivity.

During our firings, Captain Mike Barrow had a glorious, bracing idea. He obtained approval from the flagship to fire one of his primitive anti-aircraft missiles, the Seaslug, up into the Argentinian positions in the mountains. Purely a blind shot, it would have no guidance of any sort and was therefore only likely to kill rock. But the opposition would not know that and it would make a fearsome sight. When *Glamorgan* reported ready to fire, with ourselves close astern, I went to the bridge to enjoy the spectacular show which followed. The whoosh as the huge amber crescent arced up into the night sky was highly imposing from the firing end: for any troops peering seaward through the gloom, it must also have caught the attention. We could just make out the faint flash of impact as the 2,000 lb missile hit nearly 12 miles away. Post-war analysis revealed no useful results but it gave us all a lift.

On the same night, *Avenger* reported being overflown by a possible missile. Intelligence speculated that Argentinian ingenuity could have been placing Exocet launchers to fire on our ships from landbased trailers. So we plotted the position of *Avenger* with close interest before laying off the maximum firing range of Exocet and noting possible firing positions on the shore line with red circles. But trailers meant that the launcher could move a long way in one night. We resolved thereafter to cut no corners in our approach to, or departure from, the gunline — staying outside the arc whenever possible or remaining masked behind islands or outcrops. It was to be this weapon that hit *Glamorgan* two weeks later.

By 28 May, enemy air attacks on our ships in the San Carlos anchorages had declined and they were driven to attack shore concentrations that were by then largely empty of troops. Targets for high-level night bombing raids by Canberra aircraft became the maintenance area, the field hospital and the settlement of San Carlos. Although casualties were incurred they were not large, but they did increase further the load on the 'Red and Green Life Machine' — Ajax Bay hospital — which had started dealing with the wounded from Goose Green. The subsequent efforts of this medical facility were soon to save the lives of many men, from both sides. Far out at sea, attempts by the tug *Irishman* (Captain W. Allen) to take *Conveyor* safely in tow for salvage were failing. By then the great ship had blown off her own bows, as if determined to remain in the South Atlantic.

Once again the gunline claimed us that night

for more bombardment ahead of our advancing troops. We had another copybook shore firing, this time against Mount Kent, as airborne spotting and tight teamwork added up to good results. A further 100 rounds of gun barrel life were expended without a hitch. I was surprised at the semi-indifference of the ship's company until I registered that the BBC was providing soccer commentary as Tottenham Hotspur beat Queen's Park Rangers in an all-London FA Cup Final. There was a world beyond our steel home.

Winter was by then coming on fast, giving those of us on the open ocean some discomfort. Running back to the carriers could be bruising, and certainly was on the night of 28/29 May: 40-knot winds and high seas were from the east, which made our 20-knot return shattering. Having been late leaving the gunline, I had little choice — I kept up the speed.

Surging high across the face of one mountain of foaming green, *Alacrity* would stand on her tail and then hang — it seemed for many seconds — before falling with a massive impact into the next trough. Burying her nose deep into the maelstrom would send a wall of heavy water surging down the length of the forecastle before slamming into the bridge above us with a sickening crash. And then she would shake her head like a living thing, before starting her climb up the face of the next salty Everest. All the time, broken seas overran the main swell and gunshotted against the thin hull a few feet from us, making me conscious of the eyes

198

watching me to see how long I would let their only shelter take such unacceptable punishment. Feigning nonchalance, I secretly pledged to buy many drinks for Yarrow's shipbuilders if ever I survived.

Finally, I went up to the bridge to escape the gently reproving stares. Aloft it was worse. Windscreen wipers had given up the unequal struggle, every item of loose equipment was double-lashed, and watchkeepers were sandwiched into any secure corner they could find. At each plunge, a mountain would envelop the bows before boiling and thundering down the forecastle in the moonlight; cascading phosphorescence consumed both gun and Exocet launchers before smashing against windows, bridge roof and creaking clipped doors.

'Hmm, bit of a swell getting up,' I murmured lightly, but nevertheless reduced the speed by 2 knots before returning to the ops room.

Early next morning, I was called to the bridge. Amongst the mountainous seas our sharp-eyed lookout had sighted just a glimpse of orange — the colour of British emergency lifesaving equipment. We slowed, rolling heavily in the Force 8 seas as the speed came off. *Orange* appeared again fleetingly amidst the spume. I focused my binoculars and swallowed hard. It was the feet of an inverted survival suit, still buoyant with trapped air despite the weight of its occupant. We had a gruesome task of recovery on our hands.

Our main seaboat was a 27-foot motor whaler which I was loath to use in much above a

Force 7 sea. The ship had to slow to 5 knots to launch it. At that speed, hanging pendulously from its wires just above such high sea states, the boat was highly vulnerable. Men could be spilled overboard, hands could be smashed or even removed by the snapping winch wires, and even the boat shell itself could shatter against our steel hull.

Our two rubber inflatable Gemini boats with their powerful outboard engines were more durable, but even they could prove lethal in such seas. Thus I was left with our most effective way of recovering somebody from the ocean in a storm — putting another man into the water to lift him out.

Using a swimmer called for a courageous man, and plenty of skill by all concerned. Orders were given and the Swimmer of the Watch was readied in rubber diving suit, flippers and facemask, with a helicopter lifting strop designed for two people secured around him. He was lifted over the guardrails where he stood, poised and pale-faced directly below my position on the bridge wing, held on his lifeline by eight of his more muscular seaman friends. I started my approach towards the tragic pair of orange feet.

Across the line of wind and swell we rolled, slowing gently to a stop precisely abreast of the feet and 50 yards off them.

'Put the swimmer in the water — fast,' I ordered.

There was no hesitation as he plummeted 30 feet into the icy waves. Now we all had to move quickly: *Alacrity* was accelerating her already rapid drift rate down towards the feet.

The swimmer surfaced; the recovery line was paid out; and he started swiftly away from our bulk which was about to run him down. We guided him by flag signals through the water mountains but, despite his power and speed, he was only managing to match our drift rate: both ship and swimmer bore down inexorably upon the bobbing feet.

Now he's with him, and must be quick. Passing the strop around the inverted suit, he raises one thumb — and eight seamen respond. The line twangs taut — and the two embracing figures burst from the surface of the water just before they are crushed under the sliding steel.

The survival suit was only full of water and air — perhaps a spare from *Conveyor*. But our young swimmer — 19 years of age and not yet qualified as the diver he ultimately wanted to be — was rightly proud of his efforts which I felt merited a tot of rum; a privilege given rarely by a hard-hearted captain. As the boy drank his tot, I imagined that Nelson in his heaven must have smiled his approval: in our high-tech modern navy, we were probably using the self-same technique that he and his sailors employed nearly two hundred years earlier.

I had been together with many of my men for well over a year and it was fascinating to see how each responded to his greatest challenge: the young swimmer was but one of many achievers. There can be no generalization about which sort of man will shine in war: rowdy extroverts and monosyllabic introverts were found equally amongst my winners and losers. However, the men who summoned the greatest resources in pursuit of courage seemed to be the truly self-reliant, those who did not need constant support from the company of others.

Back in the force we lost another Sea Harrier, this time courtesy of the South Atlantic winter. Ready for take-off on *Invincible*'s flight-deck, the aircraft was simply swept overboard as the ship turned into the wind. Although the pilot, Lieutenant Commander Broadwater, ejected and was winched to safety, it was yet another reminder of our hostile environment. *Sir Percivale* had been delivered inshore by *Minerva*, and the last unexploded bomb had been cleared from *Sir Lancelot* by the gallant Fleet Chief Petty Officer Trotter. Yet another enemy Dagger was lost to a Rapier missile, and I was certain that the enemy could not have many left.

With our reinforcement ships now desperate to make up for lost time, the gunline became a rowdy place. On 29/30 May, *Glamorgan* and *Ambuscade* unleashed 190 rounds at Stanley, whilst *Arrow* gave Fox Bay a further 100. We ran another convoy of *Elk* and *Tidepool* into San Carlos at 18 knots with *Andromeda*, as *Intrepid* and *Plymouth* came out. It was becoming like the South Circular on a Bank Holiday Saturday.

As Intelligence insisted that the submarine *San Luis* was somewhere amongst us, we had our usual anti-submarine Sea Kings screening

Sniffing the rising wind: HMS *Alacrity* operating in the Portland naval exercise area before the outbreak of the Falklands War.

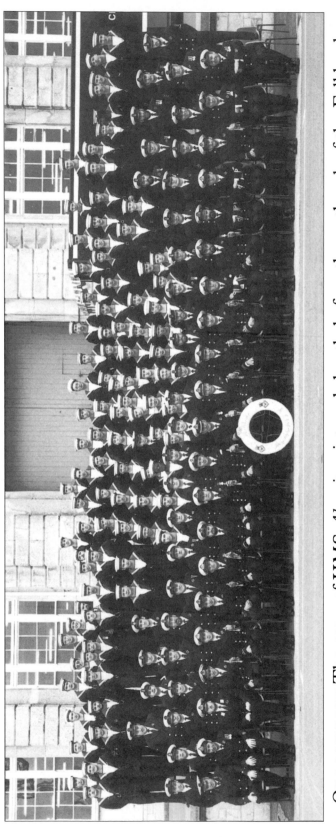

One company: The crew of HMS *Alacrity* pictured shortly before the outbreak of the Falklands War. To the author's left is Captain Hugo White, Captain of the Fourth Frigate Squadron and destined to become Commander-in-Chief Fleet twelve years later.

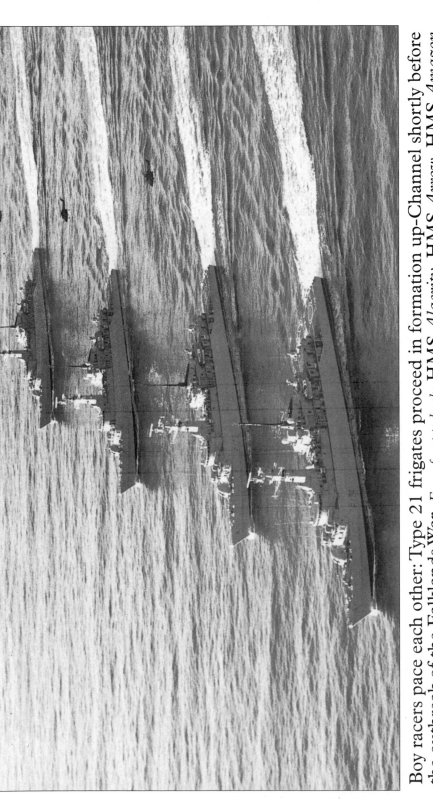

Boy racers pace each other: Type 21 frigates proceed in formation up-Channel shortly before the outbreak of the Falklands War. *From front to back:* HMS *Alacrity*, HMS *Arrow*, HMS *Amazon* and HMS *Ardent* (the photograph was taken from HMS *Alacrity*'s Lynx helicopter).

Flagship flying operations: The flagship of the British Task Group, HMS *Hermes*, conducting flight operations in the South Atlantic with Sea Harriers and Sea Kings on deck.

Helicopter delivery service: A Sea King of 846 Naval Air Squadron takes up an underslung load from the aircraft-carrier HMS *Invincible*.

Harriers a'hunting: Sea Harriers armed with Sidewinder missiles launch from HMS *Hermes* for combat air patrol over the Falklands.

The focus of attention: Stanley airfield photographed from the east by Sea Harrier on the first day of the war. Stanley and the high ground, which was to see such bloody fighting, lie in the background.

Southern seas: A Sea Harrier lashed on the deck of HMS *Hermes*. HMS *Broadsword* and HMS *Invincible* can be seen amongst typical South Atlantic seas.

Confidence dispelled: HMS *Sheffield* blazes after being struck by an Exocet missile. HMS *Arrow* goes to the rescue

THE TYPE 21 GRAVEYARD

21 May: HMS *Ardent* mortally hit in the stern by Argentinian Skyhawk aircraft. HMS *Yarmouth* takes off survivors.

23 May: HMS *Antelope* dies off San Carlos following the massive explosion of an Argentinian bomb lodged between her decks.

THE TRAGIC 25 MAY

HMS *Coventry*, photographed from one of her liferafts as she capsizes after a bombing attack by Skyhawks off Pebble Island.

Atlantic Conveyor, wreathed in smoke following the impact of two Exocets port side aft. The loss of her helicopters compelled British land forces to traverse East Falkland on foot.

en years on: The officers of HMS *Alacrity* in 1982 reunited in May 1992, just before the ship was sold to Pakistan.

eft to right, back row: Rob Sleeman, Chris Riordan, Neil Stanton, Eric Haskell, Steve Shaw, David Dyter, Tom McCrimmon.

ront: Graham Baxter, Tony Johnstone-Burt (standing in for his absent brother), Colin de Mowbray, the author, Kevin King, Anton Maguire, Bob Burrows (*Absent:* Mel Purvis, Simon Thorp, Tom Tubb, Mark Scrivens).

Victory parade: Ships of the British Task Group in formation
after the Argentinian surrender. HMS *Andromeda* leads
HMS *Bristol*, HMS *Invincible* and others.

THE GULF WAR

Into harm's way: British ships proceed to their
battle stations in January 1991.

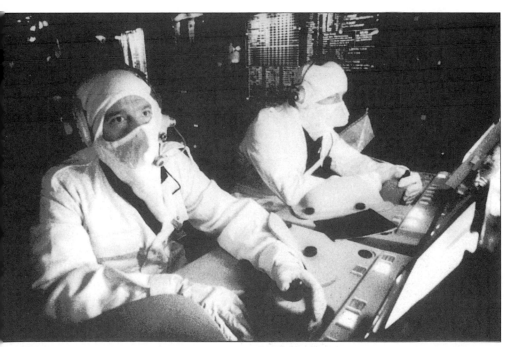

Vigilance: The men of the British flagship maintain radar
watch against Iraqi air attack.

'One eye on the holly…': 22 December 1990. The author join
the sailors and nurses of RFA *Argus* for a carol service whils
preparing for war.

'…the other on
Baghdad': Upper-
deck guncrew in
their NBC
protection suits load
ammunition under a
blazing sun.

Predator displays its teeth: A Lynx helicopter rolls to show its two Sea Skua air-to-surface missiles.

Mauled victim: An Iraqi naval patrol craft savaged by Lynx and other aircraft during the Battle of Bubiyan, January 1991.

MINEHUNTING

A diver about to countercharge an Iraqi floating mine in
January 1991.

A British Hunt-class minehunter blows up one of Iraq's sea
mines in January 1991.

Minehunters Great and Small

Mid-February 1991: The USN minehunting flagship USS *Tripoli* operating in the minefields with Sea Stallion helicopters on deck shortly before she hit an Iraqi moored mine.

Late January 1991: RFA *Sir Galahad* mothers HMS *Herald*, *Hurworth*, *Cattistock*, *Atherstone*, *Dulverton*, *Ledbury* and three USN minesweepers.

SOUR FRUITS OF VICTORY

Environmental sabotage: some of the oil wells lit wantonly
by the Iraqis during the third week of February.

A Royal Navy Sea King reconnoitres the blazing
Ahmadi oil fields, hovering alongside one of the
600 oil well fires started by the Iraqis.

The Royal Navy flagship, HMS *London*, leads the five Hunt-
class minehunters through the offshore smoke haze as USS
Missouri moves on to the gunline to answer the call for fire.

us for our transit. Frankly, we had by then become convinced that the enemy was incapable of launching submarine attacks against us. It was as well that no one knew of the torpedoing attempt against *Alacrity* by the *San Luis* on 11 May. Anti-submarine squadrons 820, 824 and 826 had proved to be the hardest worked of all Task Group aircraft: flying from the decks of both the carriers, *Fort Austin*, *Olmeda* and *Olna*, they had maintained the equivalent of four aircraft constantly on task throughout the month of May — a prodigious achievement.

On 30 May came report of a distant STUFT tanker, *British Wye* (Captain D. M. Rundell), 400 miles north of South Georgia, which had been subjected to a bombing attack by an immensely long-legged Argentinian Hercules. The dogged aircraft had heaved out eight bombs from a low level, of which only one hit — and that simply bounced off the thick commercial hull. There was a carnival air about this distant gladiatorial combat but the Master of *British Wye* did not find it amusing; after all, he was more than a thousand miles from the nearest Argentinian air base and had hardly considered himself to be in the front line. Closer to us, the hospital ship *Uganda* left her safe haven 20 miles north of the landing area and entered Grantham Sound to embark the wounded and to carry out some calm-water surgery before returning.

The same day, General Moore took over from Brigadier Julian Thompson as Commander Land Forces: the 5th Infantry Brigade had arrived.

Brigadier Thompson reverted to command of 3 Commando Brigade whilst Brigadier Wilson, newly arrived, was commanding the 5th Infantry which had been transported south in the liner *Queen Elizabeth II*. It had been decided not to risk the beautiful ship in the war zone and thus the Brigade was transferred at South Georgia to *Canberra* and *Norland*. Earlier plans for 5 Brigade to be the relieving force for 3 Commando Brigade and held in reserve were shelved: they were to be deployed on the southern flank. The British Task Force by then numbered nearly 25,000 men and more than 100 ships. 'Couldn't be done,' the sceptics had said.

That afternoon, the enemy cast their last despairing dice — the final air-launched Exocet. This time it was to be delivered by a combined flight, four Air Force Skyhawks in formation with two Navy Super Etendards, refuelling way to the south to allow them to attack from a new and unexpected direction. Though we defended primarily against the obvious threat axis of west, we were very much alive to possible attack from elsewhere, and thus they did not surprise us. Each of the Skyhawks carried two 500 lb bombs, and a single Exocet nestled beneath one Etendard — would that we had known it was their last air-launched weapon.

As with so many days off the Falklands, the welcome shroud of early morning fog all too soon gave way to rising wind and improving visibility, albeit with embedded vicious rain squalls that could take visibility from 10 miles to 100 metres in seconds. Every ship would have settled for the hazards of dense fog if it kept enemy aircraft on the runway. As we waited, the passing storms thundered against the steel deckhead: a roll on many drums, as if announcing a pending arrival.

At 1330, on their final attack heading of north-east, the aircraft were tempted into making a short sweep on their radar. Ever-alert *Exeter* called immediate detection and all ships responded instantly with Chaff, turning for the wind whilst gun and missile systems swung on to the bearing. Both *Cardiff* and *Exeter* gained radar detection of their own, allowing the latter to acquire the formation with her Sea Dart at 20 miles range — just as the lead aircraft unleashed its Exocet.

Although *Avenger* subsequently believed she killed the Exocet in flight with her gun, post-war analysis concluded that Chaff clouds seduced the missile which then ditched at the end of its fuel life. The two Etendards broke formation for their return whilst the Skyhawks pressed on resolutely with their bombs ready. As they sighted and mistook *Avenger* for *Invincible*, one of two Sea Dart missiles fired by *Exeter* destroyed the lead aircraft after ripping past a somewhat alarmed Lynx. A second Skyhawk crashed, having been hit by *Avenger*'s gun and small-arms fire, and left his last two companions releasing their bombs to splash harmlessly about the Type 21 whilst the gallant pilots made their escape to the west. Though Argentinian propaganda declared a 'devastating attack on *Invincible*', the carrier had been a further 15 miles behind *Avenger* and continued unscathed about her duties. Vigilance and impressive reactions from *Exeter* and *Avenger* had neutralized a tenacious attack. *Alacrity* had also now survived attack by five Exocets.

The gunline claimed us once more that evening. Sapper Hill was the target and the naïve spotter asked if we would like to stay around until after first light to create yet more carnage. I declined, in the sure knowledge that the only likely carnage after sun-up would be that wreaked by Argentinian aircraft upon my ship. The enemy on Mount Harriet tried to retaliate, the effectiveness of which I reported by signal with the dismissive 'active but inaccurate'. We were getting blasé.

On 31 May, Vulcans used Shrike anti-radiation missiles to destroy enemy warning radars. Damage was achieved and the RAF continued to prove it could operate at immense distances from its Ascension base. *Uganda* again entered the Sound and her Argentinian equivalent, *Bahia Paraiso*, went to Fox Bay. That night San Carlos saw outgoers *Intrepid*, *Elk* and *Tidepool*; and incomers *Brilliant*, *Atlantic Causeway* (Captain M. H. C. Twomey), *Blue Rover* (Captain J. D. Roddis) and *Baltic Ferry* (Captain E. Harrison).

And *Alacrity* went to the gunline for the last time during the dying hours of a bloody May. With our carriers and ground forces all intact, and with the Sea Harrier in the ascendancy,

there was a great sense that the tide had
turned for the Task Force. My final May
diary entry reflected four long weeks — 750
hours — of war: 'Tired but positive. The end
is near.'

6

Look Homeward

1 – 24 June

'He that outlives this day
and comes safe home'

THE small hours of 1 June were far from glorious for us. We were nearly out of gun-barrel life and it was to be our final firing. Targets were enemy troop positions to the west of Stanley, along a line between Two Sisters Ridge and the old British barracks of Moody Brook. It was a cloudless night and there was a bright moon, allowing the Lynx and spotters from 42 Commando on their bare mountain to report the fire for what was perhaps our most efficient bombardment of the war. Illuminate and eliminate: all involved were dispassionate and efficient. But I was profoundly depressed as we unleashed more than 130 rounds and listened for the last time to the spotter's quiet voice declare 'Target neutralized. End of mission.' A string of 155 mm howitzer shells splashing about us as we headed offshore for the last time did not help my mood. I signalled the flagship: 'Returning — muzzle drooping.'

We had fired a total of 587 shells in anger; but I had a good deal more anger left. If it had not been for our extended training period in the Med in February, we would have been blazing away until the end; but with only ancient Seacat and with the enemy sending no surface vessels out as targets for our Exocets, poor battered *Alacrity* was a waning asset.

My spirits were not improved by *Avenger* showing his squadron what the leader could produce on the same night, firing no less than 293 rounds in an exceptionally fine reliability performance. I was jealous of such unrestricted gun usage and felt little better when the flagship started to urge Task Group conservation — embarked stocks of 4.5-inch ammunition were getting desperately low. Later that same day, Sharkey Ward did his best to deplete the force stock of 30 mm cannon shells: he put dozens into an enemy Hercules which had no chance of survival, before making it back to the carrier deck with virtually teaspoonfuls of fuel remaining in his tanks.

As we returned to the Task Force, I remember watching Simon Thorp, my young navigator, working deftly on his charts and I imagined similar young men throughout the force, many barely out of school but all having early manhood thrust upon them. Some grew prematurely old, others thrived. I felt almost ashamed at how much I loved the heady energy of war. Far from freezing the will, it invigorated me. I think it was General Robert E. Lee who remarked whilst watching the bloody carnage of the Battle of Fredericksburg during the American Civil War: 'It is a good thing that war is so terrible, or else we would grow to love it too much.'

June began busily. Loan pilot Flight Lieutenant Mortimer was shot down by a Roland missile over Stanley airfield, being plucked safely from the water by an 820 Sea King. Reports were coming in of enemy helicopters having landed on Pebble Island but the bad weather precluded their being winkled out. This was a source of some alarm as the Argentinian Sea Kings could carry Exocets. In fact, they were engaged in a brave and very long-range casualty evacuation to the mainland.

Gallant *Norland* offloaded the famed Gurkhas, who very quickly started marching east towards Darwin, hungry for action. *Atlantic Causeway* flew off welcome new Sea Kings of 825 Naval Air Squadron (Lieutenant Commander Hugh Clark) in San Carlos. And the bustle of restocking the heavy ships ploughing back and forth, topping them up as fast as possible before their night return, was inspiring in its intensity. Stores ships *Stromness*, *Resource* and *Regent* dispensed a total of more than 12,000 pallet loads over the war, with helicopters distributing 2,000 separate underslung loads. The 'endless boredom of war' is a myth.

But there were quieter moments. A false alarm of air attack that afternoon saw me in the ops room at 1515 UK time, waiting for *Invincible* to confirm no enemy aircraft within a hundred miles. As we waited, I had Radio Supervisor Carver relay the live commentary of the Epsom Derby to one earphone of my headset. It was as well that the enemy report

210

was a false alarm as I was transported far north to the cavalry-charge descent around Tattenham Corner. *Golden Fleece* was the winner, but I had taken a sizeable ante-post win bet on the runner-up. It had been that sort of year.

The next day, 2 June, saw the start of forty-eight hours of impenetrable fog. Harriers stayed grounded throughout and I reflected what might have been the outcome if all our landings had been conducted under such a veil and the Argentinian aircraft had been similarly kept on the ground. Nevertheless, shipping movements in and out of San Carlos continued unabated.

That night, *Alacrity* departed to the repair area to the east, to be mended by *Stena Seaspread*. Our Olympus engine funnel uptakes were breaking up and the results would, if left alone, be disastrous. Lieutenant Commander Mike Townson, a founder member of the 21 Club, had his repair team weld us better inside twenty-four hours. It was Michael who had used inspired ingenuity to equip his repair team before their departure from Devonport Dockyard. Having hired a crane, he had toured the yard simply purloining anything that had even the remotest potential for use. Tour complete, he embarked the crane as well. He was a grand, resolute man.

The days were turning bitter cold; winter was coming on fast. We took the opportunity to remove some more of our topweight, shifting everything of significance to a lower position in the ship. If we were to be exposed to deep clear icing on our masts and superstructure, hundreds

211

of tons of unwelcome destabilizing weight could be added to the ship in a few hours, threatening our stability in large seas to the extent of risking capsize. The United States Navy had lost a group of cruisers in just one turn during the Second World War: they were believed to have capsized together.

On 3 June, my spirits rose somewhat at the news that divers from *Avenger* had brought up a 20 mm gun from sunken *Antelope*, christened it '*Antelope*'s *Avenger*', and set it to work. From such inspired initiatives do men draw strength in battle. Meanwhile, British heavy-calibre guns were continuing with their shore bombardment but much more selectively. Our early and profligate firing of shells had been a mistake. Somebody should have moderated expenditure much earlier, but we were all learning the realities of war for the first time.

More RAF anti-radar missile firings that night destroyed an Argentinian radar and heartened us, despite the foully clamped weather that was impairing daytime fighter operations. A cavalcade of heavy ships was by then convoying in and out of San Carlos with impugnity: Argentinian air power had been mortally hit.

It was also the night of 3 June which afforded me one of my most enduring memories of the Falklands War. There was dense fog and a comparatively flat sea — merely Force 5. We had been ordered to fuel from *Olna*'s starboard side, as she was to be replenishing another ship on her port wing. Once established on the approach, I squinted to sight my 36,000-ton fuel supply amidst the soaking grey gloom. But my first glimpse was not the usual reassuring shape; something was very different. Towering up into the swirling whiteness was an even greater bulk than that of *Olna*. Tucked in like a fighting veteran, a block of apartment flats in the night, was the unmistakable shape of the passenger liner *Canberra*. The combined 100,000 tons of steel slid on across the fog-wrapped ocean. Profoundly moved by the resolve and organization that had fashioned a fighting machine from a cruise liner in but six weeks, we set about our refuelling. But there were many lumps in throats as we stared up through frozen nests of rigging at the vast upperworks and neat rows of passenger portholes. It was a marvellous sight — grandeur and resolve in the mist.

There was a sudden stinging in my eyes that had little to do with salt spray, as I turned to my young navigator.

'We shall surely win this bloody war, Simon.'

The situation ashore increasingly indicated that we would: 2 Para's victory at Goose Green had been an immense psychological lift and had been boosted by a succession of rapid advances. No. 45 Commando and 3 Para marched (or 'yomped' as the UK tabloids preferred to call it) nearly 30 miles across the north of East Falkland, flanking the mountains, to arrive at Teal Inlet by 1 June. Meanwhile, 42 Commando advanced by helicopter over the mountains to the neck of Teal Inlet. They were poised for the final assault.

Intelligence assessments gave varying estimates

of the number of Argentinian troops confronting us but subsequent analysis revealed 2,000 men isolated on West Falkland whilst our troops were facing the remaining 9,000 men on East Falkland. Against a properly trained, motivated and proficient force, this would have been a totally unacceptable imbalance with which to move against dug-in positions. But everywhere demonstrations of British military prowess were becoming apparent. Only ammunition exhaustion could stop us.

On 4 June, *Exeter*'s Lynx trawled slowly through the murk to the south of Stanley with a large radar reflector attached, simulating a ship and trying to draw a shore-launched Exocet. But none was forthcoming. That night, Lieutenant Charlie Cantan took off in the same appalling visibility from *Invincible* in his SHAR against a suspect radar contact. He had no success other than achieving a superb safe landing in nil visibility. But, inshore, it was a night of tragic mistakes and near mistakes. *Cardiff* fired a Sea Dart at a suspect air contact, downing one of our own Gazelles and killing four men. And then, in quick succession, *Arrow*, *Cardiff* and *Plymouth* each challenged small surface craft with a view to engaging them, but they were all British landing craft to whose movement the warships had not been alerted. Thankfully, these were to my knowledge the only Blue-on-Blue incidents of the entire confusing war by the British forces. But the Argentinians had shot down at least two of their own jet aircraft.

And then, on 5 June, another gale-torn day of

thick overcast, *Alacrity*'s war started to come to an end. I received a sensitive but unambiguous signal from Admiral Woodward. My ship was lacking a gun, hull and fire pump, and a Tyne engine, and was showing cracks. He needed some ships to begin returning to the UK to commence the post-war roulement after victory, and had selected *Alacrity* to start the long journey home. I responded to his signal with a request to call on him personally. With typical forebearance, the Admiral invited me to fly to the flagship late that same night.

That evening, I shared my intentions with my crew. I told them that I was acutely conscious of their desire to go home; I knew how gallantly they had fought and how well they deserved their homecoming, but I believed that Argentinian surrender was but a matter of days away. I explained, truthfully, that I had dreamt of *Alacrity* leading a column of warships into Stanley. The ship was very quiet as my voice echoed from many speakers.

'Gentlemen, you should know that I intend to call on Admiral Woodward tonight to ask that *Alacrity* be allowed to stay and fight on for the few days that remain. Though I know all too well that many of you may be disappointed, I earnestly believe that when you are old and grey you will be glad that you and your ship stayed to share in total victory.' The echoes of my voice died away: I had never felt the ship so still. I went below to don my flying suit and to be briefed for my flight. I could imagine the fearful images of a last-minute sinking that would now

215

be spinning in the minds of my men. To their credit, nobody shot me so much as a resentful stare. I like to think, even today, that they all understood.

The vast darkened bulk of superstructure towered over the Lynx as we landed on the rust-stained deck of *Hermes* and I reflected ruefully that the flagship too was exhausted. Ancient boilers were in desperate need of repair but there was certainly no way she could return home yet. As I was escorted down to the Admiral's fighting quarters, I was shocked at how tired his personal staff looked in the dim red lighting. I hoped to God that the Admiral did not view me the same way, otherwise my chance of a stay of execution was nil. He was gracious, charming and terribly patient: he too looked gaunt and weary.

I was conscious of how much I respected this very austere man who I had only really come to know through his precise signals and radio exchanges. His logic was, as ever, unerring. He was good enough to say that no ship had done more towards victory since the outset. He agreed that victory was inevitable — and imminent (presumably he had not looked too carefully at the ammunition stocks remaining). Finally, and shrewdly, he kicked my Achilles heel — my people deserved their return. Somewhat forlornly, I protested, increasingly conscious that my argument was based only upon emotion. I had lost, but he heard me out carefully and thoroughly. When I had finished, he quietly reaffirmed his judgement. It was time for me to

216

leave. I gripped his hand, wished him a timely victory, and clattered up to where Bob Burrows had the aircraft waiting on deck. Despite the lateness of the hour, I went on main broadcast immediately on my return.

'I have just returned from Admiral Woodward. He commends you for your achievements in these waters. Tomorrow he wishes us to go home. We shall. That is all.'

A brief return visit to *Stena Seaspread* for some assisted maintenance was followed by the mandatory stripping of my ship for the benefit of the rest of the Force, and a final miserable underway transfer of it all. Warshot weapons were dragged painfully across on the jackstay for four hours. Anything that might help hasten victory was passed across for use by our sister ships. I remembered the unfortunate Springtrain ships returning to the UK having given their all to the southgoers. Now it was my turn. Simon and I stood silent on the bridge wing and I thought how much older his long and angular face looked in the damp greyness of a South Atlantic morning.

'No ship could have done more,' the Admiral had said. But I did so desperately want myself and my people to have the satisfaction of finishing the job. I sighed and concentrated upon maintaining the gap between ourselves and *Fort Grange*. It was 2100 before we were finished. With the adrenalin gone, it had been an endless and sapping business. Anton Maguire had ferreted into every corner of the ship and there was little left even to take us home. I rewarded him with a thin smile, enquiring if he intended us to starve before Ascension.

As I invited Chris Riordan to bring the ship's heading to the north-east, I sent a lame but sincere signal to all the ships who were remaining. Doubtless those who did not know me well found it patronizing to receive such heartfelt good wishes from the one ship that was actually doing what all other ships wished to do — go home. As we departed, course 073° and speed 16 knots, a rising sea battered us. More gales were forecast. Victory had better come quickly, I reflected, as the full bite of the southern winter was already with us. I stayed up longer than I needed to, reading covetously the signalled reports of gunline ships, and I slept poorly for the first time since leaving Plymouth.

We followed all signals and radio transmissions avidly as the tempo of combat continued to quicken. On 7 June there were four frigates blazing away inside Berkeley Sound. Ambuscade fired 228 shells in support of 2 Para's advance, whilst *Avenger* unleashed, for her, a miserly 156 rounds ahead of the Scots Guards. Whilst withdrawing, *Avenger* lost a propeller, which posed some big problems for maintenance and diving teams on *Stena Seaspread*.

As we battered northward on 8 June, we were emotionally flattened as news of the tragedy at Bluff Cove filtered in. The loss of fifty British lives in *Sir Galahad* (Captain P. J. G. Roberts) and *Sir Tristram* (Captain G. R. Green) was tragic and wasteful with overall victory looming.

A number of sad reasons caused the deferred disembarkation of the Welsh Guards who had been brought round from San Carlos to Fitzroy overnight on 7/8 June, and the delay was critical.

Both ships were clearly visible to the Argentinians on Mount Harriet at sunrise: their flash signal to Rio Gallegos and Rio Grande brought out a mixed force of Daggers and Skyhawks. Air-defence Sea Harriers had been drawn off by an initial attack against HMS *Plymouth*, leaving the attackers with a clear run at the Cove; for Rapier missile sites, though in position, were not yet serviceable. In bright sunlight, the five Skyhawks ripped into the exposed and vulnerable LSLs with their precious human cargoes.

Tristram took two bombs starboard side aft, killing two Chinese crewmen. *Galahad* then received the brunt of Argentinian aggression. The high-angled attack proved catastrophic, as three bombs arced into the defenceless ship. One fell squarely into the open tank deck, packed with Welsh Guards and 20 tons of ammunition and fuel. The combined effect of the ensuing inferno was horrific. Heroic rescue work by naval helicopters of 846 and 825, backed by landing craft, thankfully kept the death toll lower than it might have been, but the nature of the injuries and burns to the survivors was truly awful: 159 casualties were flown to the hospital ship *Uganda* to the north of the TEZ. Captain Phil Roberts had been the last man to leave.

Earlier on the same day, *Plymouth* had

become the victim of a flight of Daggers that punched four bombs into her in seconds, but she fought her fires successfully and survived. Three good Skyhawk kills by Sea Harriers late in the day — the last of the war — were no recompense. It had been a tragic day afloat in the midst of so much success ashore. Though it did not check the advance to victory significantly, I understood how TV pictures of Bluff Cove were so agonizing for anxious families at home, hungry for news of victory.

Our return journey was to require a series of planned fuellings from waiting tankers: *Appleleaf*, *Pearleaf* and *Brambleleaf* — it sounded like a country wine orgy. On 10 June we topped up with fuel from the first of them, *Appleleaf* (Captain G. P. A. MacDougall), before slowing our pace to 10 knots in order to escort her and MV *British Dart* (Captain J. A. N. Taylor) northward.

News of further losses reached us on 12 June. A shore-launched Exocet from Port Harriet hit the after-section of *Glamorgan* at a distance of 17 miles, not far short of its maximum range. The enemy had indeed employed the great ingenuity suspected by our Intelligence sources in offloading missile launchers from the A69 warships, flying them to the islands, fitting them to motorized trailers, and linking them to shore-based radar for guidance. Improvisation worked. The impact of the Exocet demolished hangar, helicopter, galley and a main machinery room, killing thirteen men. The Flight and some young chefs were the victims of this last loss.

Thankfully, our last musketeer — *Arrow* — was to survive the war unscathed.

My personal chagrin at returning prematurely to the UK had been magnified by the knowledge that I was leaving all but one of my fellow Type 21s behind me, even if two of them were on the cold and murky bottom. Only a very frustrated *Amazon*, driven by another good friend and highly capable officer, Ian Garnett, had missed out by being deployed to Singapore. Nevertheless, even *Amazon* finally made it to the Falkland Islands in August 1982. In the event, no ship squadron suffered more losses during the short but bloody conflict. When, on cessation of hostilities, Admiral Woodward was sent a captured Argentinian sword from Captain Hugo White, he responded: 'My gratitude to the Fighting Fourth in this vicious six weeks is boundless, and their press-on spirit has not gone unnoticed. I am sad only at the cost in men and ships, and I am proud of you all.' He returned the sword to Captain White. There was eventually to be a simple cross, called the Campito Memorial, set high on the wind-whipped hillside above San Carlos, which will look down forever over the resting places of *Ardent* and *Antelope*.

Ashore, virtually all of General Menendez's defending forces had initially been positioned on the assumption that the British would land near Stanley. Indeed, the assumption had precluded his being able to move against the distant beachhead of San Carlos. But the result was that by then he had all his best troops massed close to the west of Stanley — and this was the final, high hurdle for our advancing land forces.

Plans were for 3 Commando Brigade to take Mount Longden, Two Sisters and Mount Harriet overnight on 11/12 May; and for 5 Brigade to take Wireless Hill, Mount Tumbledown, Mount William and Sapper Hill on 12/13 May. The total of eight British infantry battalions by then on the Falkland Islands represented the greatest military force we had deployed since the Second World War, exceeding even our Korean contribution. Argentinian defenders packed on to this series of peaks faced formidable opposition.

By 12 June, British land forces had indeed rolled up the long-established enemy defensive line which stretched north/south along Mount Longdon, Two Sisters and Mount Harriet. The bloody determination of these attacks has been well chronicled elsewhere but remains admirable. Our Royal Marines had circled south around Harriet and surprised the enemy from the rear, whilst fierce fighting by 3 Para resulted in heavy casualties on both sides before Mount Longdon was taken. No. 45 Commando made a direct approach from the west against Two Sisters, which was gained at a cost of two dead and eleven wounded. The enemy had now been compressed on to the last significant high ground before Stanley. They held Wireless Ridge, Mount William and Mount Tumbledown, which were all to be the subject of final attention.

Late on the evening of 13 June, the delayed last gallant assaults of the Falkland War began. They commenced with attacks by 2 Para against Wireless Ridge and by the Scots Guards against Mount Tumbledown. Though 2 Para rapidly punched the enemy clear off the Ridge, it was a different matter on Tumbledown. Savage fighting ensued as the Scots Guards encountered some of the stiffest opposition of the campaign from Argentinian Marines. Notwithstanding intense fire support from *Avenger* and *Active*, the Guards'advance was held up for a lengthy period. Counter artillery fire was also making life miserable for 2 Para in their new stronghold on Wireless Ridge but, by daylight, the enemy was crumbling. As the Gurkhas advanced against Mount William, the Scots Guards rolled up the last of the Tumbledown defences and, at last, British forces looked down upon Stanley. Only the promontory of Sapper Hill stood between them and their objective; it too soon fell to 40 Commando transported by Simon Thornewill's Sea Kings. Victory was ours.

On the evening of 14 June, Galtieri rejected General Menendez's request that sanity should prevail and Argentina should sue for peace. But, within half an hour, Menendez had sensibly come to his own decision in the face of the inevitable, and surrendered. British forces were ordered to cease fire and the long fight was over. A total of 12,978 prisoners were taken. The Argentinians had lost 780 men as against our 255, and more than 100 aircraft (32 of them to the Sea Harrier) against 34 of ours.

But, though the *Belgrano* and several smaller ships had gone to the bottom, it had been our Navy which had lost four ships sunk and many more damaged, and 87 of our 255 dead had been lost at sea. Though short, it had been a bitter and intense fight.

We followed the final stages of the capture of Stanley and the Argentinian surrender with a flat sense of anti-climax. It was all massively remote to those who had put their will out to grass through exhaustion. Triumph and exhilaration were for others. At midnight on 14 June 1982, as the surrender document was being signed, the first really heavy snows of winter started to fall. Victory had come not a moment too soon.

Way to the north, as we entered the tropics, I was shocked to see the drawn and haggard pallor of my team when they first appeared blinking in the tropical sun. Had I been deluding myself that we could have fought on for months? The duration of our conflict paled into insignificance compared with that of the Second World War, but ours had been without any respite. And ours was fought by men drawn from a softer, more self-indulgent society in which few receive the hard conditioning that prepares one for combat. I envisage this gap, between the harsh demands of warfare and the cossetted ease of day-to-day existence, widening as the years pass.

I had no hesitation in granting our men every afternoon off for recreation, much to the First Lieutenant's chagrin. He had hoped to get the chance to wash and paint our ugly duckling. Graham Baxter unwrapped his crooked smile whilst we sat on the bridge roof and surveyed rows of very pink, semi-naked sailors all over the upper deck. 'Nothing to be heard but the sound of bursting jock-straps: I hope the girls at home are in similar strict training.' There was not a man who did not have his homecoming date of 24 June circled on the calendar.

At Ascension, there came the penultimate fuelling, and the simplest, but it caught me out. The Type 21 remains a glorious ship to handle, with propellers that can translate 13,000 shaft horsepower into nearly instant astern stopping power. With brakes so good, fortune favours the brave. A fast approach, followed by a large burst of astern power was ideal, giving wind and tidal stream little chance to deflect our bulk from its correct path. Approaching a stationary *Brambleleaf* (Captain M. S. J. Farley) lying at anchor, I misjudged a stiff cross-wind and let our delicate bow swing with a crunch on to the tanker hull. With a steel hull so thin that a heavy blow with a stiletto heel can deeply mark the surface, there is no room for mistakes in a modern warship. A year earlier I had brought *Alacrity* back from a world deployment with only one manoeuvring shaft and propeller; I had kept her safe for nearly two years; I had taken her through a bloody war; but here, on my penultimate alongside, with no challenge, I had hurt her. Though the dent was small, I was bitterly disappointed.

When I went below, I asked Simon Thorp to let me have the blank form on which the Royal Navy reports collisions. A knock on the door of my day cabin revealed not Simon but Colin de Mowbray instead. He stood looking at me, his slow infectious smile lighting the stark interior.

'Such a shame, that collision with *Atlantic Conveyor*, sir. Do you remember when the swell punched us against her? I've only just noticed, but we seem to have sustained a minor dent on the bow. Tiny mark. Devonport Dockyard will remove it in no time. And anyway, war is war . . . ' He disappeared, with only the echo of his voice remaining. I never did get my Collisions Form but I did have a terrible crowd of disobedient officers. My collusion cost me not a minute's sleep.

At Ascension we sent home our advance maintenance party for early leave, so that they could be on the jetty to greet us on our return, allowing us to take our own deserved break. One of our Able Seamen had a broken toe, so we included him in the party, little realizing that we were guaranteeing him an amazing welcome in his home village as a conquering and 'wounded' war hero. Rumour that the village had run out of sacrificial virgins for their lad on the third night went round the ship like wildfire.

Given a brilliant starlit night on 17 June we barbecued out on the battered flight-deck. Anton produced some steaks that had been missed in his over-zealous transfer of everything else to our sister ships. Many empty beer cans were consigned to the deep in the course of the evening as, for once, Colin and I were disinclined to enforce rationing. We relaxed, and with relaxation came revelations of the true realities of war. The candour was unnerving as strained men revealed their innermost thoughts and fears, reliving loneliness and uncertainty with remarkable frankness. I reflected upon my selfish absorption with nothing but the ship's performance and rapid victory. My men would have gained much more peace of mind from consistent face-to-face reassurance from me, but I had withheld it.

Over the long evening, tension slipped away from virtually everyone and, towards midnight, there was a shift in mood. Questions, revelations, comparisons and confessions were done. It was time to restore manhood and self-respect. 'Do you remember that night . . . ' 'God, our shooting was brilliant.' 'Did you ever see such a sight . . . ' Fists pumped the air, laughter came from the belly once more, hands portrayed air attacks. More laughter. Banter. Humour returned. The evening received a further boost with the news that Galtieri had just been ousted as President.

But, for some, it would take longer to return to normality. One Sunday afternoon I was working at my desk when there was a soft knock upon the door. It was a young sailor who occupied a key position in my operations room, a Leading Hand in his middle twenties: I had met his young wife and new baby just before our departure. Having been invited to enter, he stood, tense and awkward, shifting his feet. I invited him to sit and was appalled when he burst into tears. When composure was restored via my previously unused whisky bottle,

I managed to draw out the trouble. It was, he told me, cowardice. I was stunned. It appeared that he was haunted by his 'weakness'. Night after night, this young sailor, with so much new and dear responsibility at home, had sat at his radar with his headset on and had nursed the sure knowledge that he was an abject coward who was scared to death of dying.

I conjured a feigned chuckle from a throat that was so full of emotion I could hardly speak, and I tried to rationalize his normality to him.

'You produced precise results whenever they were called for — faultless under even the greatest threat. You gave strength to all around you — including your Captain. And you did all that whilst terrified?' I paused.

'Don't you know that you are, in fact, the very bravest of the brave?' I had to pause again.

'Now, I want you to stay here for a while, vent what you're feeling, then let yourself out — when you've recognized yourself for what you really are. I'm going for a walk on the upper deck, but come and talk again if you wish. I am intensely proud of you.'

He was gone when I returned and he never came back to talk it over further: I hope that he will forgive me for sharing his frankness, albeit anonymously.

As we left the tropics, the BBC gave us news of the birth of a baby boy to the Princess of Wales — William, second in line to the throne. Our interest in the item was, in itself, a reassuring reminder that we were returning to normality and to more sensitive values. Perhaps the roving padre would not need to rehabilitate us after all.

But we had another preoccupation. We had a foul load of fuel and were contaminating fuel filters at an appalling rate. I joked with David Dyter that the wheels were steadily falling off our wagon; what was he going to do about it? When we lost the use of an Olympus during our passage across Biscay, I stopped joking. I was by then reduced to but two engines out of my four, both of which were undoubtedly contaminated and liable to be lost at any time. I yearned to be securely alongside in Devonport, no longer having to think about the ignominy of being towed in on return from war.

A signal from Flag Officer Plymouth warned us that our return might not be entirely inconspicuous. Up until then we had not really thought about any public focus upon our homecoming — our thoughts were on our return to loved ones. Apparently there would be a 'considerable' number of spectators on the Hoe and on the banks of the Hamoaze right up to our allocated berth. Thank God I did not then know the sight that would confront us north of Plymouth Breakwater: I would have turned the ship about in a display of rank cowardice. The usual excellent reception arrangements for our loved ones were being made, as they always were, by the Naval Base staff.

The Admiral also asked whether I would accept a visit from the Radio 4 *Today* team in the early morning of our arrival. I accepted with pleasure, having been a long-time listener to the programme, and made arrangements for them to be winched in by helicopter.

There is a tradition in the Royal Navy, when returning from distant deployment, called 'Up Channel Night'. On the night before homecoming, certain latitudes can be taken with alcohol: excesses and occasional tragedies have been known. What the whole ritual has to say about the forebearance of naval wives and girlfriends who then have to spend the following night coping with the hungover passions of such jaded brutes, heaven knows. I was concerned that, with so much repressed post-war tension still to disperse, we had the perfect formula for tragedy. Colin de Mowbray exercised an enlightened but unambiguous series of cautions and restraints; and we all made it to the grey and still dawn of 24 June 1982.

I completed my final report as we turned the ship's head into the approaches to the English Channel. One hundred ships had gone south, carrying 28,000 men. Though I was quietly proud of *Alacrity*'s performance, it was but one of many similar successes by our warships: and my fellow ships had fought on for yet another week after we had left. Time to reflect gave me a deeper understanding of the overall maritime achievement.

Alacrity had steamed 30,000 miles at an average speed of 14 knots. She had fired her gun in anger more than 500 times and had come under attack on ten separate occasions. She had been the only British ship to penetrate Falkland Sound before the invasion — had done it twice — and had placed Special Forces undetected in the heart of enemy-held territory. She had sunk the only Argentinian vessel to be destroyed by our surface ships and had been amongst the targets of five separate missile attacks. More than seventy men had been rescued from *Atlantic Conveyor*. *Alacrity*'s Lynx had flown 100 day hours and 56 by night, completing 215 deck landings, firing 1,500 rounds of bullets, dropping a torpedo, and delivering several flares. All of it had been achieved without casualties. It was no wonder that my men felt they had something to celebrate as they prepared for their homecoming. I was indeed bringing my people safe home — but our thoughts were much with those who would never again pass through the Dockyard gates to be reunited with their loved ones.

Homecoming. Two and a half months of our lives gone which could never be compared with any others. The Radio 4 interview came and went in a blur but at least I was able to pay tribute to the achievements of our sailors, and to the love and support from the UK that had been such a source of strength to us all.

I had barely finished the interview before David Dyter appeared on the bridge with a face which told its own story. The Gods had decided, with a fine sense of timing, that *Alacrity* and her young captain were to be tested further. We had lost our penultimate engine: there was but one wheel on my wagon! Then I was advised by the harbour authority that the brand-new frigate *Brazen* was filling the berth just ahead of ours and that she would be rigged for full ceremonial with her entire ship's company ranged along the upper deck to welcome us home. Though a fine gesture, it was a thoroughly unwelcome surprise. If I were to misjudge my stop, it would be spectacularly expensive.

A much greater surprise still awaited us as we ran in at speed past the Eddystone, swung around the western tip of the breakwater and directed our binoculars upon the City of Plymouth. In twenty years of returning from seaward to our historic western naval base, I had never seen even a fraction of the crowds which were by then gathered all across the Hoe and down on to the promenade — they streamed and seethed and filled every piece of green grass and grey concrete. And all faces were turned towards *Alacrity*.

For the very last time, I spoke to my ship's company. I reminded them of their achievements and thanked them from the bottom of my heart for their comradeship. But the standards of *Alacrity* would continue right to the berth: I expected them to stand perfectly still in their positions around the upper deck throughout our entry, joined in the same unity that had brought us safe home, whatever the distractions. For I had been led to believe that their grateful nation awaited them. I switched off the microphone and nodded to the Officer of the Watch.

'Hands fall in for full ceremonial entry to Plymouth.'

As my sailors moved to take up their intervals all around the edge of the rusting upper deck,

I directed the ship towards Drake's Island. And a wall of noise reached out from Plymouth and engulfed us.

* * *

God knows what our sailors are feeling but I can hardly breathe for emotion. Despite the bedlam all around us, Simon moves lithely back and forth, taking bearings of his navigational features, and crisply passes the helm orders to the Officer of the Watch. As we swing wide around Devil's Point, I can almost imagine the lean image of Antelope *tucked in our wake as she had been when we headed out through the rain on 5 April. It is all over, and we are being overwhelmed by a grateful nation, whilst* Antelope *rots on the muddy bottom of San Carlos. I feel humble as I drag myself back to the present.*

'Admiral's Barge coming up fast from astern, sir.'

I move from the air-conditioned bridge and out on to the bridge wing — out into the cacophony of hooting ships, cheering people and distant sirens that is all for us. Every ship we pass is dressed overall with brilliant signal flags, sailors lining their decks in tribute. I acknowledge the Queen's Harbourmaster who is waving his cap with gusto, before lifting my gaze to the banks on either side. There are hundreds of people even on the far western shore to our left: behind them, carpets of green sweep up across the Cornish hillside where a tractor cuts neat ribbons of welcome in the lush slopes. The fragrance of fresh-mown grass and English summer wafts towards us on the morning air.

And all along the cobbled historic jetties to our right spreads a different mass of green. Every dockyard worker seems to be there, each apparently wearing brand-new overalls, bright in the sunlight which has just emerged through the overcast. These often taciturn men of the West, whose forefathers have served the Royal Navy for generations, are also paying tribute. These stalwarts who built and maintained our ships, and who seem on occasions to take the Navy for granted, are here to a man. For all their normal reserve they are waving and cheering like the rest. The amazing performance is unprecedented.

I look down across the long forecastle, past our weary gun and up to the shark bow with its bruised lip. My men stand motionless, slightly bent against the wind of our passage as the tumult washes about them. I look back along the signal deck beneath me, where all my senior ratings are gathered. And suddenly I am fighting for control. Like their junior ratings down on the forecastle, they too are standing absolutely motionless. But what so unsettles me, despite my responsibilities, is that every set of cheekbones seems to be running wet with tears. These men who have held themselves — and each other — together for so long, can simply no longer control themselves in the face of such a welcome. Shakespeare even captured this moment too:

And all my mother came into mine eyes
And gave me up to tears.

I re-enter the bridge and prepare to take my limping ship alongside in the midst of a sea of emotion — and bedlam.

No. 5 berth is now in sight; Brazen fills the wharf ahead, and the corner of our jetty shows the dangerous swirl of ebb tide that will carry my ship hard on to the wooden piles if I misjudge a timid approach. Royal Marines bandsmen are playing, as television cameras roam and probe, exploring expectation on the faces of our loved ones who are gathered fifty-deep, holding banners, flags — and emotions — in check. Their men — all of their men — are coming safe home.

I give approval for the sailors to 'fall out' ready to handle the ropes, wires, fenders and signals that are needed to complete the complicated ritual of taking a modern warship alongside her berth. There is an extra tension on the bridge as we all quietly measure the potential for cataclysmic anti-climax. The wise man would take a tug, with the acceptable alibi of having but one propeller. But then he would have no sense of occasion.

Taking over the conning microphone, I line myself up behind the compass repeater and start driving the ship down the imaginary line to the green flag which marks, optimistically, the precise position at which my bridge should finally arrive. Smiling at the drawn faces around

235

me on the bridge, I adopt my affectation of a slow drawl.

'Right, gentlemen. Let's put the baby to bed, shall we?' And I increase our speed: a shudder runs through the Navigator. Now we are cutting through the water at 8 knots with a neat white bow wave and the White Ensign standing out proudly in the breeze.

All is now concentration and correction, small adjustments of course to check any swing or deviation. The jetty becomes clearer, as do the features of our cheering reception committee.

'Flag Officer Plymouth on the jetty, sir,' intones Simon, quite unnecessarily.

'Thanks, Pilot; that does help.' I respond with a thin smile. David Dyter is also on the bridge, tense and expectant as he peers down through the windows at the fast-approaching jetty. Why the hell isn't he nurturing our last remaining engine, I think, savagely and unfairly. His expert team is far below, all doing just that with well-proven thoroughness.

The jetty edge is now lost to my gaze below the hurtling bow. 'Port 30.' Pause a second. 'Half astern starboard. Lever 80.' If this big swing with the rudders is not checked precisely by the surge of the single engine then it is going to be a very spectacular arrival and our stern will be flattened into the jetty.

The bow swings from the rudder bite; the massive astern power starts to arrest forward momentum — and also checks the yawing stern. The out-of-balance engine power gathers the swing of the bow and controls it.

'Moving to the bridge wing, Officer of the Watch.' I refuse to hasten. If I have got the timing of the orders right, it will all be happening correctly. I climb on to the overhanging bridge wing as the jetty disappears beneath it and the ship slides gently to a halt. The green flag is precisely below me as are, it seems, several thousand people.

'Stop starboard. Midships.'

My faithful ship sits motionless — in position. Heaving lines are thrown, wires passed, cheers are deafening; and there is a fleeting glimpse of my family in the crowd. Infernal stinging at the back of my eyes: it is all over. My delayed drawl becomes even more pronounced.

'Ring off, Quartermaster. Finished with main engine. Thank you for your efforts, gentlemen.'

I try not to notice the broad smiles of my team as we go aft to rejoin the world.

Epilogue
The Summer of '82

'Shall think themselves accurs'd
they were not here'

IT was time for well-earned leave — and for me to relinquish the command that I had been privileged to hold for an extra three months. A roisterous farewell, towed on a gun carriage by my sailors across the length of the Naval Base, gave me little chance for even a backward glance at the silhouette of the ship that would, amongst all my commands, always hold my heart.

Leave came and went. I joined the Maritime Tactical School where we distilled and taught the business of war. I tried hard not to pontificate purely on the basis of 'having been there' but the harsh lessons of combat will always be a world away from theorizing and simulation. Admiral Woodward gave of his time and we conducted a two-day seminar upon the many lessons learnt. It seemed half the Navy was gathered around the tactical floor, whilst the young Wrens moved ship symbols across a shiny surface which soon became a distant expanse of storm-tossed ocean as we talked and discussed. We turned back the clock and disseminated all we had learnt. The Admiral was typically candid and brave as he recounted the complexities of command — warts and all — in the very imprecise art of war.

In truth, I found it difficult to readapt to peace. My emotional threshold had been lowered and could be reached more readily than ever before. Minor sadnesses and tragedies frequently came near to moving me to tears. Mourning the futility of so many deaths, I eventually balanced their inevitability with the worthiness of the cause, but I made a mistake in accepting an invitation from friends to attend the summer ritual that is the Henley Royal Regatta. Hardly my scene at the best of times, in the summer of 1982 I found it obscene. After a long afternoon of self-indulgence had come and gone, I was consumed by bitterness at the frothy frivolity. It seemed to my overheated emotions that the men who had died had not even touched the consciousness of the self-obsessed, posturing, chinless nonentities who milled about the banks of the Thames. By the time fireworks ripped and spangled the night sky, I saw only gunfire and death. I remained morose and viciously angry for days. But slowly I adapted.

I was proud to be invited to Buckingham Palace to receive my decoration from Her Majesty Queen Elizabeth II, and it was a double delight to find that I would get my award on the same day that the Admiral was to be knighted. It was a happy, relaxed photograph of Admiral Sir John Woodward with his Band of Brothers that adorned virtually all the national daily papers. I sent a signal to my old ship saying that I was investigating ways of dividing the Distinguished Service Cross into 200 slivers — for it was truly theirs.

A variety of speaking engagements and lectures followed, and bore testament to the fascination of the nation with such a distant war. On occasions, I felt deep frustration at public ignorance of the part played by the Royal Navy in making the entire victory possible: giving the RAF credit for the destruction of the Argentinian Air Force which had been decimated by naval aviation left me almost speechless. I was still far too close to my subject on many counts. I could not enjoy the interest, attention and admiration, and I even found it difficult to relate the vividness of the experience to my beloved wife with whom I share most things.

Lofty ideals that I took to, and brought back from, war became somewhat tarnished over the years that followed. When I returned with *Avenger* to the Falklands late in 1985, we patrolled impotently the same seas that had seen so much fury but three years earlier, having to watch trawlers from Eastern Europe and squid jiggers from the Far East taking massive catches from waters over which we had fought. So strong was my frustration on my return to the UK that the then Commander-in-Chief Fleet, Admiral Sir Nicholas Hunt, arranged for me to visit the Foreign Office to voice my alarm to relatively highly placed mandarins. My anger deepened as I listened to the indifferent responses of my hosts who seemed determined not to restrict such trade and safeguard the interests of the Falklanders. I left King Charles Street and

Whitehall with echoes of the 'delicate balance of international relations' still ringing in my ears.

One year later, in February 1987, the 150-mile Falkland Island Interim Conservation and Management Zone was formed: an extension of 50 miles was added in 1990. Revenue from the resultant sale of fishing licences in 1991 – 2 alone totalled £26 million. Thus it is reasonable to estimate an earlier loss to the Exchequer and to the islands of £100 million over the post-war period. As for the full scale of the depletion of marine livestock, fish-heaven alone knows! Ironically, in 1993 there came news of highly promising large stocks of hydro-carbon resources being potentially exploitable off the coast, reserves that might still one day add up to compensation for the battered islanders.

Perhaps the best part of the aftermath of war was the huge volume of letters from so many well-wishers, some known personally to me and some not known at all. The desire of many to thank those who had gone south soon restored my equilibrium.

Amongst the many hundreds I received, first welcoming me home and then congratulating me upon my award, was one which had a wisdom, honesty and sensitivity all of its own. It was from an old friend with whom I had flown in the 1960s. His name was Tony Wigley, and he was later to die at the controls of a helicopter, cutting off prematurely a rare talent. His letter included the standard kindnesses about the performance of myself and my ship but it was the conclusion that gave me cause to reflect long afterwards upon the privilege that I had been given, and upon other things.

'And now you must live with the envy of those whom fate did not single out to have the chance to prove themselves amidst the ultimate challenge. I just hope we would all have done as well as you did.'

I am certain that they would.

BOOK TWO

The Gulf, 1990 – 1991

Prelude: The Call to Arms

21 – 25 September 1990

'As were a war in expectation'

IT was a rare, glittering September day with a calm English Channel telling everyone that all was well with the world. It was lying.

Daphne and I had hired a blue and white weatherboard chalet on the shingle foreshore of West Bexington, Dorset, overlooking Lyme Bay, for a few days of perfect solitude. Reality barely intruded, despite international tension caused by the Iraqi President, Saddam Hussein, having invaded Kuwait with 100,000 troops and 300 tanks on 2 August. We simply engaged in self-centred gentle excess, indifferent to events unfolding beyond the wavelets which nightly lulled us to sleep.

Two years in command of the barracks at HMS *Drake* in Devonport had cut me off from the operational navy for almost the first time, which had not delighted me. My next appointment was to be second-in-command of naval aviation, at Yeovilton, Somerset, and Daphne was relishing the prospect of two more years of stability after spending over half our married life separated. However, my appointer, Captain John Hall, had asked me to ring him during my leave — he might have some news for me.

Relaxed and looking forward to a long swim after our morning walk, I unsuspectingly inserted my coins into the Bexington pay-phone. I never got my swim, and there was to be precious little relaxation in the next ten months: I was being recalled to operations. Selected to go straight to the Ministry of Defence for three months to help co-ordinate the Gulf effort, I was then to take command of all British naval forces afloat in Gulf waters from my flagship HMS *London*, as a Commodore. The British contribution to the Gulf crisis was to be known as Operation Granby.

I felt that somebody thought it might come to war: I was going back where I belonged.

1

The Shield is Forged

26 September – 30 November 1990

'For now sits Expectation in the air'

ONCE again, regret at disrupting family expectations in no way masked my elation at reverting to active service: I was revitalized. The initial reality was rather more mundane, as we needed two homes within five days — one for me in London and one for the family for an unknown period. Commandeering the same telephone kiosk, I challenged estate agents across four counties and admired yet again the durability and adaptability of my wife.

We found our homes on our seventeenth wedding anniversary and settled with time to spare: Daphne moved into a hiring in Bridport within a sensible radius of both sons, whilst I lodged near Clapham Common with Janie Caesar, a close family friend whose husband I had flown with for many years before he was killed in a tragic flying accident. Janie was to be tolerant of my anti-social twelve-hour stints around the clock in the Ministry, an existence which was to prove high on fatigue and decidedly low on quality of life.

247

But a sophisticated lifestyle has never been part of an officer's existence in the vast, green-roofed, impersonal maze of the UK Defence Forces Headquarters which flanks the south side of Whitehall. Eight main floors are set into vertical spines, where seedy paintwork, drab offices and squalid toilets saw little daylight through greying lace curtains. During an earlier job as an Assistant Secretary to the Chiefs of Staff, I had spent two years learning much but finding endless word-play too often purposeless. To this day, I cannot enjoy the hilarious excellence of the televised *Yes, Prime Minister* without feeling a shudder of vivid recall — it remains flawlessly accurate. Nevertheless, I had encountered bright people, stimulating high-level business and subtle working techniques — albeit quickly dispelling my previous conviction that men who possess intellect must also have character and wisdom. Altogether, I had been very relieved to march for the last time in sober-suited earnestness across St James's Park, shoulder to shoulder with similarly grey men: the MOD was not for me. I had gone straight from the 'Madhouse', as it is known within the Services, to command HMS *Alacrity*. Sanity sweetly restored.

As I returned to the Ministry, I landed a sizeable bet on Saumarez in the Arc de Triomphe at Longchamps at 16-1: the omens were good. A month earlier, I would have given longer odds still against my getting back to sea.

It was time to focus upon Kuwait. The

immaculate and absurdly wealthy desert kingdom had been desecrated. Western news reports were full of excess: excessive behaviour by the brutal invaders and perhaps some excesses in the accuracy of the reporting. As in April 1982, truth risked being deafened by rattling sabres.

Nevertheless, it had been a brutal rape. Some 300 Kuwaitis had been killed and a further 400,000 had fled their homeland: only 40,000 foreigners remained out of an original total of nearly 1.5 million. The luxury shops of Kuwait City proved an irresistible lure to greedy Iraqis and, although there seemed to be some constraint placed upon the invaders' sexual appetite towards European and Kuwaiti women, there was mass rape of Asians. Wide publicity attended a claim that Iraqi troops had burst into a maternity hospital and removed fifty babies from incubators to die. Individual accounts of beatings and torture became commonplace. Millions of pounds of gold and cash were taken by the Iraqis from the Central Bank, although huge sums had been transferred shortly before the invasion. The few international friends of Iraq were getting fewer by the day; indeed, Saddam might have been more successful diplomatically if only his forces had conducted themselves with restraint. Had we but known it, we were getting our first clues that the Iraqi war machine was not the effective force it appeared to be.

Western Intelligence had started inauspiciously by forecasting no invasion, British Intelligence actually advising the Cabinet as late as

1 August that there would be no incursion. Thereafter, fears that Saddam might roll on across Saudi Arabia and into the Gulf States prompted massive and rapid reinforcement of the Saudi kingdom. In mid-August, the United States activated its Central military command organization, cut off $700 million loan guarantees to Iraq, and commenced an extensive build-up of its forces in Saudi Arabia, under the codename Desert Shield. British, French, Egyptian and Syrian forces were all following in their wake. Economic sanctions were imposed on 6 August and a full naval blockade commenced on 25 August. The UN Security Council unanimously demanded unconditional withdrawal, and even the Arab League condemned the invasion. Saddam had really miscued.

The recent history of Iraq had been turbulent. In 1958, the monarchy was overthrown and the country became a Republic, soon challenging the independence of Kuwait by claiming traditional ownership of the desert kingdom. In 1968, the Ba'ath Party seized power, their philosophy being based upon recreating one cohesive Arab state. They appointed 31-year-old Saddam Hussein as Deputy Chairman of Internal Security, a topic with which he would remain preoccupied. By 1979 he had become President. Four years later he committed his nation to eight wasteful years of war with Iran. In 1990 he chose to give back virtually all the blood-soaked territory won by his people over nearly a decade, as he sued for peace: the world was not to know that he was simply safeguarding his eastern flank at whatever price before initiating his Kuwait adventure.

His main objectives in August 1990 still remain obscure. Certainly, as a competing producer, he wished to stem Kuwait's over-production of oil, thereby increasing the world price; indeed, when Kuwait was invaded, the price rose by one-third overnight. And certainly he wished to keep his people distracted from appalling economic and internal strife. Cessation of the Iran-Iraq war had left Baghdad owing a total of £70 billion, Kuwait having refused to waive earlier Iraqi war debts and having also rejected an appeal to cede part-ownership of the north-western Gulf islands of Warbah and Bubiyan. So Saddam's 100, 000 troops replaced diplomacy, and a surprised Kuwaiti army of 20,000 men crumbled before them. Kuwait fell and Saddam was able to write off £5.5 billion of debts to the Kuwaitis, and £13 billion to Saudi Arabia.

The then Saudi Ambassador to Bahrain, Ghazi Algosaibi, in his fascinating book on the Gulf crisis, saw three psychological weaknesses impairing Saddam's decision-taking: hunger for power, adventurism and a deeply ingrained persecution complex. When one also considers his limited education, lack of military knowledge and ignorance of the world beyond his borders, one sees the origins of tragedy for his country. Of all Saddam's miscalculations, his flawed assumptions about the international reaction to his invasion were the worst, particularly concerning the French and the Americans.

251

And he certainly should have guessed that disintegration of the Soviet Union would stop it aligning with its well-established ally Iraq: the Soviet Foreign Minister, Eduard Shevardnadze, believed that if the Gulf crisis had occurred during the Cold War the USSR would have backed Iraq — probably leading to a Third World War. We had cause to be grateful for the accidents of history.

Though our Services had effectively abandoned the Gulf area in 1967 as a result of defence cuts, the Royal Navy had maintained a warship presence in Gulf waters since 1980; it was called the Armilla Patrol and gave us familiarity with the area, its waters and its local politics. And the fact that our Navy had generations of experience at balancing deterrent presence with self-restraint made it obvious that we would be in demand as international tension increased.

However, on 2 August, we had only one warship in the Gulf itself, one in Mombasa and a further vessel in Penang. They all regrouped swiftly and commenced embargo operations under UN Security Council Resolutions 661 and 662 to prevent Iraqi merchant ships entering the Gulf with banned cargo that would help their military adventurism. Meanwhile, the US Navy had provided a cruiser, a destroyer and five frigates; the French, two corvettes. And it was not just embargo enforcers that were gathering: Tomahawk cruise missiles were soon within range of Baghdad, carried by US Navy nuclear submarines, and vast American aircraft-carriers were racing to the area, escorted by battle groups of missile-armed escorts. The greatest military arsenal since the Korean War was being assembled in remarkably quick time, and maritime forces were demonstrating their effectiveness in exerting early pressure upon an adversary without any need for third-party support.

* * *

Once settled in the MOD, I lost myself in preparations and made quite sure that others did the same: people could die if we failed to pay attention. I was serving as one of four co-directors in a watch system within the Naval Co-ordinating Cell of the Defence Situation Centre, which acts as fuel and lubrication to the naval machinery of the Crisis Management Organization in the Ministry. As co-ordinators of the 'Dark Blue' cell, we four managed the efforts of a small team trying, by signal and telephone, to link the MOD to all the many naval and supply bases across the UK, and also to the newly established Senior Naval Officer, Middle East (SNOME or 'Snow me' as he was so aptly known), afloat in the Gulf. Commodore Paul Haddacks was the initial encumbent, and it was him that I was due to replace in December.

Although day-to-day operational command of our Gulf ships was then still conducted by Fleet Headquarters, Northwood, full command remained with the MOD which allocated forces, authorized their overall use and provided the operational commander with guidance as to what he could do with his vessels.

Various changes in co-ordination were planned as tension rose. Operational command of all the British forces was being drawn together in one centre — RAF Strike Command HQ in High Wycombe, Buckinghamshire. Though the Navy bridled somewhat at losing control from Northwood (which had been the tri-service centre for the Falklands), the change made good sense. However, the detailed movement of our forces and their integration with Coalition ships clearly could not take place from the outer stockbroker belt of London, so a Joint Force HQ (JFHQ) was established with Saudi agreement in Riyadh. Eventually a three-star senior officer would take command of all British forces in the theatre from JFHQ but, for the moment, the reins were held by Air Vice Marshal Sandy Wilson who had been pressed into service from his loan posting in Oman.

Out in Gulf waters, the initial British naval force, Group Whisky, comprised the destroyer *York* (Captain Tony McEwan), the frigates *Battleaxe* (Commander Andrew Gordon-Lennox) and *Jupiter* (Commander John Wright), and the tanker *Orangeleaf* (Captain Mike Farley). Commodore Paul Haddacks joined *York* on 10 August with just one staff officer.

These warships were replaced in September by Group Xray comprising *Brazen* (Commander James Rapp), *Cardiff* (Commander Adrian Nance), *Gloucester* (Commander Philip Wilcocks) and their new flagship, *London* (Captain Iain Henderson), to which Paul Haddacks and his

254

small staff transferred. He was busy setting up the command organization that I would inherit ten weeks later and directing his escorts into patrol and interception areas against the still vast number of merchant ships transitting the Straits of Hormuz, the gateway to the Gulf. Thereafter, British force levels steadily increased as the task of embargo grew and as the possibility of war became more distinct.

The key naval man in the Ministry was the Assistant Chief of Naval Staff, Admiral Hugo White, who had been the Captain of our 4th Frigate Squadron in 1982. As he was effectively the very busy chief executive of the entire Navy, he called in Rear Admiral Sam Salt, ex-*Sheffield*, to focus solely on the Gulf and run the operation for him. A tiny man of great heart and humanity, Sam was an excellent choice, making worthwhile enemies throughout that autumn in his single-minded pursuit of results. Under his authority was the Director of Naval Operations and Trade, Captain John Lang. Poised and gracious, he was destined to be my 'ear' in the MOD when I needed fast results, working unbelievably hard throughout.

In the naval cell, the daytime was a frenzy. Keeping abreast of towering piles of signals, briefing Ministers, pursuing numerous equipment modifications to our ships, and holding navy department co-ordination meetings took three-quarters of the day: preparing ministerial briefs and service papers took the rest. Most papers were for the benefit of the Defence Operations Executive which met daily to monitor Desert Shield but which had only limited delegated power and frequently needed the endorsement of the Chiefs and, sometimes, Ministers. Major policy decisions were taken by a Cabinet committee, the Defence Overseas and Policy Committee.

Even overnight periods were far from tranquil. Signalled demands from the Gulf and much of the preparatory work for the following day all had to be attended to. This did at least allow me to resume disrupted sleep patterns which I had not had to endure for four years, but I cannot say that I enjoyed the re-familiarization.

Nor did I enjoy seeing the MOD being distracted by work upon 'Options for Change', the run-down of the British armed forces in the aftermath of the Cold War. All Western nations wanted the defence savings which would come from reduced tension between the superpowers. Ironically, the demise of the Cold War had heralded a new campaign — resisting fresh regiments of reductions. The British Cabinet was naturally intent on relieving public expenditure through cuts in defence, and thus a run-down of the Services had begun somewhat arbitrarily before August 1990. Thereafter, the Treasury was appalled that the beastly Saddam was provoking additional expenditure. The result was that the allocation of men and equipment to the Gulf had to be fought through the finance branches of the Armed Forces with a vigour that would have been better deployed against the Iraqis.

The process was further cluttered by the

MOD also being engaged in its annual long-term costing which sees the Services bidding for money to pay for the year ahead and offering their proposed savings and additions. Thus we were preparing for possible war with somewhat divided aims — but at least we were spared the threat of the Soviet Union.

It was financial pressure that lay at the root of the political refusal to deploy our aircraft-carrier *Ark Royal* in the Gulf. Though it would have taken nearly £20 million to modify her to combat Iraq rather than the Soviet Union, she would have been the ideal command and control platform for our gathering naval force, a task for which she was specifically designed. The supremely single-minded Deputy Commander-in-Chief Fleet, Admiral Roy Newman, had fought to have her converted and deployed but he had not reckoned with the power of the Treasury within the MOD. The carrier never got beyond the Eastern Mediterranean.

A different debate concerned the 30,000-ton Royal Fleet Auxiliary *Argus*. New and impressive, she trained helicopter crews in peacetime but there was great demand for her and her five medium-lift Sea King helicopters to do other things. Plans were drawn up to install a containerized ward and surgery in her forward hangar — *MASH* afloat — the Falklands having taught us that early treatment of battle-torn men saves lives. But controversy attended her status with the International Red Cross. Some believed that she should be declared a hospital ship and painted white with red crosses, allegedly safe

257

from attack under the Geneva Convention: others, including experienced sailors, believed that no such guarantee of sanctity existed in a modern fighting mêlée — even the largest red cross is irrelevant to a missile radar sniffing amongst big blips in the ocean. To me, it seemed impossible to safeguard such a vessel through statute; we had to defend it by force and use it in the ideal place for our military needs, rather than be constrained to a declared hospital-ship location. Our military view prevailed and *Argus* became in all respects a fighting asset rather untidily titled a Primary Casualty Receiving Ship.

When it came to the naval case for modifying our logistical landing ships, the struggle began again. Though these vessels (the *Sir Galahad* class) were adaptable workhorses which had proved themselves in the Falklands, it was difficult to specify an exact need for such a 'jack-of-all-trades' in advance of the event. Despite impassioned exchanges with various departments of the MOD, on the outbreak of hostilities I had two out of four of these ships still being modified for war.

Nevertheless, a brave early decision was made to commit UK minehunters to Paul's direction — Hunt-class glass-reinforced plastic ships, known very unofficially as the 'Tupperware Navy'. Their slow speed and the need for them to work up in the challenging shallow waters of the Gulf made an early start important. This well-balanced little mine-countermeasures (MCM) force was headed by Commander John

Scoles and a team of minewarfare experts in their command ship, the white-hulled survey vessel *Herald* (Commander Peter Jones). Together with his hunters, *Hurworth* (Commander Richard Ibbotson), *Atherstone* (Lieutenant Commander Nick Davies) and *Cattistock* (Lieutenant Commander Mike Shrives), he commenced the long passage east from Rosyth at 10 knots. I was to come to know these men extremely well. In cost per ton, their ships were the most expensive vessels afloat — nearly £50 million for each 750-ton craft. They were soon to appear cheap at the price.

Along the 6,300-mile route to the Gulf, there also started to stretch a 146-vessel British sea supply line. These vessels were, as in 1982, chartered from many nations, even those of the Warsaw Pact, which sent a tremor or two through the odd lapsed Cold War warrior. Co-ordinated from an operations room in one of the quieter streets between Victoria Station and Parliament Square, this supply crocodile was eventually to carry 260,000 tons of general cargo and 102,000 tons of ammunition (whilst air freight conveyed but 53,000 tons). All these ships were tracked and reported by our MOD cell throughout their passage. Their vulnerability to interference was a concern which merited a number of precautions. The average transit time was twenty-one days, invariably to Al Jubayl in Saudi Arabia, and each vessel carried an Army security detachment. As they all sailed unescorted, it was as well that Iraq did not possess submarines to disrupt our efforts — the

MOD was already having to stump up an astonishing 200 per cent war tariff on most of the charters. Sadly, the Red Duster flew from only eight of these mastheads, such had been the decline in the British merchant fleet which had halved in the previous five years.

Manpower, too, was in short supply. Royal Navy strength had progressively been cut over the past thirty years to 52,000 men and 10,000 officers (the Army numbered 150,000 and the RAF 88,000). With a naval sea/shore ratio already a demanding 50:50 and our teeth/tail ratio a lean 70:30, there was little slack. Reinforcing the Gulf, readying forces for conflict and still coping with existing peacetime tasks worldwide was becoming impossible. There was simply too much to do with too few people. Accordingly, 1,300 additional naval billets were established by simply leaving gaps elsewhere or by inviting already busy personnel to undertake two jobs — 'double hatting'. I hope that those who rose to such sapping demands took justifiable pride in the final victory.

The MOD did not feel it necessary to enforce retention of those personnel who had already opted for premature departure from the Services. Furthermore,while the Reserve Forces Act of 1980 was designed for major conflict, with several demanding criteria needing to be met before the reserves could be brought forward, situations short of general war were not really covered. Thus *ad hoc* manning arrangements continued and put the Navy under great, unpublicized, pressure, whilst across the Atlantic the US Navy called up 20,000 reservists to face the Gulf challenge. More flexible arrangements for tapping enthusiastic and capable British reserves have since been evolved.

Meanwhile, away to the east, Saddam was appealing for a united Arab state under his leadership, as Nasser had done when provoking the Suez crisis in 1956. UN resolve and brilliant diplomacy by the Bush Administration was surprising Europeans more used to prevarication from the former and less subtle foreign policy by the latter. But it was an edgy process. Would the Soviets accept solidarity with their previous foes against their previous friends? Could an Arab consensus digest an American menu? Would Saddam back down before blockade and threat of eviction? Was conflict inevitable, or were we all being conned by an arch-exponent of bluff?

Our warships in the Gulf were certainly not being conned by anybody as they helped to enforce the blockade, using Royal Marines teams who rapid-roped down from helicopter abseils or leapt off high-speed boats after grappling the deck-edges of the merchant ships. But it was the US Navy, in the shape of USS *Biddle*, that intercepted the first Iraqi tanker, *Al Karamah*, on 31 August; and it was the USS *Goldsborough* that carried out the first boarding and diversion on 4 September. Thereafter, a gathering number of challenges, interceptions and boardings took place. The Coalition was exerting pressure upon the Iraqi military machine.

It was the capacity of that same machine that was by then preoccupying me. My wife, sons and close friends all received scant attention: I was utterly absorbed. Iraq possessed the fourth biggest army in the world and the fifth largest air force. Iraqi combat forces were hardened by nearly ten years of war and possessed sophisticated air defence and a proven electronic warfare capability. Their anti-ship assets included 5C Mirage fighter-bombers, 400 air-launched Exocets and 7 shore launchers with 50 Silkworm anti-ship missiles. Worse still, they had seized 6 capable Kuwaiti, Exocet-armed, fast patrol craft. They also owned a miscellany of sea mines. My interest heightened.

Their chemical weapons had been used against the Iranians and had killed 5,000 of their own Kurds at Halabja. Mustard gas, dating from the First World War, produces severe damage by blistering skin and lungs, thus allowing nerve gas an easier passage to the body's central nervous system. Most of Saddam's munitions, including his Scud missiles, were capable of delivering such substances. The prospect of Coalition forces fighting under a blazing sun in heavy protective suits against such weapons was sobering; I read with interest a post-flight report from one of our frigates whose flight observer had lost 16 lbs in bodyweight during one flight whilst wearing his chemical warfare suit.

It was a relatively small philosophical step for a tyrant such as Saddam to move from chemical to biological warfare: bubonic plague and anthrax placed in domestic water supplies and thereby infecting thousands would present our forces with indescribable difficulties. At several stages that autumn, it looked as if the Coalition was about to worry itself into concessions at the horrific prospect of biological and chemical weapons being used. Shadows of Munich, September 1938, stretched around the world: appeasers were at work. With good reason, the Americans hinted at their ultimate willingness to retaliate with tactical nuclear weapons if the Iraqis were to conduct such warfare. But, ironically, overshadowing all existing Iraqi capabilities hung the assessment that Saddam himself would shortly possess a nuclear capability.

Was it any wonder that international opinion believed Saddam would have to step back from the brink, or that some mutual face-saving formula would have to be devised? This view was fuelled by some cynics who suspected that the vigour of the West's response had less to do with the rape of innocent Kuwait and more to do with a long-standing American desire to control Middle Eastern oil. In reality, the Western economies could ill-afford blackmail by one nation which controlled a majority of the world's known oil reserves. A sentimental minority, amongst whom I was one, believed once more that by resisting tyranny we might help to establish a more stable world.

Within the MOD, the complexities of Rules of Engagement again loomed large. In fact, they were a much more important factor than in 1982: the stakes were so much higher when most of the world was engaged. More specifically, at sea, no nation wanted to share the guidance given to its ships, particularly its robust measures against Iraqi vessels resisting boarding parties. Ministers were sensitive that undue Coalition force might be used by Saddam as a propaganda tool, or might even trigger massive escalation. The US and the Australians were a particular worry, their military culture not being noted for its subtle self-restraint. Of much greater concern was the fact that nations would not declare their commitment to a possible war — a hypersensitive issue which clouded much international co-operation and planning.

By then I considered myself to be something of an expert on ROE, having spent two years teaching the subject in the Maritime Tactical School following my Falklands experience. Familiarity in the Navy with the use of ROE was now widespread due to extensive training ashore and afloat: we were much improved since 1982 and certainly ahead of the other two Services. Though good staffwork was taking place in the MOD, weaknesses remained, some of which were to pose me problems later.

Although NATO was not empowered to play a formal part in the proceedings — the Gulf lying well outside NATO's operating area — the Western European Union (WEU) nations had agreed to co-ordinate their efforts in enforcing the UN embargo; France and Italy in particular wanted to establish the Union as a significant military organization. Altogether, some political games were going on which had less to do with efficient execution of the blockade and rather more to do with eroding American domination of NATO and the newly formed Coalition.

Out in the waters of the Gulf, the WEU Task Group Commanders had started to hold meetings immediately before the full Coalition Commanders held their monthly get-togethers. Having had their inaugural gathering on board the French ship *Dupleix* in September, their second took place on board the British RFA *Fort Grange* on 8 October. Paul Haddacks was already tip-toeing along a tightrope of international sensitivities, and specific controversy arose when the French proposed WEU patrol areas which conflicted with the efficient, well-established US zones. The British and the Dutch objected, Paul upsetting the French by highlighting wasteful duplication of effort. I admired his single-mindedness but it was clear that the effectiveness of the WEU as an additional co-ordinating agency was going to need playing up. My difficulty would be supporting this line whilst preparing for war, primarily with our American allies.

Meanwhile, the British frigate *Brazen* showed that there was proper business to be done. In late October she boarded the Iraqi merchant vessel *Tadmur* and found her to be carrying banned cargo, albeit merely flour. There followed a sapping period for her young commanding officer, Commander James Rapp, whilst diplomacy sought to find an Arab state willing to impound both ship and cargo on behalf of the UN. Finally the Omanis took the ship in, only for the decision to be reversed, the cargo reloaded, and the ship invited to sail — again escorted by the luckless *Brazen*. Thankfully, before the situation degenerated into total farce, it was agreed that the cargo could be ditched at sea. I followed events in frustrated amazement: if such a merry-go-round could stem from mere flour, what would happen to Coalition unity when the bullets started to fly? However, I was delighted to see James covering himself with credit through cool action and lucid reporting; he would still be one of my captains when I took over the Task Group on 3 December.

One cold night late in October, I met the man who would represent my Gulf interests ashore in JFHQ, Riyadh. John Cartwright was a young and bright Captain of the old school and we discussed our views at length. Detailed war plans were not yet refined but there had been endless speculation, which we rekindled over a few beers.

Though the Navy continued to be the most important force during tension, any war plan would involve unremitting Coalition air power to crush enemy resolve before massive land forces attempted to regain Kuwait. Maritime forces would, however certainly be needed — to supplement the air effort by use of the US aircraft-carriers, to neutralize the Iraqi Navy, to clear its sea mines and, possibly, to conduct amphibious assault. It all seemed beautifully simple on a sociable autumn evening in London and I wished John well as he prepared to fly out to the Saudi capital ahead of me to become the Chief Naval Staff Officer ashore.

Our mutual boss in the theatre had just been

announced as General Peter de la Billière, an SAS man with a combat record that was just the stuff to inspire us all — trench fighting in Korea; ambushing Malaysian terrorists; legendary undercover operations in Aden; heroics on a mountaintop in Oman; and directing the SAS as they stormed the Iranian Embassy in 1980. I knew him personally for he had been garrison commander in the Falklands in 1985 when I had been patrolling the islands in *Avenger*; thus I was delighted at the selection.

I had not sailed into Gulf waters since serving in my first ship, *Ashanti*, in 1962. So no less an exotic location than the Lavender Hill Library loaned me the books I needed to refresh my knowledge. Poring over dusty volumes as autumn rain streamed down the window panes, I wondered where all my preparation was leading. Was I ever to take my place out in Gulf waters or was a Saddam somersault to leave me frustrated, never again going back to sea? I studied on.

The nations which fringe the vast inland waters of the Arabian Gulf are vividly different one from another — a stimulating and diverse mosaic, etched around the teachings and history of Islam. I remembered Gulf waters as being shallow and treacherous, with shifting sands and a navigable width which is rarely more than 80 miles across. But its length is nearly 600 miles — as far as from London to Prague. These geographical constraints were to provide me with a challenge or two in the future.

As October wore on and the damp London

darkness further enveloped the MOD, there came cheering news that Coalition forces in the Gulf had grown to 300,000 men. It was followed by less cheering news from the Intelligence community that the Iraqi strength opposing them had grown to 400,000. Before military action started, the Coalition would need near parity on the ground and total superiority in the air, and it would still be a hell of a long process.

On 5 November, I ate my last tasteless sandwich from the basement cafeteria and said goodbye to the Ministry. I had arranged my own intensive programme of visits and briefings during my final weeks in the UK. I was also reading every piece of intelligence, every signal, every diplomatic telegram that might be of help, as I prowled countless corridors and sat in a succession of grubby offices to draw background knowledge from the many people who helped me. Still ring-rusty after two years away from weapons and operations, I needed updating. In my single-mindedness, I felt a little like an ageing prizefighter in his mountain retreat, building himself up for his last big fight.

Two past jobs had been of particular benefit to me since the Falklands. My time commanding *Avenger* and the squadron of five other surviving Type 21 frigates had given me a taste of what it was like to control groups of warships in major NATO exercises. If I had known that I would end up in command of twenty-six vessels as part of the biggest fighting armada assembled since the Second World War, I would have paid a lot more attention.

And then as the Flag Captain (second-in-command) to Flag Officer Sea Training at Portland, I had helped to maintain the combat preparedness of British and NATO warships, assessing them against simulated attack by enemy aircraft, submarines and surface ships. Influencing and improving many people — but not always making friends — we 'Sea Riders' checked every tiny piece of ship capability as each vessel worked up, and wore down, over at least twenty-eight days and nights before being categorized as ready for operations. I embarked in ship after ship and learnt much myself as I focused upon the performance of command teams.

Now conducting my own work-up, I returned to the Tactical School in mid-November. In 1987, Iraqi air-launched Exocets had devastated Iranian tankers and the ill-fated USS *Stark*: coping with this striking force and the miscellany of supporting aircraft and missiles would be our main focus of study. But the simple sea mine had even greater potential to deny us our ambitions, causing me to challenge the Intelligence experts' low assessment of the numbers held by the Iraqis, their capacity to build or obtain more, and their ability to lay them covertly. It was a piece of clear-headed foresight by me that owed less to deductive powers than it did to memories of tense nights in cold Falkland waters. As ever, unglamorous weapons excite no passion but can generate dangerous complacency.

As I prepared my mind for combat, I tried to do the same with my body. Always a physical fitness enthusiast, I increased my exercise routine, ate less, lost weight, and acquired an impressive English cold — my own biological warfare — to take out to Saddam Hussein. An ultra-short, businesslike-haircut prompted my unadmiring sons into disparaging remarks about my emulating 'Stormin' Norman Schwarzkopf, the overall commander of Coalition forces in the Gulf. My family have always tried to give me a sense of proportion.

On 27 November, I paid my farewell calls on the Secretary of State, Tom King, whom I found to be avuncular and affable, and on the Minister of State, Archie Hamilton, whom I found to be less so. Our talks were short-lived and of limited benefit, other than allowing each party to view the other. On 28 November, I visited Northwood and High Wycombe to meet my operational commanders. At Northwood, I re-met the Deputy Fleet Commander, Admiral Roy Newman, with whom I had served at Portland three years earlier. A workaholic, punchy and as straight as they make them, he was the energetic scourge of Gulf priorities on behalf of the Commander-in-Chief Fleet, Admiral Ben Bathurst.

The subterranean corridors of RAF Strike Command Headquarters at High Wycombe were my next destination. The combined Four Star Headquarters had settled down by then and was running Operation Granby most efficiently. Naval unease about the shift of operational command away from our headquarters at Northwood had been misplaced, and the three Services combined well under the quietly understated yet inspiring leadership of Air Chief Marshal Sir Paddy Hine, a man as fair and nice-natured as he was clear-headed.

But, for me, the most important figure in the UK was the naval officer tracking maritime operations at High Wycombe — Captain Paul Canter. Commanding officer of HMS *Active* in the Falklands, he had served with me at the Tactical School and we got on extremely well. A perennially youthful, charmingly noisy gunnery officer, he was a dedicated and energetic man who spoke his mind, could be a tenacious opponent, and was just the person I wished to see fighting my corner: he was to become my staunchest supporter and my go-between.

Several newspapers reported my appointment as Task Group Commander and picked up on my Falklands experience. One stated that I had been 'hand-picked for [my] ice-cool nerve and instant decision-taking'. Whilst wondering if the correspondent had been interviewing my bookmakers, I decided to give these alleged qualities a final test before departure and took myself to Newbury racecourse. The horses looked magnificent in the late autumn sunlight and I lost myself in admiration, in form analysis, in excitement, and in assessing the balance between risk and gain. I came away refreshed — but no richer.

More days slipped past, and Saddam engaged in the mother of all vituperative verbal attacks against two men whose responses he had entirely misread, President Mubarak of Egypt and King Fahd of Saudi Arabia. Both had become implacable enemies of the Iraqi leader's adventurism. Saddam was becoming tetchy, as well he might having once again committed his nation to mass slaughter as a result of misjudgement. Iraq's position was by then supported only by Libya, Jordan, Yemen, Tunisia, Algeria, Sudan and Mauritania — and the PLO — all of whom served self-interest in their alignment. Ranged against them were thirty-three increasingly resolute countries.

Two significant international events occurred just before I flew out to Saudi Arabia. A restive and bridling British Cabinet achieved their aim of ousting a leader whom some regarded as only one step removed from Saddam: Margaret Thatcher was savagely set aside and replaced by John Major. Then, on 29 November, the UN Security Council gave Saddam until 16 January to withdraw from Kuwait — or to suffer the consequences. The line had been drawn.

But then it was time for me to come down from the mountain. For Daphne, the anguish of the Falklands had left emotional scars. In 1982 she had been able to sublimate much of her personal anxiety by supporting other *Alacrity* wives, but this time there was no such distraction. I was to embark in somebody else's ship, with a personal staff drawn together from a variety of different units; thus we were not

272

part of a ready-made community. Nevertheless, she believed in my quiet conviction that I was headed for a job I relished and that I was equipped by nature and background to do it well.

2

Storm Clouds Gather

1 – 22 December 1990

'So may a thousand actions, once afoot
End in one purpose'

TEN o'clock at night; the aircraft starts its descent to Dubai International. The desert floor is black and bottomless after the sodium-lit symmetry of Dubai City and I wonder how new Arabia, virtually constructed in but sixty years, is coping with the huge invasion of Western military power. The night is clear, as are my faculties having denied myself the duty-free delights of the drinks trolley — except for a glass of irresistible Chablis. Across the aisle, a florid-faced trio of returning expats are somewhat less restrained. Am edgy with anticipation after weeks of hard preparation and self-denial; the American statesman Adlai Stevenson had a saying: 'There are no gains without pains.' The aircraft is on late finals with the engine note but a distant whisper, finally broken by the thud of tyres on tarmac. Committed irrevocably to Desert Shield, all too soon to become Desert Storm, I am back in the game.

*   *   *

Like so many naval arrivals before and after me, I was taken under the wing of the Royal Naval Liaison Officer, Commander Tony Horton. He and his welcoming wife Felicity were based at the Dubai Embassy, from where he co-ordinated support for naval operations in Gulf waters. His already busy job was about to become busier still.

Sunday, 2 December,was spent on board *London*, alongside the port of Jebel Ali 20 miles south of Dubai, made available to us by the United Arab Emirates. A huge area of bleak functionalism, with wharves, jetties and docks carved out of rock and desert, the facility is the largest man-made harbour in the world, and the Royal Navy's borrowed corner was rightly cherished. Our warships were virtually lost amongst the miles of angled wharves which surrounded deep, cool docks, warehouses and workshops, all soon to be used by several other Coalition navies. Jebel Ali made Devonport Naval Base look like a corner shop.

Though Paul Haddacks was kind and patient, I did not enjoy the handover: I was introspective and gave little back in return. Having re-established Royal Naval influence, he had to pass over the truly exciting business to another. Were positions to have been reversed, it would have frustrated me profoundly but I now console myself with the knowledge that he was, very rightly, promoted to Rear Admiral two years later. Although he and his staff had achieved a great deal, I was surprised by the absence of war plans against an enemy who would, on past record, think nothing of attacking us at any time. There was little doubt about what would be my initial focus.

During the morning, the newly established communications system to warn of a Scud missile launch burst into life, punctuating our discussions with an exciting surge of reality. Surely Saddam had not pushed the button? The infra-red detectors in the American reconnaissance satellite had worked correctly but it was a great relief when it was revealed that the salvo of firings had been a test, deep in Iraq. It was a timely reminder to me of the possible outcome of so much preparation, though it did not stop me sleeping well despite time-zone changes and challenges ahead.

The next day, 3 December, a brief change of command ceremony for the British Task Group was held with a feudal Arab pipe band, considerable media attention, and traditional naval trappings of dress uniforms, medals and piping party. Blazing sun and brown faces behind musical instruments added a bizarre quality to the event: the Arab version of 'Hearts of Oak', played as I was piped aboard my flagship bedecked in my finery, was memorable. Despite the kindness of the gesture and obvious efforts by the flagship to formalize the event, I was restless to have done and be off to sea where I belonged. An hour later Paul departed for the UK — and I had command of the dispersed British ships.

Uniforms and medals were stowed for sea, replaced by sombre combat wear, berets and personal battle bags containing protective clothing, chemical defence kits and respirators. No peppermints this time. In a short interview with the Press, I stressed my primary aims for the Task Group — we would be combat-ready as soon as possible and would aim for the closest possible co-operation with our maritime allies, particularly the US Navy (USN).

I felt no misgiving at singling out the United States amongst the fourteen nations by then in the Gulf and Red Sea — we were natural bedfellows. Most of the war-winning capability at sea was going to come from the sophisticated American forces. Their aircraft-carriers, cruise missiles, capable escorts and perhaps their Marine Corps amphibious forces were all destined to be decisive factors. But they still had need of our fighting experience, air-defence destroyers, mine-clearance vessels and missile-armed helicopters.

Though my Task Group command still had some way to go in approaching the scale of that of Admiral Woodward in the South Atlantic, it was growing fast — and there were more ships to come. Already on station were two destroyers, two frigates, three minehunters and their own command ship, a maintenance and repair ship, two tankers, a stores and ammunition vessel, two transport-cum-landing ships and the newly conceived casualty receiving ship. I was about to get to know them all exceedingly well.

My warships and auxiliaries were by then

well-established in a cycle of eight days out on patrol, followed by four days stand-off for maintenance. At sea, they were allocated patrol areas which spread Coalition warships and auxiliaries evenly across the choke points of the Gulf of Oman and the Gulf itself. As the maritime embargo area covered 250,000 square miles of the Gulf, the Red Sea and the Arabian Sea, the Coalition also needed the long range air-search capabilities of a number of maritime patrol-aircraft: we gratefully used the Royal Air Force Nimrods that had been deployed to Oman. No merchant ship could pass undetected and unchallenged.

The Coalition embargo was clearly impressing Saddam Hussein and was costing his economy more than US$30 million each day, over half of it in lost oil revenue. He had imposed rationing upon his people as early as September, offering free oil to any nation supporting him by sanctions-busting. There were no takers, and I was having to modify my usual cynicism over the effectiveness of embargo in a greedy world where alternative suppliers will always be found at a price.

To support the embargo effort, Allied ships were already fuelling each other when required and limited multi-national exercises were already taking place, some in patrol boxes and some in a discreet area known as the Play Pen. And now I was to take my flagship out to join the games.

The whine of gas turbines running up had a familiar energizing effect upon me, as the bark of orders across the upper deck contrasted with the quiet tones in the cool, air-conditioned interior of the bridge. My pleasure was great as the raked bow of *London* bisected the departure channel and swung northward to our first patrol area. At last I was back at sea.

As we headed north through the clear waters, flying fish arced in formation alongside us, gliding, glittering and frozen in flight — little aerodynamic masterpieces that humbled our thrashing helicopter. Dolphins twisted and turned under *London*'s bow while sea snakes dozed lazily among fronds of weed out on the motionless surface. The flat and featureless northern shores of the United Arab Emirates — sombre, sun-baked hues of brown, yellow and grey — unwrapped endlessly to starboard as we headed for our patrol area. We were a long way from the shattering force of a South Atlantic winter.

On the following day, having joined up with HMS *Cardiff*, we commenced boarding operations against five tugs evacuating a Dutch dredging operation from Umm Qasar at the head of the Gulf. The low-freeboard vessels, bucking in the heaving swell, made boarding by Lynx rapid-roping the only safe solution, six men sliding to the deck within fifteen seconds. They searched *Mr John*, *Sinbad* and *Aladdin* before authorizing them to proceed; *Cardiff* dealt with the others. Thereafter, the tempo for the flagship markedly increased as we patrolled our areas, hurtled to intercept all unidentified merchantmen and challenged everything that moved.

In our command centre on board, I introduced an intensive preparation schedule, conducting daily intelligence analysis of enemy capability followed by table-top tactics to anticipate how, when, where and in what sequence the Iraqi war machine would make its move. I insisted we start by morbidly trawling every possibility, no matter how grim, such that we might never be taken by surprise, before assessing more realistic scenarios which did not credit the enemy with divine powers. Though the latter sessions were altogether more cheerful affairs, we still tended to presume that the Iraqis possessed greater ability that they were ever to demonstrate in practice — not a bad shortcoming in preparations for war, provided it does not so inflate your respect for the enemy as to paralyze resolve.

The Iraqi aircraft radii of action, air-to-air refuelling capability, missile arcs, radar- and radio-jamming capacity, command and control all became as familiar to us as our own. How resolute were the combat-hardened pilots? Would they choose to transit over Iranian territory and surprise the carriers off the coast? Were their missile patrol craft capable of mounting co-ordinated night attacks against our surface ships? I ordered a similar focus throughout the Task Group and reduced in-harbour time: there was to be no complacency.

On 5 December, I signalled a short series of guidance notes entitled 'Command Focus for December'. In them I stressed some points of emphasis and encouraged ships to increase their internal exercises. I wanted no one to be in any doubt: their new boss was thinking war. In particular, I encouraged them to think through the realities of severe damage and casualties, as the unthinkable always has the potential to become the incurable. My signal concluded: 'Having spent weeks admiring your efforts from the MOD end . . . it is my pleasure and privilege to command an already highly effective Task Group in which you are all contributors. I am sure that you will continue to use every available hour to prepare for the ultimate challenge.'

The signal reminded me of how, when inspecting ships at Portland, I would always 'kill off' the CO to see how his team coped without him. Once I invited a spirited young commander to 'die' spectacularly in the midst of simulated air attacks. His piercing shriek froze his entire ops room (as I had intended that it might) as he fell from his chair with an awful thud. The face of his warfare officer was a picture. After many seconds he seized the main broadcast microphone: 'Do you hear there, the Old Man's dead. First Lieutenant to the ops room, please. Oh, and the First Aid Party had better come too.' After but seconds, the door burst open and four earnest young men in red cross surcoats and carrying haversacks rushed in and stood looking down at the silent starfish that had once been their captain. Just as they were about to descend on him with their ministrations, his glacially clear voice echoed from the floor.

'Nobody,' he intoned, 'I repeat, nobody, is to kiss me!'

Success in a busy life hinges on allocating

priorities and acting on them tenaciously, whilst staff training advocates pursuit of only a single aim at a time. This gave me problems. I could think of a dozen aims, all meriting immediate emphatic attention. I needed closer links with my allies, my COs, my people, the littoral states and my General in Riyadh; I wanted more war preparations for my ships; and I wanted much more detailed war planning. Establishing priorities was indeed going to be the trick, and thus I was utterly delighted with the choice of my Operations Officer who was to help me.

A purposeful man, Commander David Teer and I thought the same way: a no-frills, get-things-done individual, he was a past specialist in the cool-headed game of fighter control, where a wrong judgement can kill a distant pilot in seconds. Like so many self-made men, he was self-reliant, brimming with initiative, and possessed of a superbly brusque style of leadership which was quite rightly adored by my staff. David was the type of man you sensed had taken a pounding in the sea of life, and had emerged the stronger. We got on, and he was to be invaluable to me.

Another key man was the Captain of HMS *London* and my Flag Captain, Iain Henderson, who had fought in the Falklands and had been a naval pilot. Whereas David Teer and I possessed many common personality traits, Iain could not have been more different. He was a boyish, bright, humorous and entertaining yet gentle man, given to low-key self-projection. On my arrival I explained that I intended to

282

minimize the impact of myself and my staff upon his command, and that I would play down my contact with his ship's company: I would never insert my personality between him and his people. On board *London* there could be only one leader with whom men should identify — their captain. I would involve him completely in my decision-taking, seek his advice where appropriate, and leave the precise fighting of his vessel to him — once I had made clear what I wished him to do with it. He would have my total support, and if I had his then I believed we would get along famously. And we did just that. Our close and happy relationship endured many pressures.

My embarked staff numbered seventeen, an immense disruption to a Type 22 frigate which, though designed as a flagship, could really only cope with half that number. They were mongrel in composition, drawn from the dedicated teams of several Admirals and selected on the basis of their specialist expertise. Other than David the officers were all Lieutenant Commanders, most of them in their early thirties. The conduct of war is a young man's game.

My officers comprised an aviator, Paul Collins; a communicator, Paul Daykin; a gunnery/missile officer, Brian Lambert; a planner, Martin Lander; a logistician, Roger Ireland; RFA First Officer David Gilzean; and an information officer, Anton Hanney. I had asked for additional staff with knowledge of land operations and intelligence, for whom I was awaiting nominations.

Embarked with the minehunters was my mine-warfare expert, Lieutenant Commander Brian Mansbridge. I had no complaints about the talents I had been given — they were all highly gifted, energetic and committed.

I came to respect and admire this *ad hoc* group as I watched them cope with immense work loads and a great deal of stress. Had it been known at the outset that we were headed for a major war, then it would certainly have been an Admiral and his entire staff that would have commanded the Task Group from one of our carriers. My fear was that the increase in international tension would cause Their Lordships to direct just such a shift in naval command, leaving me out of a job.

Some ship's officers had been evicted from their cabins to provide sleeping accommodation for my more senior staff, an inevitable move but not one conducive to harmony. I inherited the accommodation arrangements of my predecessor who had rejected the traditional commandeering of the Captain's living quarters and had banished himself to a tiny cabin, one deck down. It was spartan — six foot square with no shower and a main passageway outside the sliding door. I had to accept its remoteness, use Iain's shower, and try not to invade him whilst he had callers. Although I am not a great one for privilege and self-indulgence, there was no doubt that the arrangement was a lousy compromise for a one-star officer commanding many ships on the brink of war. Nevertheless, it was irrefutably democratic. I had a simple choice: either endure it, or insist on my rights and impose a similar load upon the man who had to fight his ship under such a handicap. So I settled into my tiny hutch and yearned for the small comforts of *Alacrity*.

I also quickly settled into my personal routine. Ever since I first took sea command in 1973, I have remained essentially 'dry' when 'wet': I do not drink alcohol. I discovered early on that command at sea is better for all if booze does not feature. Nothing prudish drives this habit, merely the certainty that constant decision-taking and deprivation of sleep are worsened by alcohol. (Another factor over which I had no choice was celibacy — it, too, helps focus the mind.)

As in the Falklands, I also needed to cut myself off from the self-indulgence of memory. After but one reading, all letters from home were placed in a deep bottom drawer — and there they remained.

In my tiny cabin, I slept with my face turned to the steel bulkhead which always glowed red from the emergency lanterns. In the brief seconds before sleep, my thoughts often went back to childhood. For a considerable period, my mother and I lived in a one-room flat and, as a young schoolboy needing his sleep, such close co-existence gave me a problem at bedtime. Thus I always slept with my face turned to the wall, whilst my mother read quietly by the light of a shrouded lamp. A loving and wonderfully determined woman, she was utterly ambitious for me, having been deserted by her husband

285

in the depths of bomb-blasted London when I was but 2 years old. As then, my imagination played games with the imperfections upon the surface in front of my eyes before I dropped off to sleep.

Outside the flagship, I was becoming preoccupied with other balances of strength and weakness. After a miraculously short conversion by Devonport Naval Base, *Argus* had arrived on station in mid-November, under the command of Captain David Lench. She now sported additional accommodation for 200 personnel and a two-storey 100-bed hospital insulated against chemical attack in her forward hangar. The embarked medical team of 136 included two surgeons, two anaesthetists, a support team for the operating theatre, and laboratory and nursing staff. The Senior Medical Officer was Surgeon Commander Paxton Dewar — bright and adaptable. The air department, headed by a forceful Commander Ian McKenzie, possessed four helicopters drawn from 846 Naval Commando Squadron, under the inspired command of the swashbuckling and direct Lieutenant Commander Les Port. These Sea Kings would provide me with a flexible stores and passenger delivery service until they were needed to evacuate casualties.

The normal RFA crew was therefore far outnumbered by specialist pilots, aircraft maintainers, meteorologists, Royal Marines bandsmen turned stretcher-bearers, surgeons and doctors — and a large group of naval nurses at sea for the very first time, having been plucked from military hospitals ashore. I was uneasy about these girls who lacked the seagoing training of the Wrens by then serving in our warships — despite the splendid choice of their leader, Chief Nursing Sister Gillian Comrie. I had no misgivings over their likely performance in dealing with wounded men, but a damaged, smoke-filled ship, with friends dying all around you, is another matter. Accordingly, I gave the forward commitment of *Argus* undue personal attention, whilst my staff openly speculated that the Commodore's interest was in fact related to the pretty young nurses themselves. My snarling response was said to be singularly unconvincing. Nevertheless, though *Argus* gave me great reassurance, she also gave me some anxiety.

The stores ship *Fort Grange* also carried a Surgical Support Team which was headed by Surgeon Commander Mike Farquharson-Roberts. A frustrated would-be seagoer from a naval family, he was a well-motivated enthusiast. *Fort Grange* had two more adaptable Sea Kings embarked, but her much smaller flight-deck only allowed operation of one aircraft at a time. All in all, the Royal Navy in the Gulf had magnificent medical support: Falkland blood had taught many lessons.

But some other lessons were also necessary: I was becoming conscious of a few gaps in war readiness amongst some of my RFAs. British naval support afloat is provided by more than twenty auxiliary ships, predominantly tankers and virtually all helicopter-capable, manned by

RFA officers and men who are aligned with the merchant service from where they are largely drawn. RFA sea-training is shorter and less frequent than that of warships and they have much more broken programmes. Thus their busy COs, trying to maintain standards, had my sympathy, but not so much that I would tolerate second-best.

My two staff experts on the Royal Fleet Auxiliary, David Gilzean and Roger Ireland, supported recent assessments by our visiting teams from the UK which highlighted areas needing improvement. Accordingly, I requested a command visit from London to provide the final conditioning. Before the ink was dry on my signal, Commodore Dick Thorne, RFA, and his team were with us. He and I had known each other for years. Strong-minded and intelligent, he was a born warrior who did not take kindly to being desk-bound. The finishing touches were quickly made.

Task Group engineering needs were being provided by the commercial organizations at Jebel Ali and Dubai, and by our Forward Repair Ship *Diligence* alongside the harbour wall in Jebel. An ugly but functional vessel, originally intended for North Sea oil rig support, *Diligence* had been bought by the Navy in 1982 and had alternated between Gulf and South Atlantic ever since. Her 10,000 tons provided workshops, cranes, electrical power, boiler feedwater, fuel, air and fresh water to ships needing assisted maintenance. Four massive anchors and electronically controlled bow and stern thrusters allowed her to hold an exact position in sea states of up to Force 9. She had but two handicaps — not enough time at sea and a best speed of only 12 knots. Routine replacement of her captain at such a time was something I could have done without, but it was a reminder that the RFA replacement cycle of COs every four to six months would go on remorselessly unless I challenged it. The new man was Captain Sid Kemp.

I varied *London*'s patrol areas to allow me to fly to my dispersed ships by helicopter. Although only the Sea King was fitted with dual controls that allowed me some piloting to brighten lengthy transits, time in the Lynx did at least permit me to chat with the crews, many of whom I had commanded at Portland. Flying personally or not, these flights were all delightful small escapes.

★ ★ ★

Clearance to engage rotors — slip the rotor brake — slide down my tinted helmet visor — stabbing gesture to remove lashings — ground crew race in under rotor disc, holding lashings high as they retreat for my reassurance. Take-off time. Thumbs up — lock harness — ease off control frictions — gently squeeze up the collective lever — take the weight off the wheels — and the heavy aircraft unsticks from the blazing hot flight-deck. Sweeping rotor blades chop greedily at the thin tropical air. Slide sideways over the glittering water — ease over the nose — gently pull more power — and downwash vortices spin across the stagnant surface. Airspeed increasing — vibration fading — sunlight already searing my exposed neck. And now the glorious moment: speed sufficient — ease up the nose — keep the power — and allow the fuel-heavy aircraft to surge skywards — leaving restraint and responsibility far behind. Ah, the magic of flight.

* * *

In the first few days of December, I visited *Argus, Cardiff, Herald, Cattistock, Hurworth* and *Resource*, always adopting the same pattern. Initially I would talk with the CO, hear his concerns, tell him all I knew, and highlight future priorities. Then I would chat with the Heads of Department — all highly capable young Lieutenant Commanders carrying much individual responsibility. A tour of the ship to meet the sailors would follow, allowing me to make a pretty accurate assessment of ship capabilities. Finally, I would hold a talk with all available personnel and address the issues of the international scene, our allies, embargo operations, Task Group preparations for war and what I wanted from them personally in the weeks ahead. I would then answer questions for as long as required.

Our sailors were always animated contributors, questioning me responsibly. General de la Billière later told me how mature and responsive he found naval ratings. Whilst I uttered some flippancy at the time about them not always being so lucid or sensible when they staggered back incapable from shore leave, I was proud to hear such an assessment from this wise source. Yet the willingness to talk with your men should not be overdone. I recall a particularly verbose Admiral commanding a shore establishment. As part of some modernization, an electric hot-air hand-dryer had been placed in the wardroom cloakroom. On the first morning of its operation, a small notice appeared on the machine: 'For a personal message from the Admiral, simply press silver button.'

Refreshingly more concerned with likely chemical and biological warfare than personal priorities, our sailors still wanted to know when they might get home. And curiosity existed over preparations for land and air assault by our sister Services ashore, thereby reflecting that their only sources of such information, other than my flying visits, were the *Sandy Times* (a glossy newspaper produced by the British Forces in Riyadh), newspapers from home and the BBC. All of these seemed to have a preoccupation with the Army and the Royal Air Force to an extent which irked my restless and hard-worked teams.

Gathering unhappiness at the lack of publicity for the Navy's activities in the Gulf drew my gaze more firmly to media matters. Naval public relations policy was being directed from the MOD by Captain Peter Voute. Peter had helped co-ordinate the Falkland offensive in London in 1982 whilst married to an Argentinian girl. I had no doubt that a man who had been able to cope with that dilemma should certainly be able to handle the media. Though he worked hard and did well, I was somewhat peeved when I learnt that a late bid from the BBC to embark with the Task Group had been rejected, apparently on the grounds of overkill. I was even more peeved after the war to read a book by the BBC's thwarted television correspondent which gave, I thought, a less than comprehensive picture of the Navy's achievement. I should have taken a stand and had the decision reversed.

Co-ordinating massive UK media interest (nearly 200 resident correspondents) in the Gulf theatre of operations was the task of the Joint Services Information Cell in Riyadh, controlled by Colonel Nick Southwood. On the Gulf coast, looking after specific naval interests, was Stu Reed from the staff of CINCFLEET Northwood. And newly embarked in the flagship as my public information officer, Derek Plews from our Polaris submarine base on the Clyde was experiencing quite a change from handling emotive nuclear issues.

Our media teams were divided into five groups embarked in ships decided by me. Without hesitation I put *The Times* and BBC Radio in the flagship and placed our only television team, Michael Nicholson reporting and Eugene Campbell filming for ITN, on board *Gloucester*. I reckoned that a suitable ship could, through her publicized achievements, act as a symbol for the efforts of the dispersed Task Group. *Gloucester* was destined for the front line and struck me as an ideal choice.

Hugely outnumbered by their colleagues, often in comfortable hotels covering land and air operations ashore, our embarked media men deserved my sympathy. Though they were allowed access to satellite communications to file their stories, relaying video and still pictures was much more difficult and the source of some friction. Nevertheless, I intended to seek the publicity that I had so shunned in the Falklands, and which the Navy still had not learnt to exploit; but I was equally determined that no life would be lost under my command by the imprudent pursuit of a gratuitous headline. The governing rules for the release of information were many and complicated but I had the final power of veto upon 'sensitive or classified' information. The fundamental conflict of interest between the media and the commander afloat is never easy to resolve. And so it proved.

I had not started too well. The *Scottish Sunday Mail* team visited the Gulf and asked to stay on board the destroyers overnight on 8 December, in the tense forward air-defence line. The team included one woman, Fidelma Cook. As neither ship was equipped for females (no separate accommodation, toilets and so on), and as both ships were in a vulnerable forward position, I said I could not agree to the overnight stay but would co-operate as far as possible in every other way. As a result, I received instant front-page coverage in the *Mail*. '*Mail* Girl Banned from the Gulf', screamed the headlines. I felt it might prove to be a long war.

I imposed one other restriction on the media. I insisted upon our embarked media representatives being excluded from my chat sessions with the sailors, which I saw as being private: I did not want these talks played up as 'fire and brimstone' reports to the UK, thereby devaluing my personal links with my people. Only on one occasion did this restriction fail when the media crept in at the back. Sure enough, the result was a steely photograph, glamorizing text and a headline that read: 'James Bond has nothing on this guy'. I was unamused and not the slightest bit flattered.

★ ★ ★

On 6 December, it was time to visit JFHQ Riyadh: my fellow land and air commanders had several advantages by dint of being ashore, the greatest being ready consultation with General de la Billière. So I had *London* close the coast, the Lynx fly me to Bahrain, and one of the three RAF HS 125 executive jets allocated to the General whisk me across the vast expanse of the Empty Quarter. Great tracts of desert slid below me unappreciated before we landed 250 miles away in Riyadh. On the concrete aprons as we arrived was more military hardware than I had ever seen on one airfield before — endless lines of aircraft shimmering away into the heat haze.

In Riyadh, General de la Billière's rapport with General Schwarzkopf was already the talk of Headquarters, as was the calibre of the big American. The UK media had done him no favours in presenting him merely as a larger-than-life cliché — a sort of bovine John Wayne. How our view of him was to change. As I was ushered into General de la Billière's company, I reflected that we seemed to have the right men running the show — I just hoped he was feeling the same about me.

Before we commenced discussions, I was amused and entertained to see the General turn up the volume on both the air-conditioning and a hi-fi playing Mozart — a highly effective anti-bugging device, and a very restful one.

He gave me his views on the likelihood of war, the rightful dominance of the US, the building land/air warplan, and his uncertainty over a matching maritime plan. I gained ready endorsement for my intention to visit all my ships and work them hard for war, and to establish US naval intentions and meet with all their key commanders forthwith. I was left in no doubt as to his willingness for our forces to play a prominent role on all fronts, as befitted our expertise and experience, but not to the extent that the British alone would have to take disproportionate casualties. This delicate subject — proportional risk — was then addressed at length.

Some nations were keen to take credit for participation against Saddam but unwilling to commit forces forward and risk significant losses if it came to war. Whilst we were not constrained by such political sensibilities, the General did not wish us to risk putting our people in a position where we might incur excessive casualties unmatched by our allies. I had no difficulty with such a stipulation and I adhered to it when we came to war, albeit with occasional judicious exceptions.

We talked at length about many other subjects before parting. I was heartened by his willingness to delegate much responsibility to me, provided I kept him closely informed and sought early endorsement for decisions about the forward commitment of my ships. It was a nice long leash, and it suited me.

After discussions with the Air Commander, Air Vice Marshal Bill Wratten, and the General's Chief of Staff, Air Commodore Ian Macfadyean, I re-met some friends, including the General's newly appointed military assistant, Commander Colin Ferbrache. I was also keen to meet the Army Commander, Major General Rupert Smith, who had been selected to take charge of the British Division, comprising the 7th Armoured Brigade and the 4th Armoured Brigade. But it was to be many weeks before our separate busy lives allowed this to happen. Thankfully, he was a strong-minded and combat-proven fighter.

I left the General's Headquarters wondering how the concrete and glass magnificence of Riyadh would cope with chemically tipped Scuds hailing down upon it: I guessed that civil defence did not feature greatly in Saudi life. The HQ was in an unused office block in the very heart of town; thus the basement cafeteria was known as the Scud Dodger's Bistro. I was disappointed that the naval cell was across the road and thus separate from the main HQ, and hoped that out of sight was not out of mind.

On the flight back, I reflected on the complexities of managing 'proportional risk'. At that time I had little idea that others were to experience a good deal more difficulty and that some national maritime commanders were to be personally devastated by their government's reluctance to commit them to fighting. One or two were traumatized at being consigned to a watching role, far from the centre of operations where their abilities and equipment might have been of real assistance. Had I known, I would have given greater thanks still that I at least did not have to fight with my political masters before I could even join the battle. Nevertheless, the need to consider proportional risk and national contributions was a novelty.

The early days of December were to include many lengthy journeys out of the flagship. As they often involved staging through the littoral states, it was logical that my Flag Lieutenant, who co-ordinated my visit programme and often accompanied me, should also be my Staff Aviation Officer. Lieutenant Commander Paul Collins was self-assured and sharp, excelling in Gulf airport transits as he bluffed his way through Arab bureaucracy. Local airport control was amazed that a man called Craig kept flying out of the country, never having entered it! Arab logic never quite caught on to my flying in from seaward by military helicopter and departing by civil airline without an entry stamp in my passport. Thanks to Paul, I was never arrested and rarely delayed.

During a short visit by my flagship to Dubai, I gave a dinner and a lavish lunch to foster local working relationships and to thank several loyal supporters. Guests included the Consul-General, R. A. M. Hendrie; the General Manager of Port Rashid, David Gibbons; and the captain of USS *Bunker Hill*, Tom Marfiak, who I was to come to admire more than any other ally in the Gulf. But the port call reminded me that, if fighting started, I wanted ships to stay where they were needed — at sea. Logistics would be vital.

Our needs ashore were met by a small team in Jebel Ali, receiving, sorting and delivering the mass of stores and provisions being shipped out to us by sea and air. They operated out of a protected warehouse in the dockyard, under a highly resourceful Stores Officer and co-ordinator called Jarvis Humby. He was an energetic and skilled improviser, and I quickly learnt not to delve too deeply into how he got things done — at that stage results were all. Doubtless, Eisenhower would have liked to have had the credit card of 'Wheeler Dealer Humby' in hand as Allied forces started outrunning their logistical tail across Europe in 1945. But it was a bizarre way to go to war.

Stores were flown out from the two main UK RAF bases, RAF Lyneham and RAF Brize Norton, to our forward airhead in the United Arab Emirates, Min Had airfield. They then went on first to Jebel Ali, and thence to our stores ships *Fort Grange* (Captain Barrie

Dickinson, CO of *Stromness* in the Falklands) and *Resource* (Captain John Orchard). The latter was already committed to carrying the Army's reserve of ammunition together with 8,000 man months of food for general use. We were not going to starve. *Fort Grange* also carried adequate food for the force until nearly April, and a full load of stores and ammunition. Given the man that I knew Barrie to be, I had not the slightest worry that he would deliver his load wherever it was needed. Thus it was no surprise to me later that *Fort Grange* proved to be outstanding.

These vital stores ships were provided with additional air defence by elements of our 200 Royal Marines, armed with hand-held Javelin missiles. In addition to conducting boardings, the marines protected our stores shed and the RFAs in harbour. The Navy's own army was certainly demonstrating its versatility. Their shore-based young commander, Simon Pritchard, was about to be replaced by Captain Mike Wills, who remained with me until the war ended.

On 11 December, I flew to the Dutch combat tanker *Zuiderkruis* out at sea for the meeting of the WEU Maritime Commanders. Introductions, ritual photographs and lunch preceded several hours of programme planning and discussions. As details of each nation's fighting contribution and their peacetime ROE all remained obscure, I could see what had irked Paul Haddacks and was forced to be patient. Had it not been for such reluctance to address the unacceptable face of war, I would have thoroughly enjoyed myself. Seafaring men have a similar outlook and mix well together.

They were a good crowd and I liked virtually all of them, in particular the Italian, Admiral Mario Buracchia, and his Netherlands compatriot, Commodore Ton van Gurp. It was ironic that both these men were about to become controversial as a result of their outspokenness. Mario later confided candidly to his national Press Corps in an off-the-record interview that the embargo should be given plenty of time to work, thereby avoiding war. Clearly 'off the record' is subject to a variety of Italian interpretations — he made many front pages at home and was replaced with great rapidity. It seems that Ton was later almost as forthright in expressing some rather personal views about the effectiveness of the WEU afloat. I wonder how Nelson would have coped, juggling operational priorities and delicate international diplomacy with the government and the media peering over his shoulder. That is the lot of the modern-day fighting commander.

We allocated Gulf patrol areas and discussed the balance of in-harbour time: my decision that each British ship should have only a short Christmas or New Year break contrasted with a number of other nations who could see no reason to deny their vessels port calls in the festive season. Perhaps they were right. With hindsight, Saddam did not pre-empt, no ships were bombed by terrorists alongside, and their people might have been that bit fresher when it came to combat. How I wish I possessed hindsight! For me, command often involved the gloomy business of anticipating the 'worst case': there were many Christmases ahead and Saddam was not to be granted additional celebration by our complacency. I was unrepentant.

Embargo planning was carried out by Martin Lander. Painstakingly thorough, he reduced the diabolical complexity of programming sea/harbour, patrol/standoff and work-up/replenishment to neat calendar-based charts. However, obtaining diplomatic clearance for port visits from Gulf nations drove him to distraction. Perhaps Arab bureaucracy was the reason the British liked staying at sea?

Zuiderkruis had British Sea Kings embarked; they came from 826 Naval Air Squadron and the detachment was commanded by Lieutenant Commander Keith Williamson. They had been loaned from our tanker *Olna* which was by then detached to Singapore for long overdue maintenance; such interoperability reflecting the very close ties between our two navies. Though these were the anti-submarine variants of the Sea King, they were being 'misemployed' to search for embargo breakers and to deliver stores and equipment. It was their newly fitted Demon video camera, designed to allow them to detect shallow moored mines, that would shortly cause them to be detached right to the head of the Gulf.

On my return to *London*, I gave a lengthy interview to our defence correspondents, Jamie Dettmer of *The Times* and Steve McCormack of

BBC Radio. Because of the security classification of our planning work, my briefing was higher on rhetoric than facts but they were patient and I liked them both — although some of Jamie's reporting was rightly upsetting Iain Henderson as he seemed intent upon finding any controversy there might be.

My next visit that day was to Bahrain Island, where the expanding military network was threatening the infrastructure with breakdown. Muharraq airbase was full to capacity with fighting aircraft, drab without their peacetime livery, and the RAF Station Commander, Group Captain David Henderson, was coping with quiet equanimity in the face of potential chaos. I started my calls with the British Ambassador, John Shepherd, and continued with local Bahraini officials, who were all immensely helpful. I was candid, making no secret of our resolve to be ready for conflict if it came, but I was surprised to meet some underlying complacency that the problem would somehow go away. Given that Bahrain was within Scud range, I had expected a different philosophy. When, later, I took a much-needed stroll in the backstreets and saw bright-eyed Arab children playing unconcernedly, my thoughts became increasingly gloomy as I recalled the anthrax and plague variants of Saddam's biological arsenal. As in Riyadh, the apparent impossibility of organizing effective civil defence led to virtually nothing being done. But at least the British community was being issued with respirators!

The same walk included a more amusing

interlude. My hair was embarrassingly long and, having viewed the handiwork of the ship's barber, the 'Happy Hacker', I decided to chance a backstreet haircut. I entered beneath the first striped pole I sighted and settled into my chair. Communication was impossible, but by sign language I indicated with finger and thumb the small amount of hair I wished to see removed and then fell asleep to the soporific clicking of scissors and the murmur of Arabic. Awaking to the fawning smile and inclined handmirror of my barber, I was confronted with a Craig who would not have looked out of place storming the beaches in company with the US Marine Corps — I was almost totally bald. The young man grinned for both approval and tip, indicating the length between finger and thumb to which I had wanted my hair reduced. I hoped that communication with our Arab Coalition partners might be more successful as I returned on board, trying not to notice the incredulous glances of my officers. Later, I was delighted to see a number of my more conscientious staff returning aboard with similarly gleaming skulls. Clearly the single-minded professionalism of their boss was infectious. Our US liaison visits went even better thereafter.

On 12 December, there followed a second major conference between the coastal nations of the Gulf. They met, under the aegis of the Gulf Consultative Council, with the Coalition Maritime Commanders on board the Canadian supply vessel HMCS *Protecteur* in Bahrain Port. Invaluable face-to-face contacts were made but it was evident from the meeting that rapid communication between the littoral states and their big cousins in the event of combat was going to be impractical. Thus the spectre of Blue-on-Blue — the unwitting engagement of one Coalition member by another — was going to be a recurring nightmare. Furthermore, fears of an Islamic terrorist threat to our military bases were heightened by an intelligence brief which highlighted the fact that the true sympathies of thousands of non-indigenous Arabs employed by the Gulf states might soon become apparent through sabotage. In discussion, I cheered up the meeting by explaining my organization for resisting possible attack by Iraqi Special Forces from the many dhows still filling the southern Gulf. I brightened them still further by bringing to their attention intelligence reports that the enemy possessed chemically tipped anti-tank rockets that could readily penetrate the skin of a warship. Much note-taking went on.

There were eighteen other nations with ships in area: Argentina, Australia, Belgium, Canada, Denmark, France, Germany, Greece, Italy, Kuwait, the Netherlands, Norway, Poland, Portugal, Spain, the USSR, the UK and the USA. All remained under their own national command as the need to integrate under direct American tactical control had yet to arise. The US Navy would have to shed some of their traditional insularity in the interest of compromise if Coalition unity was to be held together — particularly with the WEU snapping at their heels.

After the conference, although we were only on the island for the day, the Defence Attaché reserved a room at the Diplomat Hotel to allow me to save desperately needed time by drafting post-meeting signals in privacy and comfort. Accompanied by David Teer, I drove to the Diplomat and checked in at reception, intent upon an hour of work before we flew off to our next destination. 'Ah yes, Mr Craig. I have a reservation for you. And also for a lady called Sue?' exclaimed the receptionist in a too-loud voice. Colouring slightly despite my tan, I asked if I could see the reservation book, feeling his somewhat disapproving stare at what was clearly a carnal arrangement.

The words were neatly printed: 'Mr Craig, and SOO may be with him'. Military initials for a Staff Officer Operations meant little to a receptionist better versed in the ways of the world so I smiled through thin lips and reassured him.

'No, there is no lady, just this gentleman.' I gestured vaguely to a now grinning David Teer. The receptionist's frown of disapproval deepened.

'How many nights do you now wish to stay, sir?'

My response administered the *coup de grâce*. 'Merely using the room for a couple of hours, thanks.' The venom with which he hit the desk bell to summon the porter to lead us away, luggageless, proved to me that we had just confirmed his worst expectations of the dissolute English.

After my return to the United Arab Emirates on 15 December, we were visited by Rear Admiral Peter Abbott, Flag Officer Second Flotilla, accompanied by his designated relief, John Brigstock. He had responsibility for the Royal Navy's world-wide commitments outside the NATO area but he lacked a direct command and control function over the ships in the Gulf. Nevertheless, he was showing support and interest, offering to help where he could. Were the aircraft-carrier *Ark Royal* to be deployed, he would almost certainly have embarked with his staff, thereby sidelining me. Thus the visit had a certain tension. As for John Brigstock, I was already well aware that he had been lobbying anybody and everybody to take over the British maritime forces as soon as possible, preferably in 'his' aircraft-carrier. We were all scrupulously polite to each other throughout the visit, but somehow I felt they had come to measure the carpets.

As *London* was on patrol, *Gloucester* acted as the Admiral's flagship, hosting his official dinner for local dignitaries. The style and verve of Philip Wilcocks and his people were much in evidence and showed them to be a heavyweight team that I intended to use to the full. The excellence of dinner reminded me of one of the nicer compliments I have received about the Royal Navy. It was given to me late one night by a US Navy colleague. 'The thing I love about you Limeys', he intoned in a voice already gravelly from my malt whisky, 'is that you take so much trouble over the little things:

306

one somehow knows when you get to the big issues, you'll do them bloody brilliantly.'

Then it was time for me to visit the Hunts, where I enjoyed the informal spontaneity of their close-knit crews. Between decks the little ships were blazingly hot and humid, despite the fact that many lights had been extinguished in the vain pursuit of lower temperatures. I also visited two of the logistical work-horse ships that I had fought so hard to acquire: *Sir Galahad* (Captain Brian Tarr) and *Sir Percivale* (Captain I. F. Hislop, soon to be relieved by Captain J. M. Summers). As ever, I enjoyed my discussions with them but also found some complacency over the likelihood of war. There was precisely one month left before the expiry of the deadline laid down by the United Nations for Saddam Hussein to take his forces out of Kuwait, and there was still much to be done.

General de la Billière made his own short-notice visit to the minehunters on 18 December. He too reminded everyone that there were by then only twenty-eight days remaining to the expiry of the deadline — midday on 16 January our time — which might mark the outbreak of war.

I then attended the change of command ceremony for the Dutch ships in Jebel Ali. Peter Kok replaced Ton van Gurp, who went straight to command the Standing Naval Force Atlantic — the six warships who are the symbol of NATO's maritime efficiency and cohesion. They take equal pride in entertaining each other ashore in a liver-killing schedule. I have had two appointments at sea with STANAVFORLANT and remember them both with vivid, if exhausted, pleasure. Ton and I engaged in a bet before his departure, his £5 saying it would not come to war. His debt was later promptly settled. At the same ceremony, I also met Admiral Bonneau who commanded all French ships east of the Suez Canal. A likeable man, possessing immense charm, the Admiral and I were destined to get along less well professionally than we did socially.

Another man of immense charm was Sir Harry Secombe, by then visiting British Forces on a welcome morale-raising tour. He was given a dramatic moment when he flew ashore in *Cardiff*'s Lynx after a visit on 17 December. The aircraft received an indication that it was being locked on by a missile radar and the resulting violent evasive aerobatics gave the tenor a stimulating few minutes. The radar was finally identified as belonging to an edgy Coalition warship which was giving its defence crews some radar detection drill. For a few seconds, Sir Harry had been anticipating a different kind of drilling.

I had now been in post for nearly three weeks, had a reasonable grip on my ships, felt at home with my links to Riyadh, and had directed new emphasis upon war planning. What I still lacked was close consultation with the Americans.

The US Navy command structure devolved from their President to the Chairman of the Joint Chiefs of Staff, General Colin Powell, who defined the war strategy, objectives and forces necessary to achieve their aims. He delegated to the Commander-in-Chief, General Schwarzkopf, in Riyadh the freedom to build his own operational plan and smooth out the vested interests of the Services involved. Within the US Navy, the line of authority started with the Commander USN forces in the newly established Central Region (COMUSNAVCENT), designated the Commander of the Task Force (CTF): he was Vice Admiral Stan Arthur, on board his command flagship *Blue Ridge*. Beneath him were a series of Task Group Commanders dispersed east and west of the Arabian peninsula. I needed close links with three of them: Rear Admiral Fogarty, who would take charge of inshore operations and mine-clearance to the north; Rear Admiral Sutton, who headed the huge logistical organization at sea and who had need of all the extra tankers and transport ships he could find: and finally, and most important of all, Rear Admiral Dan March, CO of the aircraft-carrier *Midway*, who controlled aircraft-carrier operations and was thus the axis of any naval advance up the Gulf.

As a start, we managed to get one of my staff, Brian Lambert, into the *Midway* for a few days, where his plain-talking charm paved the way for better co-operation. In particular, he was able to stress the abilities of our forward air-defence units though he did encounter some ignorance of NATO procedures which could have been embarrassing if left uncorrected. It was no coincidence that *Midway* was from the US Pacific 7th Fleet — well removed from NATO. Brian was impressed by Admiral March and his appropriately named Chief Staff Officer, Captain Van Sickle. It sounded like a taut flagship which I needed to visit. Much to Brian's chagrin I recalled him to *London* only hours before he was due to be introduced to the movie star Brooke Shields, who was touring the Gulf as a motivator of considerable influence. I dismissed his protests brusquely. 'They probably only wanted you to distract her chaperoning mother,' I snapped. I sense he never really forgave me.

But it was personal contact that I needed, so I packed my bags once more and flew to Bahrain on 19 December. First I arranged to meet Vice Admiral Stan Arthur, having been well briefed by my liaison officer, Commander Colin Hamilton, who had been embarked in *Blue Ridge* for many weeks and had melded well with the Americans.

I was piped up over the side of *Blue Ridge* by a pretty blonde Duty Officer of the Deck and, though I still had some difficulty adapting to the sight of women serving in fighting ships, I was far from impervious to a feminine smile. I felt a long way from home.

A spontaneously warm welcome by the bluff and genial Stan Arthur left me instinctively liking him and looking forward to doing business with him. Immense experience flying Intruders over Vietnam had given him greater combat familiarity than many other USN surface officers. Over an excellent lunch, served by an impassive Filipino, our talk was marked by

310

typically American candour.

He too had been frustrated and disappointed to find war planning immature on his arrival in late November. He explained subsequent developments. The heart of the USN combat effort at sea would be the six carrier battle groups. Elimination of the Iraqi surface navy missile patrol craft would be the separate responsibility of Admiral Fogarty. At this point I interjected by highlighting the effectiveness of the Lynx and Sea Skua, and my willingness to allow full use of them. He was enthusiastic when I declared my firm intention to commit them all right up against the Kuwaiti coast at the earliest possible moment.

He went on to confirm that the coastal area was unsuitable for large-scale amphibious assault over the beaches, although close-in heli-borne assault was a possibility. But the Americans had an amphibious task force of more than twenty ships and nearly 18,000 marines raring to go: there would be great pressure to use such forces, despite analysts' assessment that a full amphibious attack would entail too many casualties. The US Marine Corps had just conducted their own large-scale amphibious assault exercise on the coast of the United Arab Emirates before the gaze of the world's media but sadly the evolution had suffered from a rare heavy swell. How much of the exercise was intended to deter, to delude, or merely to prepare, was unclear. What was clear was that the only area where the Coalition might be able to land was just south of Kuwait City.

Scrutiny of a chart and knowledge of the factors necessary for a successful amphibious landing left the clear impression that such an operation would be extremely risky. As the only naval forces likely to be committed as a precursor to such operations would be my own, I was disquieted.

Our talks ranged on over the separate capabilities of my forces and the difficulties of liaison with so many disparate allies. Only when we turned to command arrangements did I again feel some concern. The Americans would be using a complex command organization, better designed for dispersed operations in deep oceans. Such a structure would certainly have its limitations within the northern Gulf, which was virtually another San Carlos, and it worried me. I was also concerned that the complex business of eliminating Iraqi surface vessels, minefields and coastal defences might lack both appropriate high-level command attention and simple command and control. Sadly, I was correct.

I left the Admiral with my commitment to aggressive forward support, provided both I and my staff were fully involved in planning the high-risk coastal phase. He concurred and thanked me.

Disappointingly, my visit to Admiral Fogarty and his senior staff in *Lasalle* did little to fill in the gaps in my knowledge. The ship was known as the White Ghost of the Arabian Coast due to her all-white paint and her many years of Gulf service. Converted from amphibious transport and first commissioned nearly thirty years earlier, she showed her age in every corner and was vulnerable, even against an unsophisticated opponent, having only four 3-inch guns and one Vulcan Phalanx gatling gun. But it was her primitive watertight and gas-tight subdivision that really worried me: the thought of her in the middle of a chemical and biological threat area was sobering.

Accompanied by David Teer and my liaison officer, Lieutenant Commander Tim Stoneman, I met first the Admiral and then his senior staff officers. We shared our frustration at the understandable reluctance of the politicians to allow fighting ships into the extreme north — waters that the Iraqis saw as theirs. Both of us had been pressing separately to thrust our forces forward. The refusal handicapped our war planning and preparations. Sophisticated US strategic intelligence was incapable of tracking the enemy forces that were laying mines in Iraqi territorial waters, and probably farther out in international waters. British and American reconnaissance units remained barred from proceeding north of latitude 28°, which left thousands of square miles of ocean dominated by our future enemy.

In the event of war, I explained my intention to provide all British Lynx for anti-surface operations. *Gloucester* and *Cardiff* had been working up helo co-operation with *Bunker Hill*, exploiting the co-ordinated strengths of the Lynx armed with Skua and the USN Seahawk radar. Joint attack plans had been devised and distributed amongst ships and their flights. Their potential targets were nearly fifty Iraqi vessels — of which only twenty possessed missile capability — amongst them ten Russian-built missile boats, a Soviet-built salvage minelaying tug, a sizeable minelayer, fifteen minesweepers and utility craft (all capable of minelaying), five light patrol craft, and five TNC 45 missile craft, won from the Kuwaitis in early August, and capable of 41 knots. It was the TNC 45s, armed with Exocets, that were our primary surface threat.

On the subject of mine-clearance, I stressed that I and my MCM force were waiting for planning discussions. In return, I received little clear detail as to the sequence and form of their war plans: I was 'to be advised'.

From *Lasalle*, I next visited Rear Admiral Sutton, in charge of logistics. Considerable allied co-operation was already taking place but the Admiral was grateful for my offer of *Orangeleaf*, and *Olna* when she returned from Singapore. He understood my need to keep control of the RFAs carrying British Army ammunition but what he did want was the use of some of my logistical landing ships. There I could not help. Even whilst we were speaking, my sailors were transferring one-quarter of the ammunition from *Resource* into *Sir Percivale*, and would soon be doing the same into *Sir Tristram* (Captain B. J. Waters, OBE) to spread risk and give me more flexibility. *Sir Galahad* had by then embarked the support team that was to go forward with the minehunters; and I wanted *Sir Bedivere*, soon to arrive in the Gulf, to act as my stores delivery boy. If anything, I could have done with more of them myself.

The Admiral was bullish about using the two American 70,000-ton hospital ships, *Mercy* and *Comfort*, in the north in pre-declared locations. I disagreed, highlighting their vulnerability once Saddam's hotshots started flinging Exocets around. I was mightily relieved when I learnt three weeks later that they were to be kept south of Bahrain for the duration of hostilities. I left him with the reassurance that I would be taking *Argus* into the very front line and that her services would be available to all.

My various meetings had reminded me how good it was to do business with the Americans: frank, plain-talking, friendly and uncomplicated, I enjoyed their company. Indeed, I would still have done so — even if there had never been the Marshall Plan, the formation of NATO and forty-five years of paying Europe's life insurance premiums. They exhibited a genuine collective and individual philanthropy on a scale which shames us bickering Europeans. But somehow they always seemed to be much happier with simple bilateral consultation, rather than the complex multilateral variety. I shared their preference.

Nevertheless, I still lacked a clear picture of their detailed concept of operations and was worried that there might be a bigger planning vacuum at sea than I had imagined. By then I had liaison officers embarked in all the key USN flagships, *Blue Ridge*, *Midway* and *Lasalle*, but was far from happy with my links to the USN key commanders once war started. The absence of a personal secure-speech network left me isolated. We were in desperate need of a CO-to-CO 'natter net' such as Sandy Woodward had established in a different war. It was more important still within a multinational maritime operation.

Later, David and I stole a drink in the nightclub of the Diplomat Hotel before flying out. Three willowy and sensuous Filipina girls were on stage doing dynamic vocal justice to Tina Turner's 'Simply the Best'. I smiled, being a considerable fan of Miss Turner's vitality and having used the song to light one of my previous commands with the fire of self-belief. On reflection, it seemed a trivial device to spark the will. But it worked.

Before we departed, I got into conversation with a group of young RAF airmen and women. Remaining incognito, as was my wont in such situations (I was 'in shipping'), I was surprised to find virtually all the Muharraq RAF contingent living in the Diplomat on generous expenses, with bar, swimming pool and nightclub on tap for the duration of their deployment. Until then I had been lecturing my sailors that I wanted no complaints about their conditions afloat, as they did not have to 'contend with the deprivations of our sister Services in the desert'. It was as well that I was about to visit the Army, north-east of Al Jubayl, where I would be confronted with a different sort of reality.

In order to reach the main resupply port

316

on the east coast of Saudi Arabia, I flew to *Gloucester* and took passage with her overnight: she was to be my temporary flagship for the short visit to Al Jubayl, and she would be accompanied by *Argus*. I detested imposing myself on any CO overnight at sea — it was always intrusive — but Philip Wilcocks took it with gracious calm as we slipped northward, leaving the mysterious aloofness of Saudi Arabia spread impassively away to port.

Al Jubayl made Jebel Ali look like a sepulchre. The influx of men and *matériel* was at its height and hundreds of trucks were winding away to their military destinations in the west at a rate of more than one a minute. I was about to take one of them to see how the Army was surviving in the desert, but first I hosted a visit on board *Gloucester* and *Argus* from the Minister for the Armed Forces, Archie Hamilton, who was accompanied by General de la Billière.

I found the visit disappointing. Whilst touring *Argus*, Minister Hamilton remarked — in the presence of the captain and several sailors — that he did not see the part that the Navy would play if it came to war. As I had just spent the preceding three weeks and much energy trying to inspire our sailors to face up to conflict with resolution, I was concerned that such remarks could be misunderstood and might dent morale.

I then briefed the Minister in the presence of the General and Philip Wilcocks upon embargo operations and our preparations for war. I also chose to address Rules of Engagement

317

in some detail, particularly the importance of synchronizing our rules with those of the Americans as we would be operating shoulder to shoulder with them in high tension. I stressed our likely need to fire upon unidentified jet aircraft that could be missile-firers closing our exposed forward ships at high speed: our air-defence destroyers were my preoccupation.

Whilst acknowledging that we always had the inalienable right of self-defence, I stressed its use solely as a last-ditch recourse, it being potentially random and weakened by being merely dependent upon the heat-of-the-moment perceptions of a CO likely to be under some pressure. In no way was it a substitute for a carefully reasoned and rehearsed set of agreed and controlled responses to a variety of threats.

Following our discussion, I was uncertain whether the way had been smoothed for later rule-change requests or not. But I wanted no more Falkland-type occasions of watching a fast-closing radar contact and simply having to wait and see.

Fortunately, it was then time for me to join one of the supply trucks heading north-west to visit the forward trenches and get a brief taste of life under canvas with the troops who were working up for war. They were spending sixteen days at the front and then four days back at the aptly named Camp Four which was no more than a bunch of Nissen huts outside Al Jubayl. Although ingenuity had gone into providing them with some contrast, theirs was a miserable and character-testing experience — not least because of the nature of some of their rations. The worst were the American 'Meals Ready to Eat' (MRE). They were known affectionately by our soldiers as 'Meals Rejected by Ethiopia' and a thriving blackmarket in British rations was soon established. I much enjoyed my time with the Army and left Al Jubayl with great admiration for the character with which they had started their training and long wait: it intensified when I read the latest piece of morbidity from our Intelligence boys — Saddam was alleged to have 450,000 men and 3,600 tanks awaiting our 'Desert Rats'.

Once back in *London*, with three days left to Christmas, our command centre briefings started trying to second-guess what was going on inside Saddam's mind: though inconclusive they were stimulating. If he was alarmed by the scale and commitment of the Coalition build-up and convinced of their ability to hurt him, then would he really wait until the UN deadline expired? Perhaps he would stall until the eleventh hour, conduct a partial withdrawal, stand his ground and watch the Coalition fragment from within through a lack of resolve. Would his highly sophisticated propaganda machine gradually erode the resolve of the Arab nations ranged against him? Or was he so intent upon humbling the USA that he would pre-empt? If so, would he do so at Christmas, when our guard was low? Surely he would hit the Israelis with every Scud he could muster to spark a response that would inflame Arab nations and fracture the Coalition? Surely he would use chemical weapons on the battlefield and at sea with scrupulous care to ensure no Arab casualties, and would not use any Scud against the centres of Arab population? Such debate served only to prove how poor fighting men are at predicting the intentions of erratic Arab dictators. Perhaps Saddam would have been better off employing any one of our favoured options rather than the course he finally chose.

But, if I was Saddam Hussein and wanted to bloody the Coalition and generate the scale of casualties needed to shake resolve in the heartland of America, I would certainly exploit surprise and pre-empt just before Christmas. I wanted my Task Group ready.

So I issued all my ships with details of the precise position in the Gulf that I wanted them to occupy come any outbreak of hostilities, together with the codeword Tigris which would signal them to proceed straight to these positions. I followed it with a transition-to-war signal, scheduling final preparations. It started: 'A man should never fight at a time and in a manner of his enemy's choosing. The foe is battle-hardened, area familiar, and may be fanatically motivated. I am not complacent.' It concluded: 'Check your battle ensign is in the locker.'

Though pre-emption remained my main pre-occupation, it did give rise to one light-hearted moment. During a conversation on secure-speech telephone between myself and Admiral Sam Salt in the MOD, I was seated at the desk in Iain Henderson's day cabin. For once, the normally supportive Admiral was less than helpful in meeting my request for a particular small enhancement to some ship's equipment. I fired my last despairing verbal shot, reminding him of the likely results if Saddam were to pre-empt.

'It may appear to be a stable situation from the cloisters of the Ministry sixth floor,' I concluded grimly, 'but everyone inside the Scud arc feels very different.'

I swivelled in my chair to seek the concurrence of Iain who had been sitting reading his newspaper and listening to the rising tempo of my appeals. I fear that my paroxysm of laughter must have scared the hell out of Sam Salt and cast severe doubt on my sanity. The baleful, goggled face which appeared as the newspaper was slowly lowered was a perfectly timed piece of humour. Unbeknown to me, Iain had quietly donned his respirator before resuming scrutiny of the editorial. His buoyancy of spirit and his lightness of heart made him an ideal companion. I apologized for the private joke and rang off, leaving Sam to reflect upon the choice of maritime commander. The Admiral never gave me the enhancement that I sought.

In fact, by then, my ships were already extensively enhanced with some specialist items to allow them to cope more effectively with the enemy. Particular equipment that earned its cost several times over included the satellite navigation global positioning system (GPS) that I had been delighted to receive in Ascension nine years earlier, the electro-optical surveillance sight (to see floating objects in the water by night), secure-speech radio (to talk privately via satellite with the UK), and data communications systems (providing the ability to pass signals back and forth without pieces of paper). All this equipment was in constant use throughout the campaign. Each destroyer and frigate was carrying about £4 million worth of sophisticated improvements to help defeat the enemy.

Our aircraft were similarly fitted with GPS, an additional mode of IFF (Identification Friend or Foe), Chaff and flare dispensers to cope with infra-red missiles, night-vision goggles to turn dark Gulf nights into day, and an evil-looking, heavy machine-gun pod. The provision of such kit at a time of severe economic cut-backs was a significant achievement and it was good to see the names of many of the people who worked so hard to provide the equipment appear in the final honours and awards list after the war.

It was then 22 December, twenty-four days to the expiry of the ultimatum, and the British Forces were about to receive a popular VIP. The Prince of Wales wished to include the Navy in a whirlwind tour of our armed forces, and I settled for an overnight stop in *Brazen*, as James Rapp had been his First Lieutenant during the Prince's command of the minesweeper *Bronington* some years earlier. The visit went off very successfully. His Royal Highness has great affection for his navy and she for him.

Another popular visit commenced at the same time. Sir Donald Gosling, a highly successful businessman and one-time navy national serviceman, had gained high-level approval to make a morale-boosting visit to all our ships. Accompanied by an ex-submariner comedian — and are they not all? — he toured every ship, providing entertainment and some highly generous contributions to each ship's welfare fund. The comic, Stan Taylor, was extremely funny and suitably earthy, each warship giving him acclaim only one step removed from that which would have been granted to Brooke Shields — *sans* clothes. It was a typically kind gesture from Sir Donald which constituted a welcome Christmas present.

Sadly we had started to receive a different sort of Christmas gift — floating mines were drifting down upon Coalition warships from the north. Initial feelings that these were but left-overs from the crisis of 1987 broken away from their rusted moorings were soon disproved — many were brand-new. Iraqis were placing them in the northern Gulf to come south on the coastal current and make life extremely difficult for us. The demands of having to avoid collision with these infernal weapons never let us relax at sea thereafter.

On the evening of 22 December, I went out to sea through Dubai to join *Argus* for her Carol Service; some of my staff and media team accompanied me in the harbour boat. A creek bisects the heart of the city from seaward — an ancient waterway plied by a thousand dhows, each heavy with the most amazing Aladdin's cave of deck cargo. Along the waterside, tiny alleyways slither away from the waterfront and into the well-ordered symmetry of the city, whilst all is abustle with the vigour of commerce. We could smell the fragrance of spices, coffee, tea and perfume which wreathed the banks. The entry point for so much of the shipping that normally plies its trade into the Gulf is Port Rashid which welcomed us with the pointed fingers of vast cranes, jutting and shimmering in the glare, before we headed out to sea.

Thanks to our plunging progress through a fierce coastal swell, several of my companions were feeling decidedly unseasonal by the time we climbed the high side of the would-be aircraft-carrier. After a convivial supper with David Lench and Paxton Dewar, I walked around the ship chatting with personnel before we all gathered on a totally black flight-deck. Dozens of candles were lit, turning the night into a kaleidoscope of flickering gold and amber. I left the seated group of senior officers and mingled with young sailors and nurses as we sang our carols. Emotions were high and many a voice quavered as cupped hands sustained the guttering candleflames. They were all far from home, potential risks were fearsome and most of the fresh faces glowing in the candlelight were barely out of school: 'Silent Night' never moved me more.

The final words of the Naval Prayer echoed around the silent flight-deck: 'That they may return in safety, to enjoy the blessings of the land with the fruits of their labours.' We were all suddenly alone with our private thoughts.

When the service was over, I gave a radio interview in which I was asked to explain how the Task Group Commander felt as Christmas approached. My response was swift and sincere: 'One eye on the holly; the other on Baghdad'. We were not about to be surprised by pre-emption and, when the UN said go, we would be ready.

A huge tropical moon was rising as we climbed down into our launch. And as we smashed and splashed our way back through the battering swell to shore, I was strengthened by the sense of community that I had detected throughout my Task Group. That night my diary recorded that, each day, I was working for sixteen hours, sleeping for six, handling 800 signals, and had sixteen ships under my command. It also recorded that I was loving it.

3

Sands of Time

23 December 1990 – 16 January 1991

'Famine, sword and fire
Crouch for employment'

BY 23 December, with twenty-three days remaining, I had programmed at least half my force to be at sea throughout the 'holiday' period. Each ship was to be at short notice for recall, even when they were ashore. Only the minehunters were granted special home leave, the tiny vessels not being designed for constant running far from home support: the crew of their UK-based sister ship HMS *Quorn*, under the command of Lieutenant Commander Nigel Williams, flew out and replaced their colleagues in rotation. Nobody in the Task Group resented this exceptional treatment and, in the light of what they were shortly to achieve, it was all the more deserved. *London* 'drew' Christmas in Jebel Ali, which offered Iain and myself a small chance of contrast.

But first I had to meet the last of the USN commanders — Admiral Dan March, CO of the carrier USS *Midway* and Vice Admiral Arthur's choice as Battle Force Commander of the main group of warships in the Gulf. He had taken his vast flat-top down the coast to Abu Dhabi, where he and his men were engaged in 'rest and recreation'.

As returning behind the wheel of a car after weeks at sea can produce a performance of numbing incompetence (indeed, my wife refuses to drive with me during the first few days after my return from deployment), I rightly decided to let David Teer handle our hire car. The arrow-straight coastal road ran through 70 miles of empty desert to the old Trucial State of Abu Dhabi.

Inland, the featureless terrain gradually rose as we moved further south. Stark and scarred wadis, old creek beds and ancient pool scallops increasingly littered the sandy backdrop. In tiny Arab villages, never more than one storey high, dogs scattered and dark-eyed children squinted as they watched us pass. In the shadows, old men sat and chewed on leaves of qat to divorce themselves from the reality of their meagre existence. A miscellany of vehicles roared their way back and forth, producing a collision of cultures, if not one of a more serious variety. Huge Japanese off-road vehicles crossed with large-finned, chauffeur-driven gas-guzzlers. Purposefully fast European cars and pick-up trucks were driven by expatriates, guardians of the work ethic in the land of plenty.

Rocketing through a dust-shrouded and deserted Arab hamlet, David and I failed to see a large traffic-calming hump in the road, with the result that we hit the black escarpment at about 60 m.p.h. Our Scud launch profile was only marginally less impressive than our metal-grinding landing much further down the road.

'I know you mentioned you could just do with a damned good hump . . . ' I intoned as I massaged my very tender scalp. We drove in silence the rest of the way and never dared check the underside of the hire car.

Predictably, the elegant Admiral was enshrined with his personal staff in the penthouse suite of the Hilton at the southern end of the bougainvillaea-clad Corniche. I half expected to see dusky young concubines being ushered out as I entered, but perhaps David's driving was having a delayed effect. The view from the heights of the Hilton was sensational — palms, eucalyptus, acacias and the sparkling waters of the sea front lay spread out below us. The city was a mass of coloured fairy lights, its gleaming glass and concrete buildings floating in pools of floodlighting.

The Admiral was an imposing man: young, fit, alert, utterly self-confident; and, from his conversation, as single-mindedly absorbed in aircraft-carrier operations as I had suspected. He was candid about the risks of bringing his huge carriers into the shallow, constraining waters of the Gulf but showed little interest in any likely coastal surface action, making it clear that the carriers would only advance north when both air and surface threats had been neutralized. I expected nothing less.

He was also intensely suspicious of Iran, either as a low-level break-out area for the Iraqi Air

Force or ultimately as the launch platform for Iranian aircraft themselves. Thus, he was interested in the overland radar performance of *Cardiff*, a factor which dictated much of her subsequent positioning. Indeed our air-defence focus as we looked up-Gulf was to remain somewhat skewed right of centre for the entire duration of the war. He was therefore delighted at my offer to give him tactical control over my two destroyers as soon as we could rationalize our ROE. I left with much belief in the man who would direct the carrier effort, but with limited confidence that my priorities might be at the forefront of his attention. As we drove back, the darkness was lit by countless fireflies and enlivened by the clatter of crickets which matched my clamorous thoughts.

On 24 December, I hosted the next routine Coalition Maritime Commanders' meeting on board *London*. The flagship's Executive Officer, Lieutenant Commander Rob Farmer, had made a particular effort to ensure that all went well and much constructive work was done — even including some debate on possible war. This time I largely kept my peace, reassured by the knowledge that I had set up a face-to-face liaison with all the USN hierarchy and by the fact that, whilst I still lacked a number of answers to outstanding questions, I had a clear vision of what I and my forces would be doing come any war. The Dutch, the Australians and several other nations were destined to escort the American Carrier Battle Group, whilst the Canadians would be further back, escorting the logistical ships and monitoring the supply vessels entering Hormuz. A more purposeful air prevailed amongst my colleagues and some useful detail was explored.

On Christmas Day I helped serve the ship's company lunch, noting again how much they enjoyed the boyish naturalness of their young captain. That day also marked just three weeks to the UN deadline and my last relaxation for more than two months. Thereafter, my only subsequent indulgence was massive portions of custard whenever it was on the menu — if Iain did not beat me to it — and one delightful private video showing of the legendary three tenors' concert with Pavarotti, Domingo and Carreras: refinement in the midst of carnage.

That evening, we had a splendid homely dinner with a generous local family called the Jarmans but the incongruity of charades in dinner jackets whilst many of my force patrolled the moonlit waters left me feeling that it was I who was living the charade. Nevertheless, we all worked hard at normality and, in spite of my over-developed professional conscience, I enjoyed myself. No harsh reality was being allowed to break through to the consciousness of the locals. Sipping my port, I reflected upon the radius of the extended-range Scud missile that neatly enveloped the gracious house in which we sat. By the time we left the kindly Jarmans, a dense fog had rolled in from seaward.

★ ★ ★

The glow of our sociable gathering was quickly dispersed. Just before Christmas, Saddam had directed his merchant ships holed up in ports around the world to run the gauntlet and return home; a number sensibly ignored him, which was hardly surprising given the success of the Coalition embargo. Nearly 1,000 boardings had taken place, in which the Royal Navy had played a full part, most conspicuously against the *Nada* (*Gloucester*), the *Amuriyah* (*Brazen*) and the *Tadmur* (*Brazen*).

But now we had word of two important vessels on their way to the Gulf. The USN particularly wanted the first, the *Ibn Khaldoon*, to be the subject of a truly combined operation, well south-east of Hormuz, the better to defuse any propaganda ploy by the Iraqi vessel which had been declared a peace ship carrying emotional and humanitarian support to the Iraqi people. So I gave *Brazen* the task of going to help. But, as *London* also needed open waters in which to conduct some Sea Wolf firings, I accepted the invitation from Admiral Fogarty to go the Ball and also to take my princess — the flagship.

Fog delayed our sailing by an hour on 26 December but better visibility offshore allowed Iain to make up the leeway. As we sailed out through the Straits of Hormuz, I scanned the signalled lists of Christmas provisions which kind and thoughtful folk at home had provided to brighten the British Forces' festive season: 11,000 lbs of turkey, 4,000 Christmas puddings and 55,000 mince pies. I eyed the list feeling like a Dickensian

331

Spirit of Christmas Past; the Task Group were certainly getting damn-all yo-ho-ho from their single-minded commander. But my spirits were lifted by the knowledge that the General was by then submerged in 20,000 home-baked cakes sent out by a grateful populace for him alone, as a result of urgings from a national tabloid. God knows what he finally did with them all.

Whilst heading south-east from Hormuz, *London* was overflown by one of the RAF Nimrod detachments from Seeb in Oman. These three large maritime patrol aircraft had been ranging far to the south, reporting incoming merchant ships and marshalling warships to ideal intercept positions. We continued on south-east along the coastline of Oman, which stretches for hundreds of miles. Visible to the south-west were great craggy mountains; to the east lay the flatter, sandier expanse of Iran sweeping across the horizon; and away to starboard stood the grand natural harbour of Muscat.

The boarding itself was something of an anti-climax but if the Iraqis had intended *Ibn Khaldoon* to be a lure they could not have been more successful; at one stage a total of seven Coalition warships were clustered round her, whilst gaps were left in the patrol locations back in the Gulf. Thankfully, most of my remaining ships were neatly tucked into their designated war patrol areas. But I was keen to get back to them. A search of the ship revealed no contraband, merely a team of apparently well-meaning people intent on preventing war. Their intentions were better than their planning — the

332

ship lacked medical supplies and adequate food and water. The 'peace ship' was allowed to proceed without further incident and I was surprised that the superb Iraqi propaganda machine failed to make some political capital out of this transit. But they were working on other things.

Ibn Khaldoon was followed by *London*'s target, the tanker *Ain Zalah*, a huge lady who was boarded simultaneously by a combined US, Australian and British party from three types of helicopter — presentational togetherness. Our embarked and highly talented ITN cameraman, Eugene Campbell, produced footage of *London*'s rapid-roping, deck search and crew muster but this, the last allied Gulf boarding, spawned claims of brutality towards Iraqi crewmen and wanton damage on board. Though I suspected exaggerated propaganda, we ourselves had some misgivings over pugnacious international boarding teams whose efforts had prompted our strong and silent Royal Marines into disparagement. War can be such a frightfully competitive business.

Still south of Hormuz, we fired our Sea Wolf missiles, bringing roars of relieved acclaim from the ship's company as the towed sleeve target disintegrated before a direct hit. Thus we felt good as *London* creamed back through the crystal blue waters and re-entered the Gulf on New Year's Day, 1991 — ready in all respects to go to war. It seemed inconceivable that such clear skies would soon be obscured by the filth of battle, but the clouds of war were at last recognizable to the world: civil sea and air movements in the area had died.

As we re-entered the Gulf, I helicoptered into *Midway* and *Bunker Hill*. Though they originated from different eras, they were the pick of all the allied ships that I had seen. A huge grey city of over 67,000 tons, *Midway* carried 2,500 men and more fixed-wing aircraft — F18 Hornets for air defence and A6 Intruders for attack — than we had been allowed to retain in the whole of our navy. Having watched camouflaged Hornets being punched off the flight-deck at a rate of well over one per minute, Dan March took me into his command centre to view his coloured screen, where all one hundred US ships currently positioned in the Gulf were on display. I was envious of such an accurate surface picture but noted that many allied ships were not shown — a somewhat symbolic omission.

The *Aegis*-class cruiser *Bunker Hill* had been launched forty years later than the *Midway*. Displacing 10,000 tons and capable of 30 knots she was, with her long elegant bow and slab-sided superstructure, imposing. Her 350 men had control over the most sophisticated modern warfare systems — Standard, Harpoon and Tomahawk missiles, anti-submarine rocket launchers, two Sea Hawk helicopters, two triple torpedo launchers and the best air-defence system in the world. Wherever US aircraft-carriers go, so too does at least one of these elegant killing machines. Her commanding officer was Captain Tom Marfiak who had lunched with me in Dubai.

For thirty-six hours I let *London* operate with the *Midway* whilst the next US carrier, *Saratoga*, transitted Suez, followed shortly thereafter by *Theodore Roosevelt* and the *America*. There were so many damned aircraft-carriers converging on *our* strip of water it was beginning to look like Walt Disney's dawn patrol of the elephants in *The Jungle Book*.

And then it was time for a last visit to Bahrain where we were to stay from 2 to 5 January. A breezy port entry saw us berth under the gigantic shadow of the US flagship, *Blue Ridge*. Security in Mina Sulman port, Bahrain, was superb. US Coastguard patrols raced everywhere in high-speed boats, loving the action, whilst constant radar watch detected anything that moved on the surface; and acoustic sensors and diver patrols gave little encouragement to any would-be underwater saboteurs. USN ships, like ours, maintained a high state of readiness against possible underwater explosion. I never felt the slightest misgiving when my ships were in Bahrain.

On arrival, during another sun-baked, smoke-hazed morning, I watched our divers start their daily search of the ship's bottom for limpet mines or signs of underwater intruders. After final checks upon their compressed air sets, seated upon the inflated rubber sides of their launch, they exploited the mystical demisting properties of human spittle in their facemasks, before tucking and rolling backwards into the oily water. A quick vent of surplus air through the tight wrist seals of rubber suits, a flurry of flippers, and they were gone — down into the shimmering depths beneath the 5,000-ton warship. I could imagine them, picking their way largely by touch along the slimy weed-covered steel, hoping the eels that inhabited the green fronds were facing the other way. Special men — divers.

On the 3rd, I flew once more to Riyadh and met the British Ambassador to Saudi Arabia, Alan Munro, before providing the General with an update upon my war plans and receiving the latest news of events in the desert. I was reassured by what I heard of the Army's training efforts which seemed to be matching ours in their single-mindedness. Of the Royal Air Force's efforts, we had seen the Jaguar ground-attack aircraft at close quarters for they had been acting as the 'enemy' attacking our ships. Meanwhile, Tornado interceptors had been integrating their efforts with the US Air Force and the Saudis, whilst the bombing variant of the same aircraft had been blowing low furrows in the desert floor as they worked up their ultra-low-level attack techniques. Interestingly, the air-defence Tornados' efforts to meld with the US Air Force were being bedevilled by the same mismatch in their ROE with those of the US as was threatening the integration of my air-defence ships with USN colleagues in the front line at sea. There was a pressing need for the UK to grant us the greater freedom already possessed by the Americans.

On the ground, units of the 1st (BR)

Division had started arriving from Germany on 10 December and were becoming fully acclimatized. But the Army was already facing problems. The General was keen to exploit the balanced capability of his forces with their own logistical support in what was generally expected to be the main axis of advance — in the desert to the west — rather than get bogged down in some bloody constrained fighting along the coast. Despite 7th Armoured Brigade's rapport with the US Marine Corps, with whom they were destined to fight along the coastal strip, the spectre of likely casualties within such a tight coastal corridor and alongside the bullish marines was disturbing. The US Marine Corps were known to be worried about their future in a post-Cold War world and were allegedly intent upon showing their utility in battle, come what may. Talk of a willingness to take up to 17 per cent casualties implied that Britain might have to expect an entirely disproportionate rate of loss amongst the Desert Rats. The answer to the dilemma was very clear to the British — they should be allowed to deploy several hundred miles to the west. General Schwarzkopf was asked to agree to such a move. Shortly before Christmas, he did so.

Late that night, after my meeting with the General, I flew into *London* and debriefed my waiting staff. There were just twelve days to go, and General Schwarzkopf had confirmed that the forthcoming operation was to be known as Desert Storm.

By then, I commanded an impressive armada:

a command ship (*London*); a utility escort (*Brazen*); a pair of air-defence destroyers (*Cardiff* and *Gloucester*); an MCM force of one command ship (*Herald*), three MCMVs (*Atherstone, Cattistock, Hurworth*) and a dedicated support ship (*Sir Galahad*); a fleet tanker (*Orangeleaf*); two ammunition and stores ships (*Fort Grange* and *Resource*); a Primary Casualty Receiving Ship (*Argus*); and three adaptable LSLs (*Sir Bedivere, Sir Percivale* and *Sir Tristram*). I had agreed to give the USN tactical control of the destroyers *Cardiff* and *Gloucester*, together with the tanker *Orangeleaf*, but I would retain control of the rest of my force. All our ammunition ships, with *Brazen* escorting them, were destined to carry dedicated spare ammunition for the British Army. *Argus* needed careful supervision — despite my offering her for allied use — as I intended to advance her in step with the foremost units and close behind them. *Diligence* was to look after British ship maintenance needs. And the MCM group of *Herald, Atherstone, Cattistock* and *Hurworth* would not be committed until I had shared in the planning of their use with the Americans.

I had told my minesweeping commander, John Scoles, that I had no intention of letting him and his brave little group go anywhere harmful without Royal Navy missile defences going with them. This was no reflection upon our allies, it merely recognized the cohesion that can only be achieved between one's own forces. The minewarfare support unit was by then well established in *Sir Galahad* which was going to have to be exposed to a good deal of risk in the very front line. I had picked her as she was suitably modified to cope with chemical warfare, and I sensed that her taciturn, no-nonsense Captain, Brian Tarr, would enjoy a scrap. I briefed him personally, and his ship was to make a great contribution — Brian's eventual OBE was hard-earned.

My Force alone in the Coalition had comparatively recent experience of fighting inshore against land- and air-launched missiles. Our prime skills lay in air defence, mine-clearance, anti-surface operations with the Lynx and Sea Skua, and our ability to sustain operations for weeks on end without recourse to base port support. We were thus the most balanced and experienced fighting force in the Gulf.

Frankly, I think we felt ready for all but massive use of chemical and biological weapons. Though decontamination, donning protective clothing, regulating safe exposure times for upper-deck weapon crews, nerve gas injections, respirator drills and detection techniques were all practised over and over again, the prospect of the real thing was another matter. The operational use of biological weapons was a whole new game — one that we would be quite happy not to play.

Falkland fighting experience was well scattered throughout the Task Group but the Gulf was a very different arena. Though high seas and cold were thankfully missing, and there was little likelihood of a submarine threat, there was a price to be paid. High temperatures for all exposed personnel made the sweaty claustrophobia of our multi-layer survival suits, respirator, lifejacket, and anti-flash hoods and gloves almost unbearable. As virtually everyone else would be committed to a watch-on watch-off cycle within the air-locked bowels of their ships, the prospect of a lengthy period of fighting was far from attractive.

During our time in Bahrain harbour, the sleekly elegant presence of the liner *Cunard Princess* became the extravagant talking point amongst our sailors. The US had chartered her — resident crew, bars, dancing girls and all — to provide their soldiers with a few days' respite from their desert vigil. As myth was infinitely more attractive than reality, I had received some lurid questioning. I parried the smiling banter but knew that marked variances in the treatment of their military personnel by Coalition countries was causing considerable unhappiness. By then several nations were offering their people large war bonuses, exemption from income tax, or a roulement which gave them scant weeks in theatre — all of which demotivated our sailors and made our six-month cycle seem forever.

I briefly entertained the Captain of *Cunard Princess* and he kindly offered return hospitality before Iain and I were due to return to sea. We were to attend their evening show on the assurance that it would be memorable. It was.

The ship towered above the dusty docks of Mina Sulman, security patrols crawling all around her. By the gangway sat dozens of smooth-cheeked, earnest young personnel all telephoning home. Between decks, we were ushered through a spreading veil of cigarette smoke by suave waiters and pretty waitresses into a teak-framed ballroom pulsating with life. Astonishingly young men and women, their skin burnt pink from the Saudi sun, were certainly enjoying their five-day furlough. Befeathered dancing girls went through a leg routine which escaped no man in the room, whilst a once-youthful male singer was leading the audience (not that it needed leading) in passionate repeat choruses of 'Glory, Glory, Hallelujah'. I exchanged quick glances with Iain as we took our seats, accepted a beer, and submerged beneath the torrent of noise and emotion. The audience was surprisingly sober and generally well-behaved. Nevertheless, they were lost in an orgy of sentimentality, anxiety and loneliness; I recognized the symptoms from long ago. Prospects of Saddam's Republican Guards and TV images of the twisted victims of chemical warfare were a combustible mix. The youngsters sought inspiration whilst wallowing in self-doubt. Shadows clouded the young eyes that were fixed on the stage, where the weary trouper was belting out a flat version of Sinatra's 'I did it my way'.

It may have been their way but it was not ours; Iain and I were uncomfortable and, as soon as we could, we made our apologies and left. By that stage they had moved on to 'Battle Hymn of the Republic' — fists thumping tables, hands waving and eyes glistening. Never has the anticipated terror of war been so thinly masked.

The night air was clean and still as we walked silently back to *London*, the ship seeming cathedral quiet as we made our way along the polished decks and sought our beds. The Royal Navy was readying itself its way. I lay awhile reflecting upon the mysteries of men and women preparing to die.

* * *

David Teer's designated relief, Commander Tony Dimmock, was being flown out ahead of his appointed time, for I had need of him in *Midway*. I knew that his deceptively diffident frame contained a fine intellect and I was delighted to have him with me. Already an exceptional promotion candidate, he was the antithesis of David Teer but a most impressive staff officer. My rapid brief to him as he passed through on his way to the carrier made it clear that he was to push British priorities and prime me on US intentions by whatever means offered.

Just before we sailed from Bahrain, I gave lunch to the British Ambassador, Admirals Arthur, Fogarty and Sutton, and Group Captain David Henderson. Although we deliberately limited 'shop talk' and enjoyed a fine meal, prepared with their usual excellence by the flagship's galley, I repeated my concern about the lack of a mineclearance plan. Once they had gone, I signalled Admiral Arthur and reiterated the prerequisite of planning with his staff before I would commit my MCM force. I think it must have got lost on arrival.

As we sailed from Bahrain, harbour waters were being ripped by a gale which had the flag hoists on *Blue Ridge* snapping taut and even swayed the bulk of *Cunard Princess* — I could imagine the servicemen and women feeling queasy as they telephoned home. The untypical blow gave poor Iain a challenge before we safely reached the open sea; the Type 22 frigate carries a lot of flat steel above the waterline which develops a mind of its own at slow speed in a gale.

Once out at sea, I sent a final 'transition to war' signal to all my COs, listing items for their close attention whilst making it clear that I regarded orders merely as a springboard for initiative. Amongst other things, I told them to conserve their helicopter flying hours — and their people. I also promulgated the final details of the initial ship positions for the outbreak of war. Carefully calculated on the basis of the earlier work conducted by the Maritime Tactical School, the plan provided the ideal basis for subsequent staged advances that would make the best use of mutual support as the separate ships pressed northward.

I then had all COs flown on board *London* at sea for extensive war briefings. I made no mention of proportional risk and casualties, for that was my dilemma. And, sadly, I could only speculate about likely minefield operations, as I still had nothing to tell them. They were calm, charged-up and ready, leaving me proud and grateful that we had been given a five-month period of systematic preparation. On completion, I flew to *Gloucester* and gave a final briefing to the media before we commenced our last work-up for war.

Much earlier, I had instructed my staff to prepare an exclusively British exercise to test teamwork before we came under fire. If chemical Scuds were to fall along the western coast of the Gulf then a huge British seaborne evacuation loomed: airfield runways and terminals could soon be smoldering heaps of highly contaminated rubble. So we chose Bahrain as a suitable setting for an evacuation exercise opposed by the enemy: the memory of those bright-eyed children playing so carelessly was still with me.

As the whole subject of evacuation was political dynamite, planning had to be covert. Discreet consultation and visits, and reconnaissance of coastal embarkation points, were all conducted by David Gilzean in three short weeks. Emergency evacuation, helicopter and ship embarkation, fast transit and an escorted departure under chemical and air/surface threat were planned. Simulated air opposition was to come from RAF Jaguar aircraft from Muharraq, and a seaborne Exocet 'threat' from three of our warships, transformed into instant Iraqis. Before the exercise took place we warned the USN and the Bahraini authorities alike as we had no desire to generate confusion. Ironically, the earlier tragedy of the *Vincennes* and her 290 Iranian airliner victims was actually a blessing;

everyone afloat, and many more aloft, were very edgy at the prospect of a recurrence.

So now it was time for the exercise which we had called, appropriately, Deep Heat. It was to be preceded by the simulated evacuation of casualties to the hospital ships *Mercy* and *Comfort*, and included battle damage to a crippled escort which would have to be defended by air as it was towed and then prepared for docking. The enthusiasm of my staff in simulating the evacuation left me decidedly suspicious — both hospital ships were packed with young female nurses.

At dawn on 8 January, with one week remaining to the expiry of the UN deadline, I ordered up the ships, tucked them into close formation and put the helos up to take our picture. It was not a success — oily still waters and the lack of dynamic movement produced a frozen tableau of dispassionate remoteness. So we committed ourselves single-mindedly to the exercise.

During the final stages, the Prime Minister, John Major, visited us. Accompanied by General de la Billière, a vast cluster of acolytes and a media train, he listened to my brief, toured the ship, viewed rapid-roping by helicopter, watched a simulated air attack from Jaguars, and admired the Task Group sailing close past him in two columns. The ships looked magnificent at speed. We had extensive coverage on British TV that night and our visitor appeared delighted with our preparedness. In turn, his interest, questions and obvious humanity went down well — 'fresh as paint' was how one of our senior ratings described him.

As we finished the exercise, I signalled all ships a detailed de-brief upon their separate Deep Heat performances. Post-event analysis was alive and well. I then ordered them to their final battle stations. *London* and *Argus* steamed to a position off Qatar, which juts out aggressively into the Gulf 180 miles north-west of Abu Dhabi. From there we could provide timely support to the exposed forward destroyers, and I had an ideal position from which to command.

As I watched *Cardiff* move forward on radar, I felt for her commanding officer, Adrian Nance. He had been on board *Sheffield* when she had been destroyed by Exocet in the Falklands. Eight years later, I had him, his memories, and his ship utterly exposed in the front line of missile defence — once more against Exocet. I wonder what nightly memories he lived with? They never showed.

The following day, I took passage with *Brazen* to Jebel Ali before flying up to Dubai for a final WEU meeting, where some infighting over draft war guidelines soon bored me. Frankly, in our intended forward position, it was only our plans with the Americans that were relevant to me, and we had those sufficiently clear from my pre-Christmas meetings with the US Admirals, apart, that is, from the penetration of the minefields. In the afternoon, when we all met with our US counterparts to tidy up details, I sensed a little jealousy over the close rapport of the US and UK.

Coalition 'trade' in Iraqi-registered or Iraqi-bound cargoes was starting to dry up, thanks to embargo efforts at sea over the previous seventeen weeks. The remnants of ordinary merchant ship traffic entering and leaving the Gulf were growing weary of answering a succession of our challenges on VHF radio but we let such overkill continue — the deterrent effect was not unhelpful. We had a stranglehold upon all seaborne routes but not, sadly, upon some of the overland entry points north-west of Iraq: 165 Coalition ships from nineteen nations in both the Red Sea and the Gulf had challenged 6,920 ships, conducted 832 boardings and diverted 36 embargo breakers.

And so it was down to 10 January, with five days remaining to the deadline. I provided a working breakfast for the French Admiral on board my flagship, prior to *London* conducting a final Sea Wolf firing and scoring direct hits on both high-level and low-level targets. Work-up, preparation and conditioning were complete. I gave a final, bullish interview to Jamie Dettmer: the initiative would soon be ours, with devastating consequences for Saddam. As much as any Force could say with confidence, I believed we were ready.

Nevertheless, inhibitions remained upon our ability to respond to surprise attack. I had been signalling ROE quizzes to my COs for weeks and marking and discussing their answers. What rules we had, we knew. But we wanted more delegated freedom to ensure our survival against surprise pre-emption. Our dilemma was demonstrated on 11 January, when *Gloucester* declared Air Raid Warning Red. Unidentified air contacts on radar showing Iraqi characteristics were coming straight towards her from the north. If she failed to engage the contacts at extreme range with her Sea Dart missile, they would have the chance to unleash Exocets against any of the picket ships. Thereafter, her remaining defence was the limited 4.5-inch gun and finally the Phalanx revolving-barrel gatling gun which would throw up a wall of steel against a foe in the final 1,000 yards of its attack. As we had set up a communications link to cope with such an eventuality, my appeal to the General to allow *Gloucester* to engage when the aircraft were within Sea Dart range was answered with typically forthright agreement. His vigour provoked a backlash from Whitehall but did at least, after three more days, spur the last delegation of ROE that I and my captains needed and which finally aligned us with the USN. In fact, the enemy aircraft turned away and were never identified, but I was grateful to them. Over the next few days, we continued plenty of air-defence exercises with the help of the RAF Jaguars. Countdown had started.

The last helicopter movements were shuffled, the issue of anthrax and plague vaccine organized and final drills scheduled. Intelligence and warning signals had become deafening. Drifting mines were sweeping down upon us all at an increasing rate. I made final adjustments to ship positions and readiness. My diary chided me to top up on some sleep while I had the chance.

As once before, pacing myself was going to be the trick.

A final preparations signal went out to my ships. It concluded by telling them to prepare their battle ensigns, and finished: 'You no longer need good luck — you will undoubtedly make your own.'

Amidst rough seas on 14 January, I deliberately ordered *London* and *Argus* to practise more 'goalkeeping' — the demanding manoeuvres in close company that had so exhausted *Alacrity*. I then passed tactical control of *Gloucester* and *Cardiff* to the USN, though I continued to monitor their every order with solicitude, retaining the right to veto anything I did not like: *Brazen* was ordered to fly her Lynx forward to double *Cardiff*'s air capability. I noted that our little minehunters had already spent 150 days at sea since leaving the UK.

I also started to send a comprehensive daily signal report of all Task Group events to the MOD, Riyadh, the USN commanders and all my COs; my subsequent candour and informal comments, intended primarily for my ships, were not appreciated by some mahogany-desk drivers, but what the hell — when men are risking their lives they deserve a little 'open government'. And at least everybody knew what was going on.

And then we were down to the last twenty-four hours. International news reports and speculation upon war had become a clamour. I signalled that my ships (by then grown to nineteen with the arrival of *Sir Bedivere* and *Sir Tristram*, with *Olna* closing fast from Singapore)

349

were 'ready in all respects for war' and requested a suitable codeword for the Task Group when hostilities commenced. Keyed up and always in favour of inspirational tones, I offered the MOD the resonant 'Agincourt'. Their lacklustre response told me to take the next alphabetical codeword in their military handbook, and I could hardly believe my eyes when I saw that we would engage in the Mother of all Battles on the starting signal of — 'Walkman'. Henry V turned in his grave; my teenage sons would have been delighted; and my staff knew better than to approach me for an hour or two. Irked by our bloodless bureaucracy, I immediately penned the following signal to my ships:

We are about to engage in the greatest endeavour of our lives, on behalf of most of the nations on earth. After weeks of preparation, you are entirely ready — with a spirit and resolution that are remarkable. Over the days ahead, total concentration and sustained application will ensure an emphatic victory. May God go with you as you move in harm's way; my best wishes will be with you throughout. Without further orders, all Commanding Officers of Royal Navy ships are, on the outbreak of hostilities, to hoist battle ensigns.

Bugger Walkman!

The UN ultimatum expired at midnight New York time — midday on 16 January, Gulf time. Early that evening I took a secure call from General de la Billière. The long wait was over:

350

quoting the agreed code, he gave me a series of figures — clearly the start time for the commencement of hostilities. I thanked him, told him we were ready, wished him goodnight, and sat staring at the cluttered bulkhead in my private corner of the communications office. There was only one snag — I was unaware of any agreed code. Somehow, something had been missed. I toyed with the idea of ringing him back but quick assessment of the figures left me with the obvious conclusion — the date-time group was merely reversed. The first cruise missiles and aircraft were to be launched early on the morning of 17 January 1991.

After due reflection, I requested a shake at 0200 and went to bed. I knew the demands we would all encounter over the days ahead, when sleep would be cherished. My Task Group was ready. Anyone who had just been told that the end of his world might commence in six hours' time would not sleep at all. Thus I told no one, not even Iain Henderson and David Teer. In my narrow, sweaty bed, with ship noises murmuring about me, I experienced the one totally disturbed night of both the Falkland and the Gulf Wars. I was waiting to transmit Walkman. Wasn't I just!

4

Storm Breaks

17 – 25 January 1991

'Came pouring like a tide into a breach'

FREERIDER one loose!' crackles the radio — the first batches of cruise missiles soar from their shipborne launchers, and we are comprehensively at war. It is just after 0300 local time — 2300 Zulu — on the morning of 17 January and I cannot believe what is happening to my radar display: amber symbols obliterate the screen, hundreds of them, almost superimposed one upon the other. I am watching the greatest single-wave assault of destructive power since the Second World War. A mass of aircraft inch their way implacably across the display towards the top left-hand corner — Kuwait and Iraq. Cruise-missile tracks mesh with carrier-launched and shore-based bombers. In sophistication and scale, it is simply unprecedented.

* * *

First across the border had been 12 US Apache attack helicopters with laser-guided missiles: they gave two critical early warning radar stations no chance at all. A vast air armada then arrowed through the resultant gap in Iraqi radar cover. The arrowhead comprised eight F15 Eagles; the shaft was made up of 700 Allied attack and defence suppression aircraft; and the feathers were 30 F117 Stealth 'invisible' aircraft, bound for Baghdad and intent upon levelling Saddam's palace. From seaward, carrier aircraft catapulted skyward, adopted battle formations and flew north-east for their targets. Cruise missiles were being launched from above and beneath the sea on both sides of the Arabian Peninsula. And B52 heavy bombers laboured in from their distant bases, wings sagging from the weight of free-fall bombs.

Though in some places our fighter patrols were stacked up four deep over the same position, they were superfluous on that first moonless night — only Coalition aircraft with empty missile rails and bomb racks would be coming down the Gulf. We imagined the tense men in each symbol on our screens, all of them intent upon wreaking the greatest possible destruction in the first pulverizing surprise attack. I returned to my command centre at 0320 to ensure that Walkman was being transmitted through the Task Group, although anyone with a radar set had no need of the alert. We remained at Action Stations for some hours, in case of return attack. We were, most emphatically, committed.

In the first twenty-four hours, the Coalition launched 1,000 combat sorties and 151 cruise missiles. Of the fifty or so that were fired from Gulf waters, all but one hit their targets of command, control and communications systems, the Defence Ministry and Baghdad Television. A total of 18,000 tons of high explosive — the equivalent of the Hiroshima atomic bomb — was dropped in three hours alone. The first volume of the 'Air Tasking Order', the huge document which scheduled every single aircraft movement from tanker to attack aircraft to air-defence fighter, filled me with wonder.

Dawn on 18 January was symbolically gloomy with extensive haze and full cloud cover. I spent the morning in my command centre, analysing the immense volume of incoming Intelligence and raid assessments. A report of 100 per cent damage by F111 bombers upon Umm Qasr Naval Base and its missile patrol boats was very heartening but proved to be only one of several inflated claims in the heat of the moment. Typical problems of modern Intelligence were already showing: immense quantities of unrefined raw data were being pumped into my flagship, though our Northwood Intelligence boys were trying to crystallize it down to something I really wanted — damage assessments upon Iraqi airfields which housed the aircraft with anti-ship missiles. But it was wasteful lunacy to send valuable manned aircraft back over the target merely to report damage, so we remained frustrated. There were no other sources. In contrast to the Falklands War, the enemy was offering us far fewer signal interception opportunities, and we had virtually nothing coming from inside their camp.

Our embarked newshounds were understandably insatiable for information, but they too were elated. Although Jamie Dettmer had covered several wars, he was afloat in anger for the first time, whilst Steve McCormack was now in his first shooting war. I briefed them with some non-releasable information about our initial deployment dispositions, how we were likely to be used, and the interdependence of land, sea and air. I also warned them that it could be a long job. Having choked off the Iraqi economy over four months and safeguarded the sea train, naval forces were now needed to dominate the Gulf and destroy all aircraft which came out against us. Steve interviewed me for Radio 4 and I tried to relay the confidence that flowed from seeing the 'endless conveyor belt' of aircraft on our radar screens.

On 17 January the Americans had taken the brave early step of putting the frigate *Nicholas* right forward by herself — isolated and hopefully inconspicuous — for clandestine operations and to rescue any ditched Coalition aircrew. Given the massive complexity of the air battle going on above and around her, it was a reasonable risk to take. Though far from tiny at 450 feet and 4,000 tons, her air defences comprised merely a single missile and one small-calibre gun. *Nicholas* had expendability written all over her. Like *Alacrity* she was fulfilling an important role and her loss would not be catastrophic. Her aggressive captain, Commander Dennis Morral, had some anxious hours as his ship slid in amongst the oil wells, depending solely upon keen-eyed lookouts and mine detection sonar. The fact that she was the same class as the ill-fated *Stark*, struck by Iraqi Exocet four years earlier, could not have been reassuring.

Right at the outset, on 18 January, in collaboration with Army helicopters and the sole surviving Kuwaiti patrol craft, *Nicholas* eliminated a force of Iraqis who had been directing anti-aircraft fire from eleven oil platforms. She killed five and took twenty-three prisoners of war. 'Where are the mines?' must have been the first question on any interrogator's lips: it was certainly on ours. But no information was forthcoming.

On the same day USS *Worden*, who was also probing north, reported twelve enemy patrol craft operating up against the Kuwaiti coast; *Cardiff*'s Lynx was directed in for Skua attack but found nothing. As it was the Americans alone who possessed the integrated suite of command, control and communications equipment needed to co-ordinate all forces, they ran the show. Painstaking and often dangerous efforts to gain positive identification of enemy surface vessels before attack caused us to yearn for a Total Exclusion Zone and the freedom to eliminate anything that moved. But thankfully there was little confusion in the vast air co-ordination scene being delivered to all ships on data-link by *Bunker Hill*. Their talented CO, Tom Marfiak, had taken a grip.

Amazingly, over the first forty-eight hours of the conflict, the Coalition lost but a handful of aircraft. Three of them — a Hornet and two Intruders — were from the US Navy. I knew how the sailors would be feeling in the close-knit air groups on board the carriers. But why such tiny losses? Had we exaggerated the threat? Where were the battle-hardened Iraqi air defences? Was Soviet-built equipment inadequate? Had the embargo denied the Iraqis key spares?

As the rain of aircraft and Tomahawk launches continued, the bemused *Olna* re-entered the Gulf from Singapore, her crew sporting suntans that they were soon to lose. I allocated her a replenishment support position in the now cluttered southern Gulf and could sense her incredulity at what had erupted during her absence.

Her fellow auxiliary *Argus* was getting a clearer glimpse of the war since her commercial aerial array allowed her to watch the American TV news company CNN. The crew would listen to the firing of a cruise missile on the tactical net, watch it go by, and then race below decks to see the missile hit. Or so it seemed. I understood from their Captain, David Lench, that it did wonders for morale. The TV image of a cruise missile proceeding down the white centre-line of a Baghdad main street became the definitive image of the Gulf War — much more positive than sad *Antelope*'s disintegration.

Less encouragingly, the cruise missiles had an unsettling characteristic; they needed to recognize a point of land before they could start their terrain-hugging transit to their targets.

Accordingly, they often started off going south-west — straight towards us or friendly territory at more than 500 m.p.h. This always caught the attention. Thereafter, I felt happier when the 1,000 lbs warheads were racing across the desert floor at never more than 300 foot, silently ticking off their navigational calculations — accurate to but a few metres — but all well away from us.

In addition to the Tomahawk, the USN were blooding their new land-attack missile called SLAM. During one firing against the doors of a hydro-electric power station, the second missile went precisely through the hole punched by its predecessor. It was a very high-tech war.

Although the Coalition was being scrupulous in avoiding civilian collateral damage, Saddam was less fastidious. On 19 January, three long-range Scuds were fired at the heart of Tel Aviv. These versions of the missile had reduced-size warheads but could travel longer distances: the Al Hussein went 350 miles and the Al Abbas 450 miles. Though damage from the Scuds was minimal, we were grateful for Israeli self-restraint: they had wanted to launch a 100-aircraft counterstrike, followed by assault helicopters and special forces, but international pressure dissuaded them. Riyadh and Dhahran were also soon receiving Scud attention but there were still no major casualties and, mercifully, chemical warheads were not forthcoming.

Obviously, Scud-busting had become vital to the Coalition. If Saddam's ballistic missiles brought Israel into the war, then historical enmity between Arab and Jew would certainly sever the Coalition. Just before the birth of Christ, the Chinese military strategist Sun Tzu wrote: 'Of supreme importance in war is to attack the enemy's strategy. Next best is to disrupt his alliances.'

Allied aircraft were by then repeatedly striking the twenty-eight Iraqi fixed Scud launch sites, but their thirty mobile launchers were much more elusive and needed targeting by US and British Special Forces. Ironically, Scud sites were to attract 10 per cent of all Coalition air attacks, despite the missile being a relatively ineffectual weapon. Eighty-eight were launched, killing 32 and wounding 250. If the enemy had not got lucky on 25 February when a single missile hit a US barracks in Dhahran, killing 28 and injuring 101, the Scud would have been militarily insignificant.

Though our early warning system to detect weapon launch was working well, it took several more minutes to hear the likely target; not reassuring when ballistic missiles were arcing back into the atmosphere at several thousand miles per hour. But the Patriot defensive missile system was already earning its phenomenal price tag and had been provided to Israel.

When we received an early report, subsequently proved as false, of a chemical attack upon Al Jubayl, I ordered the Task Group to start taking their Nerve Agent Prophylactic tablets (NAPS) ready for our inevitable move north. Also in readiness for such a move, allied aircraft sought to destroy another key missile along the Kuwaiti coast — the anti-ship Silkworm. These ugly yet primitive rockets could not be ignored; with a range of more than 80 miles and with a warhead of 1,000 lbs of explosive, they would ruin an unsuspecting ship's day. Sadly, they too were mobile.

On 20 January, I signalled Admiral Fogarty, asking for information upon the move forward to the north, as neither I nor my MCM commander had yet been invited to join USN mineclearance planning. Although I also pressed Riyadh, who pledged to maintain pressure from their end, nothing was forthcoming. I consoled myself with the thought that the allies were clearly anticipating a long period of air attrition before advancing upon the enemy. Reports of but seven Coalition aircraft lost seemed unbelievably low.

Having started *London* inching north from the tip of Qatar on 20 January, attended by the fat shadow of *Argus*, I focused upon *Cardiff* and *Gloucester*, 70 miles up-threat of us, maintaining air defence for the carriers. They had been at the highest level of vigilance since Christmas and would be in the front line longer than any of my vessels: nobody would be going home while we were still opposed by a capable enemy. It would be easier to destroy his aircraft in the air rather than on the ground, and we wanted to draw the teeth of his air capability before we moved against his navy with our missile-armed helicopters.

On 21 January, a House of Commons vote formally endorsed the role of British Forces in the Gulf by 563 votes to 34: as during the Falkland War, the national consensus was holding up well. On the same day, I helicoptered in to both *Cardiff* and *Gloucester*, taking with me our media men to give them some contrast. They seemed happy to come, clearly not having registered that there was virtually no friendly force interposed between the Iraqi air force and our Type 42s. The ships had settled into a good working rhythm with the USN on either side and were controlling USN fighter patrols well. Utterly exposed and never knowing when a surprise missile attack might hit them, they were festooned with shrouding radar-absorbent material (RAM) which reduced the radar returns of the ships to attacking missiles. They still looked lonely and vulnerable. My diary recorded: 'Purposeful bunch — still clearly ready for anything.'

That day I also put out a signal in which my staff and I had tried to grade the many potential threats that faced us. Surprise air attack, including a launch from mainland Iran, remained our chief concern.

The next day, I was invited to bring *Sir Percivale*'s load of Army ammunition forward to Al Jubayl, so I ordered *Brazen* to act as her shotgun and gave them a helicopter on minesearch ahead. This meant that *Brazen* had to desert her charges in her British patrol area to the south, which by then numbered five ships, but I was happy to risk them being unescorted for a short period. Just south of them, the minehunters had completed every element of their work-up training and were turning over their organizations ready for the call forward. The tanker *Orangeleaf* was getting low on fuel, having topped up many allies as well as ourselves, and thus I had her replenished and she started the cycle again. *Sir Tristram* had finished taking her load of United Kingdom Army ammunition from *Resource* and was ready for her call forward. As the enhancement of *Sir Bedivere* was at last complete, I decided it was also time for *Diligence* to shake off her shoreside cobwebs and ordered her to sea to commence her own shake-down.

The orchestration of separate ship movements, their placement in their 10-mile-square boxes of ocean, and the subsequent movement of them to deny anybody sure knowledge of their location took a great deal of time, but I had started the first of our pre-planned leapfrog movements up the Gulf, all the ships synchronized as if they were each tied by miles of invisible string.

On the same day as the tanker *Olna* took station under British escort to the south, I directed *London* to try our first replenishment of fuel at sea from *Argus* in a flat calm and on a very hot day. If the unwieldy two-ship combination was to go into combat, it had to be as self-sufficient as possible. The fuelling rig was swung out by heavy crane, Iain tucked the flagship in close, the hose was connected — and we had proved our own mobile filling station. After the replenishment, I asked Paxton Dewar to come across and brief me upon his plans for getting plague and anthrax vaccine into us all. Before these unfamiliar drugs were administered to our high-price bodies, I obtained reassurance on the testing they had undergone.

Considerable air effort was at this point being devoted to neutralizing enemy airfields, mainly through the RAF's airfield attack bomb. The weapon was about the size of an office desk and discharged a mix of nearly 250 cratering bomblets that penetrated deep before exploding: the accompanying delayed action mines made airfield repairs an unpleasant business. I followed attempted runway-busting with close interest, Operation Black Buck and Stanley airfield having left me cynical. Nevertheless, I felt great involvement with, and admiration for, the RAF Tornado aircrew as they pressed home their ultra-low-level attacks. It was disappointing when their loss rate forced them up to medium-level.

The futility of trying to keep such large airbases closed soon dawned upon the air planners who then shifted their attacks to the 600 Iraqi hardened shelters, using 2,000 lb laser-guided bombs to penetrate and take out the aircraft within. The accuracy and cost-effectiveness of laser-designated bombs had already been demonstrated by the F111s and the F117 Stealth aircraft. But even unguided munitions had a certain influence: each B52 bomber operating from Diego Garcia, Spain and the UK would pour 20 tons of bombs upon Iraqi ground forces from a high level before starting its long ride home. Though lacking in accuracy they shattered enemy morale. It needed shattering: Coalition Intelligence was now crediting them with 530,000 troops, 4,300 tanks, 3,000 guns and stocks of ammunition and stores that could last for thirty days of intense fighting.

By the end of the first week of war, the Coalition had launched 15,000 air sorties (8,000 combat, 7,000 support) and 220 Tomahawk missiles. Massive defence suppression was still being conducted against enemy radars, guns and missiles, despite gathering certainty that enemy air defences were in tatters. The allied air forces would soon be able to pick off radars, missiles, AA guns and fighters with virtual impugnity. Iraqi hopes of victory against the allies had died with their air defences — unless they could exact a large-scale military reverse on land or at sea.

And so the Coalition commenced a long aerial war of attrition before considering the use of its land forces. General Schwarzkopf had clearly read his Lenin (or perhaps not!): 'The soundest strategy is to postpone operations until the disintegration of the enemy renders the delivery of the mortal blow both possible and easy.'

The following night, 23 January, having moved up close inshore by Dhahran, we viewed the Scud at first hand. The reported launch, detected from the heart of Iraq, set everyone on edge and we waited for the likely target. 'Dhahran!' came the transmission. And all our lookouts gazed inshore. On a rare clear night, it was not long before we were treated to our own fireworks display. Patriot anti-missile systems soared into life, a pause and then two Roman Candles lit the distant sky: two confirmed kills. A third Scud had not been destroyed and overshot its target into the sea. I ran the line-of-fire bearing across the chart and noted with a smile that it passed very close to our present position. Dumb weapon though Scud was, it still packed a big bang. The thought of being eliminated by a mathematical chance in a million did not appeal. We pressed on northward and lookouts resumed their all-round watch.

I was having trouble with the British reinforcement sea train: not unnaturally they wanted information and guidance upon risk as they entered the Gulf. I spent hours on secure-speech radio with the MOD and Riyadh. It was a confidence tightrope: we did not want captains to baulk at delivering their loads but they had to have accurate advice upon the real hazards. I assessed the floating mine to be their prime threat.

Communications traffic had erupted with the outbreak of hostilities. In the flagship, we were handling more than 1,000 incoming signals each day and transmitting an average of 70 — a totally unacceptable load for our team of Radio Supervisor Mark Hoar, Chief Communications Yeoman Paul Fewtrell and seven young ratings. Cries of 'minimize signal traffic at sea' achieved nothing. Ready-formated US signals with hundreds of addressees threatened to clog the system. To help ease the load we flew out from the UK a most capable Chief Radio Supervisor, 'Mac' McIver.

Each day I spent much time in our Special Intelligence office on board with my newly joined and very experienced expert, Lieutenant

Commander Martin Butcher, who had replaced Paul Daykin. He was, like so many of my team, inspired by combat. Tireless, intelligent and drily humorous, he was a source of great strength as he leafed through thousands of pages of signals and spent hours analysing information from the Intelligence communications nets. Equally loaded were the anti-submarine crews of *London*, who had been detailed to support myself and my 'mongrel' flag staff. Their converted sonar room was our war command centre, compressing six or seven personnel into a space the size of a mini-bus. CPO Cunningham was a particularly patient and supportive man, who must have been deeply frustrated at having no submarines to kill.

But it was the enemy in the air that we really wanted to kill; a retaliatory attack from the Iraqi Air Force had still not come. Complexities of co-operation were demanding and radars remained cluttered by a thousand echoes; it was the ideal time for an enemy air attack. Indeed, at the rate we were destroying their aircraft, they simply had to strike while they still had the capability. Was the enemy ever to chance his arm?

On 24 January he did. Early warning aircraft (AWACS) were usually the first notifiers of enemy detection; and so it was that day. At 0927 came a Flash signal from the AWACS to the north-west that enemy aircraft had just gone 'Feet Wet' (departed the coast) by Bubiyan Island — heading south, straight towards us. Iain hit the Action Stations alarm as I ordered the enemy report to be signalled to our vessels

366

down-threat of us. As I peered through my respirator goggles at the busy radar screen, calculating how our ships could best counter the threat, I was thinking of the Falklands. If Iain was doing the same, he did not show it as he settled at his radar display and started directing his teams.

I had agreed that our embarked media team could come into the normally restricted ops room when appropriate: the poor chaps had to report something of substance — mere briefings would not keep their editors happy. They stood, hooded and tense in the ultraviolet lighting, notebooks poised and shoulders hunched, for what could be their first and last experience of missile attack.

★ ★ ★

The noise level is rising, speakers crackle, fingers point; London is still learning. Respirators are on and anti-flash hoods mask identities. Bunker Hill is counting down the raid in a constant cool commentary as the enemy aircraft symbols, relayed on the data-link, blip down the screen towards us. I order Argus to be advised of the raid, put in the 'Action State', and positioned squarely down-threat of London's Sea Wolf. I order our second enemy report to be transmitted to Riyadh — I rather hope it will not be our last.

Quick calculations are made — visibility range, wind direction, and the ideal course on which to deploy Chaff decoys. I seem to have been doing this business for ever. Are we about to regret being the most north-westerly of Coalition ships in the Gulf? The enemy aircraft have been reported as Mirages and are tracking straight down towards us. The raid is just beyond our radar range, and parts of the data-link picture and commentary from the Air Co-ordinator no longer match. I hope the system is not about to break down under pressure. Coalition fighters are being called down from their patrol stations west and east to take the attackers. Dozens of ship missile-heads search northern skies for a possible lock-on. I find myself smiling, despite the tension. We have a lot more going for us than nine years earlier.

Iraqi air raids against Iran during their war suggest they will probably use high-level 'lure' aircraft, pretending to be the raid itself, whilst the real ship-killers slip through the radar arc at a much lower level to fire their Exocets and then scram home. This raid is certainly adhering to the pattern. USN Hornet interceptors escorting an outgoing raid have obtained radar detection from 30,000 feet and are going for the high-level pair — two Soviet-built MIG 23s. As the Hornets swoop for a firing run, the Iraqis light up afterburners and escape. The Mirages, coming in from a lower level, are not so lucky. A short pause; and now I hear the reassuring tones of Bunker Hill — a Saudi interceptor is engaging them. Our correspondents scratch away at their pads; the ops room is totally silent. For the moment the attackers are somebody else's battle — if they fail, it will soon be ours.

'Grand Slam! Grand Slam!' the radio crackles again in my earphones. Both enemy aircraft destroyed. It is still many minutes before the air-raid warning is reduced from Red to White and we can stand down from Action Stations. The air is rancid and the wet rubber of our respirators is slimy with sweat as we remove them. For many in this darkened space, it has been their first time under attack.

* * *

It was a lone Saudi F15 fighter who had shot down the Mirages with tailshots from his Sparrow missiles, despite being exceptionally low on fuel. He reported that the enemy aircraft had not wavered as he locked his missile radar on them: the pilots were either preoccupied with their search ahead for targets or they were on a suicide mission. However, the Saudi pilot, Captain Ayedh, was more adept as a flier than he was as a communicator — in a subsequent interview, he described the critical interception thus: 'I just rolled in behind them and shot them down.' Clearly another Sandy Woodward.

We speculated on whether the neutralized raid would give the Iraqis the information they needed to mount a co-ordinated mass attack, or whether it finally convinced them that our defences were impregnable. We awaited a follow-up. Next morning, the 25th, we received our first Intelligence reports of enemy aircraft disappearing over the border into Iran. Totally unexpected, the move left us confused. USN analysis suggested a regrouping for mass attack against Coalition ships at sea. Our air-defence guard tightened, and we re-measured the short reaction time available if enemy jets emerged suddenly from the radar shadow of Iran. What other reason could there be for such movements? What high-level understandings might have been reached by these two former protagonists?

That night, as *London* held her slow patrol position north of Bahrain, an F18 fighter pilot, returning to *Midway*, ejected from his failing aircraft into the sea 8 miles ahead of us. Our Lynx, two Sea Kings from *Argus* and the USN rescue helicopter all sprinted towards the lonely airman. I urged caution; it was a classic formula for mid-air collision. I needn't have worried: our young helicopter controller was already directing height separations as all the radar blips converged.

'The combined helicopter downwash will probably kill him anyway,' morosely commented the Petty Officer at my elbow. The USN won by a short rotorhead and, as a dripping young pilot was whisked back to his carrier, all the British medical teams on board *Argus* disappointedly stood down. They had been training hard for weeks and were desperate for some real activity.

Some maritime advantage — and useful propaganda — was gained when USS *Curts* and USS *Leftwich* recaptured the first Kuwaiti soil, the island of Qurah, on 24 January. I thought of my piece of Falkland Rock and, in truth, Qurah was about as significant. But it certainly made us all feel good — and CNN coverage of the event would have delighted John Wayne. After a five-hour exchange of fire with the enemy holders of this tiny, barren and totally exposed little island, three Iraqis lay dead and fifty-one prisoners were taken. Also from the north, we had reports of a Saudi missile patrol boat being lost just west of the Dhorra oilfield. Subsequent reports indicated a Blue-on-Blue, which was never confirmed or denied.

Meanwhile, I was restless to see tighter and more precise control of our Lynx in the oil-rig cluttered waters to the north. The number of craft needing identification was declining — even the dullest dhow captain had by then discerned that there were better places to be in January 1991 than meandering around the sandy waters of the northern Gulf, aspiring to become a 'kill' transfer on a Coalition fuselage. Nevertheless, radar propagation in such a hot and humid area was producing spurious contacts galore and the picture remained poor. Fixed-wing post-mission reports had already claimed the destruction of twice as many Iraqi ships as the enemy actually possessed!

To be fair, there were unambiguous successes. I listened to a USN attack aircraft completing positive identification upon an Iraqi vessel, followed by a direct hit with bombs. The pilot's laconic summation, when asked to make a damage assessment, was masterly: 'He appears to have a major stability problem. Oops, correction, his problems have disappeared. So has he!' The allies were settling down.

On 25 January came first reports of a massive crude oil dump from the Sea Island Terminal in Kuwait. Initial uncertainty as to whether it had come from a US air attack upon a large tanker moored alongside was dispelled far quicker than the slick: it was Iraqi hands that were opening control taps to contaminate Saudi desalination plants further down the coast. Eventually stretching 35 miles and containing 120 million gallons of oil, the slick was fortunately to disperse much faster than expected.

Meanwhile, a different grade of oil — diesel fuel — was being daily dispensed by *Orangeleaf* to Coalition ships under the control of the Canadians, commanded by Commodore Ken Summers, a punchy bundle of energy who had a good grip on the Combat Logistic Force (CLF). Our destroyers 'up front' were refuelled every few days by a delivery-boy tanker sent forward from the CLF before it retreated underneath the carrier air-defence umbrella. Ships were patrolling at slow speeds as defence against the floating mine and so the need for nightly top-up as in the Falklands was not necessary.

Though fuel was essential, the arrival of fresh provisions and regular stores was an important morale-booster. Determined not to bring the invaluable *Fort Grange* right forward from Jebel Ali, I was left with the dilemma of bridging the 200-mile gap between us and her. Though our Sea Kings valiantly carried key stores back and forth across the vast tracts of water, it was clear that we needed a low-value vessel to provide delivery-boy service to our forward units. Like

Nicholas, my choice of *Sir Bedivere* relied upon her being only a single inconspicuous radar blob if enemy aircraft were to appear.

I was also by now becoming conscious of how small my staff was. I was getting little rest and David Teer was getting less. I could only delegate so far and thus our junior Lieutenant Commanders frequently needed to turn to one of us for counsel or a decision. After all, we were by then controlling twenty ships in a major war. Before appealing to the MOD to open yet another box of officers, I looked around to see if I could make better use of those I already had. My liaison officers embarked with the USN had, with the outbreak of hostilities, become a greatly reduced asset, being virtually unable to communicate with me. I therefore recalled them both, and established them as my supervising senior watchkeepers, thereby reducing the load on David and myself and improving the quality of our advanced planning. They spent much of their watches analysing potential future problems, anticipating weaknesses, and putting up carefully thought-through options for my deliberation. Defence of the minehunters in the minefields was a particular challenge. I settled down with my newly balanced team — and slept easier.

5

Lynx on the Prowl

26 January – 13 February 1991

'The gates of mercy shall be all shut up'

DURING the second week of war, more Scuds fell on Israel, Riyadh and Dhahran, allied air raids continued unabated, and cruise missiles went on streaming past us — largely courtesy of *Wisconsin*, *Leftwich* and *Caron*. Recent heavy bombing raids on Basra cheered us, as did claims that there were more than one million refugees from Iraq poised on the Syrian and Jordanian border. On 26 January, I was at last invited to join conference with Admiral Fogarty's staff on board *Tripoli*. I flew myself in by Sea King, my good-hearted pilot very tolerant of my boyish desire to have time at the controls.

We gathered in the large wardroom; I was accompanied by John Scoles and his key staff. Numerous commanders of USN ships and of the Australian clearance diving teams were present, and I renewed acquaintance with the USN mineclearance commander, David Grieve, a likeable professional with impressive minehunting experience. He and John Scoles got on well together but they had still not joined in any detailed planning with Admiral Fogarty and his staff.

The meeting was conducted by Admiral Fogarty's staff, who apologized for their Admiral's absence due to ill health but indicated that they were about to 'outline' future plans for an advance upon Kuwait. I was disquieted but remained silent.

The plans which followed struck me as so ill-conceived and immature that I could not believe that the USN had been their architect. Around me the mood changed rapidly to one of similar incredulity, not least among the senior USN officers. We were apparently to move north in a combined group as early as 4 February, with my minehunters leading the way. We were then to advance through the Iraqi minefields, whose position and density were frankly unknown, at an unrealistic speed for precursor mine detection to within 4 miles of enemy gun, missile and rocket-launcher positions. There the minehunters were to commence their clearance operations at dead slow speed in full daylight under the admiring gaze of the enemy. When sufficient water had been cleared, the battleships would come close in behind the hunters, commencing bombardment of enemy positions prior to 'possible' full-scale amphibious assault.

No one had yet been asked to contribute to this briefing *tour de force*. Nevertheless, pointed questions were coming from the USN commanders. What softening up of shore defences would be undertaken from the air? Would dedicated air cover be maintained over the ships in their exposed positions? What percentage of mines could possibly be cleared in the limited time on offer? Answers were few and unconvincing. One senior USN officer, a delightfully blunt and forceful speaker, was most vociferous in speaking out and provided me with one of the quotes of the campaign. As he was, in his judgement, at the 'zenith of his career', he was not afraid to 'put his pecker in the pudding' by saying he thought the plan 'crazy'.

David Grieve then spoke well and critically of the planned timings, given the likely presence of a sophisticated mine called the Sigeel. The weapon contained smart sensors that made its hunting a laborious process; and with nearly 2,000 lbs of explosive it was a true big-ship killer. The drifting mines we had encountered were deadly enough, containing only 300 lbs of bang, so pity the fellow who took a Sigeel. Our estimate was that it might take thirty-three days to clear the area if Sigeels were present: ironically, USN estimates were more pessimistic — they reckoned on forty-two days. However, if it were not present, we agreed we might be through in sixteen to twenty days.

At last I was invited to address the gathering. I did so briefly and much to the point — I rejected the plan. Based as it was upon an 'in to out' exposure to enemy defences, my forces would be at highest risk — quite unnecessarily — from the outset. Intelligence indicated 50,000 enemy troops dug in along the coastal strip, with extensive weapon systems covering the intended operating area at virtually point-blank range.

Loss of even one or two of my Hunts would slow clearance to an unacceptable degree and might risk failure of the entire operation. And I could not accept the staff claim that attack helicopters and bombardment with 16-inch guns constituted adequate defence suppression for twenty-four hours each day. Though I was disturbed that so much unsound planning had taken place without the involvement of myself and my staff, I reaffirmed my willingness to join in proper planning as soon as possible in accordance with my earlier arrangement with Admiral Arthur.

Some fences were mended when we rose from our places but I was profoundly saddened. I have a great fondness for the American people and have always enjoyed Navy-to-Navy contacts over the years. Many aspects of their Service are admirable, and the power and sophistication of their equipment are outstanding. But it appeared that their occasional propensity to ignore the priorities of their allies had surfaced once more. Even a modicum of consultation could have avoided a quite unnecessary confrontation.

I was pensive during the flight back to the flagship. Although I had always been determined that Royal Naval escorts would accompany the MCMVs in amongst the minefields, I had not previously intended taking my £150 million flagship into the maximum-risk area. One briefing had changed all that. I alone would need to decide the proper balance to be struck between risk and gain, and there was to be only one place to do so — in the heart of the minefields with my vulnerable Hunts. *London* was going to have some excitement. Once back on board, I spent a long time on secure speech to Riyadh, High Wycombe and the MOD.

I also had a long talk with John Scoles over my refusal to commit him and his forces until we had a plan we could believe in. As ever, he was full of pragmatic good sense, agreeing with the firm position I had adopted. He returned to his group to debrief his COs and await the call to join me in some proper planning. On 29 January, I was winched down by helicopter to the Hunts. Desperate for action and content with the risks, they gave me an exhilarating few hours and hardened my determination that they should be used emphatically but correctly. I then diverted many miles to call on the newly joined *Sir Tristram* who struck me as one of my more impressive RFAs. It was a shame that I needed her only for more mundane duties as a reserve ammunition carrier.

In the short pause which followed, we were reassured to hear that the Basra-to-Baghdad rail line had been cut, which would limit reinforcements to the coast. I let integrated work-up between the US and UK MCM forces continue. Sadly the Belgian Government had circumscribed the degree of risk that their capable minehunters could incur, with the result that they spent most of the war 400 miles from the front line, out beyond the Straits of Hormuz.

Our Lynx were by then patrolling the northern waters with increasing arrogance. Each Sea Skua missile weighed 320 lbs and each aircraft took a patrol load of two weapons, enabling them to carry extra fuel to fly more than 100 miles to reach their targets. With pilot and observer working as one, the potent weapon system went into battle at ultra low-level at 140 m.p.h., their eyes and ears being the USN helicopters hovering high above to obtain the greatest possible electronic horizon. We were now into the critical stage in the fight for sea supremacy — it was time to remove the Iraqi Navy from the board.

As I returned to *London* from *Sir Tristram*, I received reports of Iraqi land forces having mounted a series of attacks across the border around the town of Khafji. Some heavy fighting was in progress with the US marines, and Coalition aircraft were firing on the Iraqi armour.

It was then that *Gloucester*'s Lynx reported seventeen surface units looping south around the town to seaward — high-speed launches and small vessels packed with men, doubtless intent upon outflanking the Khafji defences. Both *Gloucester* and *Cardiff* Lynx were given clearance to attack with Skua. On a crystal-clear day, the Lynx pressed home their first significant attacks at low level, televised by Eugene Campbell from the *Gloucester* Lynx: he produced a compelling record as the Sea Skuas cut low furrows across the glittering waters before impacting. Several hits were obtained. Follow-on attacks by Jaguars and helicopter gunships left four vessels sunk and twelve severely damaged.

The convoy had been decimated. The following day the enemy withdrew from Khafji, leaving 160 prisoners of war but having killed 11 US marines.

This single action at sea seemed to uncork the bottle. Over the next 36 hours, all our Lynx conducted multiple missile attacks upon several Iraqi patrol craft which had emerged from cover around Bubiyan Island. There was no intelligence to indicate why so many of their boats tried to run the gauntlet of our formidable air capability. If they intended a co-ordinated attack, it is unlikely that they would have chosen to transit over 100 miles south to hit us in broad daylight. More likely was a coast-wise dash to the shelter of Iran, thereby emulating their colleagues in the air force. Whatever their intention, they were unlucky.

Reconstruction of this turbulent phase was complicated. Poor visibility, uncertain radar propagation, and the wheeling, diving attacks of the aircraft did not lend themselves to dispassionate reporting. Contacts mixed with oil rigs, wove in and out of haze banks, floated as burnt-out hulks, and sometimes lay doggo avoiding attack. Add to this the number of potential attackers and the scope for confusion was immense. Nevertheless, when cooler assessment took place, the results were still impressive. Twenty-five Skua missiles were fired; eighteen hit targets, seven Iraqi vessels were certain kills, and several others were incapacitated. A 73 per cent lethality rate had included the sinking of, or severe damage to, a minelayer, three TNC 45 patrol craft, two small patrol craft, one landing craft, two unidentified smaller patrol craft and the much-wanted minelayer. It was entirely appropriate that after the war the tiny Lynx force were awarded three Distinguished Service Crosses and five Mentions in Despatches.

The Sea Skua has never been a sinker of major ships but it is a stunningly accurate neutralizer of small vessels. Subsequent photo reconnaissance included a side view of a TNC 45 missile boat which had seen both its bridge and its missile area almost surgically removed by a Sea Skua. Days later, as we moved north, *Argus* recovered a number of bodies in Iraqi uniforms whose wounds contained pieces of Skua casing. The bodies were all buried with full military honours by *Argus*, who kept a video and photographic record of the quietly dignified ceremony. War protagonists often have an involuntary bond with each other, history showing that atrocities are more often launched by second-echelon forces moving up after the main exchanges of fire, rather than by front-line fighters. Those in the fight have mutual respect — perhaps they can too readily identify with each other.

In the aftermath of the 'Battle of Bubiyan', as the Americans proposed it should be called, several aircraft conducting low-level reconnaissance along the Kuwaiti coast were fired upon by shore AA batteries — including a surface-to-air missile launched at Lieutenant Commander David Livingstone, the aggressive Flight Commander of *Gloucester*. Overconfidence following success in battle amongst our aviators — 'the immortality syndrome' — prompted me to issue a directive calling for more prudence. I had no desire to see young lives squandered needlessly. On one of my flying visits to the destroyers, I was also disquieted to see the effects of the high work-rate upon air and ground crews; flying rates were by then four times those of peacetime. I encouraged both Adrian Nance and Philip Wilcocks to give their crews a short stand-down.

As we moved into February, I repositioned *London* and *Argus* well forward to just off Al Jubayl in order to stay close to the slowly advancing air-defence line. This also allowed me to monitor sea-train arrivals and provide helicopter mine searches off the port. My move north prompted a hint of a finger-wag from Riyadh concerning risk, relayed by John Cartwright. I fear my response was sharp. My Force — my responsibility — my judgement — my neck! Any questions? NAPS tablets were making me irascible. Poor chap, it was probably just a spot of solicitous concern for us all and, to be fair, it was the only hint of back-seat driving throughout the war.

Attempts at a different type of back-seat driving were also emerging from the media. Our embarked teams were restless at missing minute-by-minute action to the north, and imagined that another media team was scooping them elsewhere. The increasingly voluble Michael Nicholson of ITN was getting sick of producing a good TV 'take' and then not being provided with an instant helicopter to take his material inshore for relay to ITN. As he seemed to overlook the astonishingly high work-rate of our helicopters upon war-winning activity, I was not overly sympathetic and directed Philip Wilcocks to ensure that flying hours were not expended needlessly.

An understandably frustrated Mr Nicholson radioed the flagship one day and, in my absence on *Argus*, Iain took the call. Having repeated his complaints about inadequate transport, he concluded by saying that he intended contacting his Director, who was 'a personal friend of the First Sea Lord', as if that would improve the situation! Iain said he doubted that such a prospect would have the slightest effect upon his single-minded Task Group Commander. On hearing of this, and as there had been a couple of earlier exchanges with Michael, I signalled the Ministry that night and gave a brief summary of events which included the reference to the First Sea Lord. I concluded: 'If this nonsense continues, Mr Nicholson shall not.' The following day I received a sympathetic signal from Peter Voute which said that the First Sea Lord, Admiral Sir Julian Oswald, had made it clear that, as in all other things in the Gulf, he would support my judgement absolutely. Michael Nicholson continued to get the best release of film facility that we could offer in the circumstances. Perhaps we were all getting a little edgy.

Whilst the Fleet Air Arm was demonstrating its effectiveness, the Iraqi air arm continued disappearing into Iran. The daily flow of aircraft simply melted into the vast land mass to the north-east, and the Intelligence community remained bemused. By the end of January, eighty aircraft had flown the coop. So we maintained our exhausting schizophrenia: one glance at Iraq, and one towards Iran. But by then I doubted the likelihood of air attack from Iran: if they had the will and the ability to do so, they would already have hit us.

As I moved the Hunts forward to continue training off Qatar, we saw the welcome arrival in the Gulf of reinforcements from the UK. The destroyers *Exeter* and *Manchester* were accompanied by the Type 22 frigates *Brave*, my next flagship, and *Brilliant*, notably carrying the first females in a British warship. The Royal Navy had only started to allow women to serve in warships a year previously and there was much reorganizing going on. Several ships were modified to take them and training for sea service was proceeding apace. Nevertheless, as with those on *Argus*, these young women were having to adapt to something for which society and upbringing had not prepared them. Before I placed them in the heart of battle, I needed reassurance that *Brilliant* too was a capable ship. It was soon to be forthcoming.

As ever, there were four completely different characters in command of our new warships. The most senior was *Exeter*'s, Captain Nigel Essenhigh, known appropriately as 'the Pirate'. Blackbearded, tall, bright and outgoing, he was a natural leader whose sailors thrived on his style and high competence. His ship had arrived ahead of the others to facilitate a high-speed change of a defective engine with the help of *Diligence*.

In contrast, *Brilliant* was in the charge of a submariner, Captain Toby Elliott. He led his people with great verve, quirky originality and some ingenuity. Far less experienced in surface ships than many of the other COs, he had commanded several submarines and would rightly trust his instincts if background knowledge ever failed him. Composed and relaxed, he seemed just the right man to cope with the subtleties of girls going to war.

My designated flagship was commanded with uncompromising certainty by Captain Bob Williams. No CO could have been more intent that his ship should succeed. Fit, articulate and possessed of many strong convictions, his style of leadership was utterly different from that of Iain Henderson. Knowing Bob of old, I was interested to see how his powerful, hands-on style would adapt to working under my command.

The 'Canteen Boat' — the traditional title for the junior boy — was Commander Andy Forsyth. Though I did not know him well, his abilities had just won him early promotion and his own command. He would have the ultimate challenge of proving himself in a new rank, a new ship and a new environment. His First Lieutenant, Chris Mervik, was well known to me from his time as a helicopter squadron CO at Portland and I felt sure that *Manchester* had good balance at the top.

My determination that none of them should be pitched into the front line until they had soaked up the tempo and complexity of the air effort was helped by a request from the WEU Area Commander for ships to assist with operations to the south. Accordingly, I loaned *Exeter* and *Brilliant* to the Italian Admiral in his flagship *Zeffiro*, escorting newcomers in from Hormuz. Having hurtled from the UK, these two frustrated COs were thus held 250 miles from the front line whilst the war seemingly slipped past. Nigel was marvellous in his self-restraint but kept finding excuses to ring me on secure speech and drop heavily weighted hints that his utterly capable ship was entirely ready to 'mix it'! 'The Pirate' was getting restive but I was determined to hold the short pause. Very soon they would be entirely ready.

As for the other two, I had little choice. *Brave* had to come forward to our new position, by then well north of Al Jubayl: as my new flagship, I wanted her entirely ready to take my staff in case *London* was sunk beneath us. With her came *Manchester*, who would be needed as an additional air-defence picket. I was not shy about exposing their fresh Lynx crews to engage the remnants of the Iraqi patrol boats, so I declared them available to the USN. Within a couple of days, *Manchester*'s aircraft was lucky enough to sight two small craft off Faylakah. She identified one of them as a Vospers patrol craft and achieved a kill with one Skua. I flashed her a signal: 'Welcome aboard!'

The arrival of our reinforcements set a number of our ships that were overdue for a return to the UK speculating hopefully. Roulement of personnel had already become a preoccupation throughout the three Services. War had prompted the need to modify the peacetime patterns of deployment for all, but the staged build-up saw personnel trickling into the theatre with different expectations of time on station. This was particularly difficult for the RAF, as a large number of their personnel had come from secure jobs in the UK, in which they had no expectation of deployment. Much signal traffic and some false guidance preceded the decision that there could be no roulement during combat but that the situation would be kept under 'constant review'. This caused a good deal of bitterness from those who had been waiting, bags packed, for a long-promised return. Afloat, the greatest impact was felt by the RFAs who normally rotate their entire crews every six months without fail as a contractual undertaking. I rationalized, explained and justified, but thankfully never needed to threaten. Some welcome and more enlightened relaxations were subsequently introduced and I was then given freedom to recommend the selective return to England of long-serving ships where appropriate.

On 1 February, my staff aviator Paul Collins flew home, to be replaced by a capable and intelligent Lynx observer called Alan Rycroft. On the same day, I flew a Sea King to *Fort Grange* for a visit as *Orangeleaf* came forward to fuel *London*. Hungry for information, they seemed to thrive on my candour and entirely reflected my bullish mood — they were a rewarding audience. The following day I was again up on the destroyer line with Adrian Nance and Philip Wilcocks: they were coping well with the strain but, on my return, I summoned a long-range Sea King with fresh provisions to brighten their lives. Expensive brussel sprouts.

I then heard that Commodore Doug Armstrong, Commander of the USN 22nd Destroyer Squadron, had been given the unenviable responsibility of planning and executing the inshore phase. Mature and sensible, he was a highly experienced operations man who promptly asked for my detailed modifications to the plan and for the precise contribution my forces could make. I signalled an expanded version of my earlier proposals and awaited his response.

On 3 February, *Missouri* moved forward under escort to commence bombardment of enemy bunkers just beyond the southern border of Kuwait, and well south of likely enemy minefields. It was the first occasion that her guns had fired in combat since Korea in 1953. She was later relieved by *Wisconsin*, escorted by the ever-present *Nicholas* and making the first operational use of the Pioneer, a remotely piloted vehicle, for spotting her gunfire. Though her 16-inch guns had been less than accurate when used off the Lebanon in the 1980s, the Pioneer had since transformed their effectiveness. Their 1-ton shells could accurately penetrate nearly 30 feet of concrete, leaving behind a crater the size of a tennis court at each point of impact. Both battleships were being systematically blooded.

The vessels themselves were a marvellous sight. Their gracefully balanced superstructures were set into a 60,000-ton, 900-foot-long frame, containing a potent blend of old and new weaponry. In addition to the 16-inch gun, they had twelve 5-inch guns — each one bigger than the largest carried by the Royal Navy — together with thirty-two Tomahawk cruise missiles and sixteen surface-to-surface Harpoons. Manned by 1,500 men and ringed with armour plating that was seventeen inches thick in many places, they were the pride of their navy, second only to the aircraft-carriers.

On 4 February, I flew to *Tripoli* in mid-Gulf, and thence to *Lasalle*, further south. Doug Armstrong, David Grieve and myself discussed the inshore plan with Admiral Fogarty and his staff. We still lacked encouraging damage reports against coastal defences and Silkworm launchers. Every time I asked whether we were part of a full amphibious assault or merely a massive deception plan, I was told that this was not yet known 'for sure'. The answer to that question was fundamental: I would take great risks if we were an integral part of final attack plans. However, if virtually all my forces were to be thrust against the Kuwaiti coast purely as a ruse, I would be more cautious.

This was the only gathering with the Americans that I can remember as being less than relaxed and amicable. Nevertheless, Doug and I were completely aligned in our views and my wishes for my forces were all met eventually. So, with final agreement on a sound plan, with a USN commander I could fight alongside, and with no answer forthcoming to my key question, it was time to live dangerously. Thus I committed my forces, thereby making just the disproportionate contribution that the General and I had agreed to minimize. I would be placing more than half of my expanded force of twenty-six ships into the minefields, and a further five ships in close and dangerous proximity. As a proportion of the national forces deployed to forward and aggressive commitment, it was the greatest of any nation in the Gulf.

London would escort the MCM support group of *Herald* and *Sir Galahad*. *Gloucester* and *Manchester* would act as close missile traps inside the longer-range USN systems, and *Argus* and *Diligence* would loiter within 40 miles of the minefields, suitably defended by some of my new escorts. Of course, the Hunts would be out in the van. But I reserved the right to veto the continued use of any of my ships at any stage of the operation if I was unhappy with such employment.

My visit to *Tripoli* allowed me to take a closer look at what was to be our future companion and overall flagship. An amphibious assault ship of 20,000 tons and 600 feet long, she carried 700 personnel and was well equipped for command and control. Though nearly thirty years old, she was immensely sturdy. Six giant Sea Stallion helicopters were embarked with sophisticated mine location and destruction equipment first developed for use off Vietnam. It seemed inconceivable that such vast aircraft had been flown out from the US, two at a time, in the belly of C5A Galaxy transport aircraft. They covered mined waters much faster than a surface minehunter but, I was assured, with far less certainty of success.

On return to *London*, my rather neat landing, despite a strong cross-wind, restored my spirits but double jabs of the plague injection — Cutter — soon reduced my zest. That night the General blessed my decisions made on board *Tripoli*.

Planned penetration of the minefields was simple to describe but difficult to achieve. We would cut a 2,000-yard-wide approach lane from a starting position well to the east and hopefully outside the offshore limit of the minefields. US helicopters would carry out exploratory operations ahead of the Hunts and USS *Avenger*, who would sweep, then hunt, by day and night until a clearance of 80 per cent was achieved. Next, helicopters and Hunts would clear a 10 by 3 mile rectangle of swept water for the battleships to bombard the shore — and as a possible platform for amphibious assault. Smaller boxes would then be cut towards the coast, taking the battleships' gunfire further and further into Kuwait. NATO nations usually demanded a clearance factor of 80 per cent before risking their high-value units in war. More comprehensive clearance took much longer and was unacceptable; the heat of summer was approaching.

Mine clearance is a complex blend of old and new techniques. Moored mines are cut by towing wires with explosive cutters at a set depth. Influence mines are neutralized by towing a noise generator and magnetic loop, simulating the acoustic and magnetic signatures of ships. However, pure minehunting involves using high-definition sonar to detect ground mines on the sea bed. These are then destroyed with a remotely activated countermining charge, normally placed by divers or propeller-driven submersibles. Time and patience are always at a premium.

David Teer and I spent several hours each day planning, drafting signals, conversing on secure speech and anticipating the next stage. Our separate memo pads which we compared twice daily were voluminous as we continued to co-ordinate twenty-three separate ships. I worked hard on keeping my COs in the picture and building mutual confidence throughout all ships. Dispersed operations over a wide area in the fog of war made it damned difficult.

Before closing the Kuwaiti coast, we needed to be sure that a tiny island called Khubba near the mainland would remain free of Iraqis. This barren blob of sand and rock dominated our mineclearance area. I offered Admiral Fogarty our Royal Marines to take, hold and police the target. He expressed interest and we worked up a plan. Frankly, I was conning him. Our marines, though very competent, were not SBS Special Forces. Nevertheless, I believed that our Green Berets, who had been cooped up in warships and were desperate for action, could eat an operation such as Khubba. I invited Mike Wills to form his scattered men into a group and train them for contingency operations.

Some almost comic distraction was provided when a Sea King bringing a spare Lynx engine forward to us developed a ruptured oil line and was forced to carry out an emergency landing on the stark tip of Qatar. We flew in a salvage team from *Argus*, wondering how in God's name we were to remove 8 tons of helicopter from such an inaccessible spot. Ingenuity prevailed. A long walk by the team to a remote garage produced metal tubing which was brazed into shape, and the aircraft was back in her shipboard hangar within hours. It was all reminiscent of jubilee clips around the tail shaft of *Alacrity*'s Lynx. As then, I smiled and didn't investigate too closely. When the aircraft finally arrived, it delivered the first sacks of a bumper crop of Valentine cards, most of them seemingly penned by little girls intent on chatting up the sailors.

Encouraging reports of enemy deserters having crossed into Saudi Arabia were balanced by news of Arab terrorist action in Jordan, Lebanon and Greece; I was relieved that all my ships were at sea. Off Kuwait, the Iraqis were apparently filling a tanker with explosive liquids to act as a fireship against possible Coalition amphibious assault. Old ideas are often the best.

We were not the only ones under threat: on 7 February, the BBC told us that the Irish Republican Army had fired a mortar bomb into 10 Downing Street. I hoped that security services and the police were taking their future precautions as seriously as were we. On 8 February I again flew to *Cardiff*, sharing the latest developments with them and attempting to brighten spirits.

Desultory engagements were still taking place to the north, most of them involving fixed-wing aircraft. Although *Cardiff* and *Manchester* helicopters both claimed kills, we were by then simply mopping up. On 9 February Admiral Arthur and the Intelligence community agreed to declare Sea Area Supremacy over the entire surface of the Gulf. At last we were dominant. By then in the overland war, 44,000 Coalition air sorties had been flown, the equivalent of one bombing aircraft for every minute of Desert Storm. Nearly one-quarter of this effort had come from the decks of the six USN aircraft-carriers, *Midway*, *America*, *Theodore Roosevelt*, *Saratoga*, *John F. Kennedy* and *Ranger*. Over the entire period of war these ships were destined to fly a total of more than 18,000 fixed-wing sorties.

I celebrated with further visits to *Gloucester* and *Brazen*, as my flagship and her lumbering companion continued picking their slow way north towards the Saudi border. The ships were like a staid old couple, steadfastly inseparable: matronly *Argus* and rakish *London*. We were having increasing difficulty with Saudi coastal forces. I wanted to take *London* and *Argus* in and out of the Saudi 12-mile territorial waters, making use of offshore islands to block floating mines and send confusing radar echoes to the enemy. But I was instructed to remain outside, pending diplomatic negotiations. My reactions were less than kind. Whose country had Desert Shield been mounted to protect? Some faceless bureaucrats were alive and well in Riyadh or London, or perhaps both. So we maintained our position, exposed in the coastal current, whilst our helicopter barrier patrols cleared mines from the path of the sea train labouring into Al Jubayl. By then, anxious merchant ships were being directed to approach the port only in daylight to avoid night collision with floaters; they lacked our low-light TV night-sights.

Most floating mine interceptions were in our area, as the coastal current was strong on the western side of the Gulf. Visual lookouts needed no inducement to remain alert as there had, by then, been more than 100 mines detected and destroyed. When one was sighted it was sobering to see how little of the sphere and spikes were actually visible, particularly in broken seas. We tended to advance by day and then fall back in a slow fishtail manoeuvre by night, carefully calculated to ensure that we only passed back through waters swept during the day. It was frustrating stuff and I yearned for the 30-knot surge of *Alacrity*. Our ship captains compared the safest manoeuvring profiles by signal. Some believed they were best off drifting with the current at night, their shafts stopped. But a 4,000-ton warship and a 300 lb mine drift at very different rates; without steerage-way, a ship has no ability to respond to a late sighting. Nevertheless, I refused to arbitrate upon the techniques preferred by ships' captains; each knew his own vessel best. The 'floater' was a new threat and we had no computer modelling or scientific analysis to help us — just a group of mariners using mariners' wits to keep them from harm.

My staff worked hard to increase our readiness against a mine hit. They produced a minefindings plot, showing the time and position of mines sighted and destroyed, from which we established three risk areas. How far north you were dictated your water-tight policy, the decks below the waterline that you left vacant, and the restrictions upon your night movements. Reading from north to south: 'Red' was hell; 'Yellow' was a distinct pain; and 'White' was bearable. As a result of the policy, hundreds of our sailors slept night after night on bare steel decks whilst lookouts strained their eyes, hoping for moonlight and dreading a loppy sea which would mask any floating mine.

By every man's bunk was placed an emergency lifesaving breathing set with sufficient air to get him through smoke to the upper deck — some more Falkland lessons had been learnt. Everybody existed in three layers of protective clothing, notwithstanding the temperature: cotton underwear, combat blues and flameproof white overalls. Topping off the ensemble were the white anti-flash hood and gloves. On one hip we carried our anti-gas respirators, and around our waist a lifejacket. Finally, a cumbersome battlebag contained personal protection gear. I thought of the

396

bronzed young RAF ground crew in their shorts by the pool at the Diplomat Hotel and envied them.

On 11 February, *Cardiff*'s aircraft hit an Iraqi vessel, as their talented young aviators, Lieutenants Phil Needham and Guy Hayward, sought more glory. But it was to be their last. On the same day, we received the long-awaited operation order covering the move north. Penetration of the minefields was ostensibly to mount a major heli-borne raid against Faylakah Island and to put battleship fire into Kuwait: there was no mention of amphibious attack against Kuwait itself. Five of the nine most forward positioned allied warships were by then British (the remainder continuing to be USN) and I had every intention of ensuring that the Royal Navy continued to stay where it belonged — out front.

So close to the long-awaited move north, it was a huge disappointment to receive a signal from Commodore Doug Armstrong — his farewell. After just ten days in charge of preparations for the coastal operation he had been routinely relieved and was on his way back to the States. The US Navy's zest for replacing warfare commanders with great rapidity in mid-combat left me amazed. The origins of this strange procedure were, I suspected, a hangover from Vietnam where ship activity was relatively low-key, apart from carrier flying operations, and where there was little complex interaction with the enemy. In a less frenzied setting, a newcomer could quickly adapt and produce adequate command and control without being unduly stretched. However, the complexity of a Falkland or Gulf War made different demands. Indoctrination took time, and whilst it was happening fighting performance could not help but be degraded. Degradations produce mistakes, and mistakes kill. Thus I was intent upon keeping in the front line those who were already conditioned, until only fatigue dictated the need to replace them. As in politics, a week is a very long time in war — and even a little combat experience is invaluable.

Doug's final signal to me made it clear that he did not understand the nonsense of his being relieved at such a time any better than did I. Nevertheless, I entirely reciprocated his last paragraph which read: 'Valued our too brief friendship and cannot think of an ally with whom I would feel more comfortable or confident in going forward. God speed. Very respectfully. Doug.'

I was profoundly depressed at his departure as there was to be quite enough uncertainty ahead without yet more turbulence at the top. Doug was replaced by Commodore Peter Buckeley. I worked quite comfortably with Peter but we never established the rapport I had shared with Doug; and I sense there were many occasions when I drove him to distraction with my necessary interventions over the next three weeks.

On 12 February, I had discussions with Peter aboard *Herald*. Once we were called forward to penetrate the minefields prior to land assault, we agreed to muzzle both sets of our embarked media to avoid giving any advantage to the enemy. On 13 February, the General made a flying visit to *London* and to the Hunts, with the confirmation that we were starting the last lap. 'Cor blimey, sir, I do believe he's come to bless us,' muttered an irreverent sailor.

We concentrated hard upon the complexities of minewarfare, the one naval warfare discipline that even the most experienced tactician still tends to leave to the specialist. I leant extremely heavily upon the advice of John Scoles and Lieutenant Commander Brian Mansbridge, my MCM staff officer who had been embarked with the USN minehunting force. I had also called to the flagship as my permanent adviser Lieutenant Bill Kerr, a small Scottish clearance diver of quiet self-belief and high ability who proved invaluable. Our homework upon the 80 per cent clearance factor gave cause for reflection; elation at destroying eighty mines would subside pretty quickly if you impacted with one of the remaining twenty. Life would soon be edgy.

It was to be edgier still for our divers who were about to take centre stage with the Hunts. Our Fleet Diving Group had deployed from the UK as three detachments: one to *Sir Galahad* to work up mine-clearance skills; one to *Diligence* for maintenance support; and one for anti-terrorist security duties in Jebel Ali and on the RFAs. In preparation for a move north, this last group combined with the *Galahad* team. The grouping was about to show its worth.

Against the likelihood of amphibious assault,

I requested an additional staff officer from the UK. The ever zestful Lieutenant Commander Lloyd Bridgewater arrived, and we were soon running think-tanks upon the unpalatable possibility of over-the-beach attack.

But, before we headed north, I needed to integrate my reinforcements and to decide who might commence their long passage home: we could be about to commit to quite a long and intense fight. It was only fair to ensure that I had largely fresh ships that had not been working hard for many weeks. I selected *Cardiff* and *Brazen* to return home. *Cardiff* had been up front as long as anybody and had certainly been most exposed up against the Iranian coast. *Brazen* had also achieved a great deal and, as I could not contemplate releasing her sister ship *London* at just such a time, she too could return. Nevertheless, though needing to start a ship roulement, I could not take entirely unblooded ships forward. This was tough on the two who must stay — *London* and *Gloucester*. Though I listened to the expected pleas from Adrian Nance and James Rapp, I had no hesitation in sending them home, although I recalled my own passion to remain in the South Atlantic in 1982. Both ships had been on station for twenty weeks of high-intensity operations. *Cardiff* herself had returned to the Gulf after only a short period in the UK on return from her previous deployment. In a Navy decimated by defence cuts, this type of stretch is common and, though it gets little publicity, it drains the goodwill and patience of our people and their families alike.

400

I ordered *Exeter* and *Brilliant* forward with a brusque apology to the French Admiral who controlled WEU escorts that I had more important things for them to do. Equipment, publications and modifications were transferred from outgoers to incomers: *Cardiff* to *Manchester*; *Brazen* to *Brilliant*. I also took the opportunity to bring forward the two 826 Sea Kings from *Zuiderkruis* to join *Sir Galahad*.

My designated relief for *Herald* was *Hecla* (Commander Hugh May) who had also arrived in the Gulf with much-needed reinforcement Hunts — *Dulverton* (Lieutenant Commander Colin Welborne) and *Ledbury* (Lieutenant Commander Frank Smyth). One of *Hecla*'s routine progress reports to me as she had approached the Gulf had erroneously transcribed her latitude and longitude, putting her position neatly in the middle of the Empty Quarter of the Arabian Desert: I commended her for her determination to get to us by the quickest means possible! Just ahead of *Hecla* had come the tanker *Bayleaf* (Captain R. W. M. Wallace) to replace *Orangeleaf*.

By then, my resupply line of 350 miles was unacceptably long. If we were to sustain operations in the far north, I had to establish a more forward airhead in the only location that offered security, Bahrain. After several days of signals, I flew ashore to the island on 13 February to talk to the Ambassador, Tony Horton, and Jarvis Humby. We agreed a system with the help of the Bahrain Port Authority: our stores were to be flown into Muharraq, shipped

401

by road to a port set-aside area guarded by Mike Wills and his marines, and a cycle of collection and transit by *Sir Bedivere* would be established. In the space of five days, it was all functioning, but only thanks to the Bahraini authorities, the British Embassy, the Americans and our shore team. How the British do prefer to improvise rather than plan — I should have anticipated such a transfer weeks before.

Whilst in Bahrain, I answered a call to brief the media teams ashore to explain the Navy's exploits afloat. I was keen to do so. One young sailor had summed up the feeling of many when he had pleaded with me: 'I've been out here doing the business since last September. We've blockaded the Iraqis, we've played hopscotch with their mines, and now our aircraft have sunk their bloody Navy. But every time I get the airmail papers from home, all I see are sodding tanks, waiting in the desert.' I shared his chagrin; indeed, such frustration had prompted me to allow our ever-willing ITN cameraman Eugene Campbell to fly combat patrols in *Gloucester*'s Lynx. So I held a press conference on board *Sir Bedivere*, alongside in Bahrain, for a very frustrated bunch of newshounds avidly awaiting a still distant land assault.

Captain Bill Walker had done me proud. In a wardroom bedecked with White Ensigns, TV cameras and microphones, I was confronted by an audience of fifty international reporters. Clearly 'tank pictures' were not enough. I have always relished the kick of being before TV cameras and had had some experience of it, so

I tried to convey the tensions, the excitements and the achievements of the war at sea, and they seemed to enjoy it, judging from the benign and admiring questions which were put forward. Television magnifies our joys and woes tenfold: but I knew that transitory acclaim could turn in an instant into more newsworthy disaster. Thus there can be a temptation to treat the publicity game as a cynical exercise in mutual exploitation. After an hour, I drew the session to a close, being restless to be back at sea. I re-embarked up-Gulf later that afternoon, reassured by the new support arrangement and vowing that the next time I came ashore it would be in Kuwait City. It was.

Task Group preparations against chemical and biological weapons were by this stage becoming destructive in their own right. Daily consumption of NAPS tablets, to condition our bodies against the effects of nerve gas, was getting a bad reputation amongst the sailors. Many claimed tiredness, blurred vision, dizziness and high-decibel flatulence — foul rumour also having it that we were destroying our libidos. Remembering the shoregoing habits of some of our sailors, I felt like doubling the dosage but the frivolous aspect of the affair disappeared when I learnt that, as a result of the rumours, a number of senior ratings were not taking NAPS. I reminded everyone that we were about to move into an ideal position for the enemy to use chemical weapons. Any man not correctly preparing himself would likely pay for this omission with his life.

More worrying was the unmistakable effect of the plague prophylactic injections: most people went down with severe 'flu symptoms for between thirty-six and forty-eight hours. So bad were these reactions that we were driven to inoculating in phased batches so that we did not neutralize an entire ship at a stroke — or rather a jab. I must confess to some reflection myself as to the testing process that the vaccine and NAPS had undergone. Sailors were, of course, claiming that it hadn't gone beyond pigs. It was becoming clear that the waiting process of war was getting to many. I sought and obtained medical reassurance from London which was signalled to all commanding officers.

The emotional preoccupation with chemical weapons was out of proportion with their real threat to us, but such is the nature of the unknown. We increased our already regular drills and were often unsettled by spurious alarms from the upper-deck automatic chemical alarms. On one such occasion, Martin Lander hurtled to the cabin which he shared with newly joined Alan Rycroft, who was off-watch. 'Al, put your respirator on; the chemical alarm's gone off!' he yelled at the ball of humanity under the covers.

'It's bloody well on already!' came the doubly muffled response.

Notwithstanding Coalition attempts to minimize civilian casualties during their continued massive air assault, it was inevitable that something would go wrong. On 13 February it did. After an air attack against a command bunker in

Baghdad, the Iraqis released emotive photographic evidence of between 200 and 300 dead civilians, claiming that the bunker was in fact an underground air-raid shelter. Allied photo-reconnaissance showed it to be a cordoned and secure area, which did not fit with the air-raid shelter claims. Worse still, on the following day, two RAF bombs malfunctioned and went into the centre of Fallujah near Baghdad; another seventy-three died.

Both events received a bad press at home. Just to keep our own spirits high, the BBC announced that the British minesweeping force was about to move north into the Iraqi minefields off the coast of Kuwait. I was less than amused. I just hoped that whoever had released the information was not about to inspire another Goose Green.

As we awaited the final call forward, I believe I felt my first and last fear of the two campaigns in which I fought. Some say that only a damn fool feels fear. Not so; my command preoccupations had consistently anaesthetized me against terror and I was very grateful. But now I was asking myself whether, by deciding to take my flagship and so many of my ships forward into the minefields, I was needlessly sentencing many men to death. Only the next few days would give me my answer. And I was fearful.

At last the interminable waiting and stop/start was over: it was time to move. High above us, the Coalition was completing its 67,000th air sortie. At 0300 on the morning of 14 February — Valentine's Day — I led my ships to rendezvous with *Tripoli, Missouri, Wisconsin,* their escorts and the US MCM group in the central Gulf. Having passed tactical control of my units to *Tripoli*, I then ordered *Exeter* to bring forward *Olna*, *Argus* and *Diligence*. I wanted them in the vicinity of the Dhorra oilfield to provide support from close at hand, but outside the range of Silkworm and within the radar clutter of the oil rigs. Peter Buckeley was particularly grateful for the presence of *Diligence* as the American repair ship *Jason* remained secure in Bahrain: everyone was being forced to make their own risk/gain calculations. Thirty-four vessels were moving north, half of them British. It was only the invaluable *Fort Grange* and *Resource* and the ammunition-carrying LSLs that I wanted to remain safely in the far south. As for the rest of us, the northern Gulf was about to become ours.

6

Mighty Mo and Little Glo

14 – 25 February 1991

'And teach them how to war!'

NO sooner had we started northward than a twenty-four hour delay was ordered and we paused — precisely on the latitude of 28° north. I had no idea of the reason but assumed that there needed to be some synchronization with the impeding land assault. Sadly, the control of our forces was split: both *Gloucester* and *Manchester*, as our advanced air defence, remained under the tactical control of Admiral Dan March, way to the south in *Midway*; all other ships were being directed by Peter Buckeley. Thus, for the next ten days, ships often very close together were being controlled by different commanders: the US command structure was showing its unsuitability for close-quarters work. My frustration was shared by poor Peter.

Very early on 15 February we resumed our passage north whilst *Wisconsin* diverted west to bombard the Kuwaiti coast again — presumably part of the reason for the pause. Her targets were artillery positions, command locations, boats in port, troop positions and even coastal minefields. Already there was overdemand upon calls for fire. Far to the south, *Brazen* had sailed from Jebel Ali for home. All roulement of British Service personnel had now been curtailed: clearly we were on the brink. I ordered *Hecla* to come forward to Bahrain to assist in running the stores delivery service to us in our forward position.

Our passage was painfully slow, being limited by the maximum speed of the older wooden USN minesweepers, and the need for a good mine lookout. *Brave* soon detected a 'floater' which was subsequently destroyed. Though air and missile attack remained a threat, the mine had become our main preoccupation.

As we advanced, the BBC told us, in order of priority, that the England Rugby team had beaten Scotland 21 – 12 at Twickenham and that Iraq had proposed a ceasefire. Whilst the enemy declaration was transparently a stall against the land advance, it did not stop conjecture by many that there might be an eleventh-hour reprieve from entering the minefields. Wanting was believing.

On the afternoon of 15 February, I ordered *Exeter* and her charges to detach for the Dhorra. We continued north and, at precisely 1802, *Herald* wheeled to the west and we were directly closing the Kuwaiti coast. I watched our Hunts out in front of the force and wondered about their morale in such an exposed position. Though I knew they were proud to be the spearhead of the entire maritime effort, and though British technical excellence and competence were not in doubt, they were heading for slow and painstaking mine clearance under missile threat, a drain on both courage and confidence. I sent them the following signal: 'From the platform that you are about to provide for the allied navies, we can complete our domination. You will be under my admiring gaze — and the defensive air umbrella — throughout.'

Early on Saturday, 16 February, as the Iraqis were firing Scuds into Haifa, *Tripoli* and *Sir Galahad* peeled off to their anchor berths whilst the rest of us continued west, *London* and *Gloucester* riding attendance on the Hunts and *Herald*. I felt the same anticipation as on 11 May 1982. No Falkland Sound opened up before me, but the anxious uncertainty was similar. Tension was high. Mid-morning, an air-raid warning was called which proved false. Tension became higher still with reports of *Exeter* finding another floating mine down in the Dhorra (the 110th so far, Bill Kerr reminded me) and four more Iraqi bodies, distended and forlorn as they shared the drifting waters with their own mines. They were all flown to *Argus* for checking and correct burial.

Jamming of our radio circuits commenced as we moved closer to the enemy but reports of air attacks upon Silkworm launch sites on Faylakah brightened our spirits, despite earlier revelations of elaborate dummy launchers having been attacked in error: for devious duplicity, our foes were close to being the best in the world. The Hunts divided the intended swept channel into five segments and went to work as a number of air-raid warnings were called on the strength of shore radar transmissions that could have been Silkworm targeting. I issued a caution to the Task Group not to wear out their people prematurely by undue periods at short alert; I only found out later that one of our ships in the Dhorra had spent many hours at exhausting Action Stations. Some learning curves were near vertical.

Sunday, 17 February, started well and finished badly. In the morning, our divers recovered two more Iraqi bodies to their helicopter whilst *Dulverton* and *Ledbury* detected and killed our first two ground mines, thus giving us confidence that Intelligence had got it right and that we had started in the correct place. I flew in to *Tripoli* in the morning and we had a lengthy meeting to refine our timings of mine clearance and how we would cope with opposition. We had no inkling that we were just about to support such theory with practice. Signalled reports of possible Silkworm missile-launcher activity to the north were backed by the detection of enemy radars which seemed to be targeting the force. Peter Buckeley immediately ordered complete withdrawal to the east. I was aware that the choice was not my own and that the Americans might well have collateral evidence that was not available to me but, nevertheless, given our effective missile systems and alerted condition, I felt we might have stood our ground. The Silkworm is big and slow, an ideal target for the Sea Dart. If we withdrew at every alarm we would not reach the coast before Christmas.

Thankfully, the threat was reassessed from more Intelligence received, and we started moving west again just before midnight, but we were about to regret the withdrawal. It was a gloriously calm and starlit night, so clear that we could see low transiting aircraft and the distant flashes of bombing and flares over land. We soon matched their excitement.

At precisely 0145, only a few miles off Khubba Island, *Tripoli* took a full minestrike. The reverberations thudded through *London* three miles away, leaving no possible doubt as to what had occurred. Somebody had 'bought it'. She had been hit on her starboard side forward, just below the waterline. A moored mine had clearly been responsible.

Brian Mansbridge was on board the US flagship and later described the experience. Both explosion and whiplash were unmistakable, even in such a solid ship. Damage-control reactions were fast and effective, the forward section of the ship being quickly evacuated, allowing fire and flood boundaries to be established. Two mine-lookouts had been blown over the side (subsequently they were recovered alive) and a 20- by 30-foot hole had been punched in the hull — luckily just clear of a messdeck packed with sleeping sailors. Directly above the blast, several more men had been resting around the base of a hatch which acted as a blast vent and they were completely covered in a vortex of aerated grey paint and spirit from the store beneath them.

As they rushed up the ladder, they were met by a member of the damage-control party. 'My God!' he exclaimed. 'So that's what chemical weapons do to you.' Some colourful language from the victims soon brought him to his senses. A helicopter from *Argus* collected one injured seaman for treatment and I imagined him being pounced upon by dozens of professionally frustrated doctors and nurses.

Alarmingly, *Tripoli* was well outside the estimated easternmost limit of the minefields and still 30 miles off the coast. The effect was immediate. If we could not believe our Intelligence then what could we believe? Was the entire offshore area mined? Were these delayed-action weapons placed on the bottom for a timed period before floating up to the surface? If so, we could have no confidence in an allegedly cleared area remaining safe. Or were they smarter still? Had ship-count fuses been steadily ticking off the vessels passing overhead, until exploding on a predetermined number of passings? Our confidence was shattered as surely as had been *Tripoli*'s hull. We had clearly been inside the minefields before we commenced hunting operations. As so often in combat you live — or die — by the quality of your Intelligence.

Every Coalition ship had come to a dead stop in the water. It was an eerie sight: the high-technology warships frozen into immobility, all knowing that the only safe place in a horribly uncertain world was where nothing had so far gone bang — the spot on which they floated.

The minesweepers *Leader* and *Illusive* preceded *Tripoli* slowly out of the minefields, whilst the remainder of the American ships requested the services of the Hunts to lead them away. In happier circumstances I would have been flattered by the compliment. As we waited for amplification of the damage, I reflected upon the loss of life if a similar explosion were to rip through my flagship, whose hull was but a fraction of *Tripoli*'s half-inch steel skin.

With lookouts redoubled as the first light of day appeared, the ships continued eastward, seeking safe water in which to group. As we pored over the chart trying forlornly to second-guess the significance of the minestrike position, the Hunts were ordered to investigate *Tripoli*'s position. All of a sudden, nothing was safe any more. We needed another mine fix to draw logic from *Tripoli*'s misfortune. We were about to get it.

At 0420 another massive reverberation echoed through *London* and again all ships slid to a halt, awaiting identification of the latest victim. It was the super-expensive *Aegis*-class cruiser *Princeton* who answered the call for information. She had been hit right aft, experiencing extensive whiplash throughout her length. Although her hull was intact, it was badly twisted and she had damage to her port shaft and rudder, flooding in her magazine from a ruptured firemain, and shockwave unseating of her Harpoon missiles in their launchers. Her visual lookout in the bows had been hurled more than 50 feet into the air, luckily coming down in the sea alongside to

413

be recovered safely. We dispatched another Sea King to collect him and two other victims with head injuries for ministration by the delighted *Argus*. USS *Horne* took over her duties and we all returned to our calculations on the chart table. Once again, the unspectacular sea mine proved to be a handicap out of all proportion to its cost and complexity. It was turning out to be a thoroughly bad day.

Following further withdrawal, we regrouped for a rethink. There was little choice. Battleship bombardment in advance of Coalition troops was a key part of the impending Desert Sabre advance on land: we had to move back in — and quickly. A sweep of the area around the *Tripoli* strike position revealed a line of other moored mines, running broadly north — south. Though I had always believed that mining south and east of the Dhorra would have been wasteful of Iraqi mine stocks and was thus highly unlikely, I viewed the radar echoes of the *Exeter* Group milling to the south with concern and just hoped that I was not about to be proved wrong. A report of a mine sighting from one of them — *Brave* — set my nerves jangling, until it was found to be another drifter. Gross uncertainty was starting to play upon the nerves of us all. The sapping effect of never knowing whether the next breath would be our last, despite being many miles from the enemy, was considerable.

Damage to *Tripoli* and *Princeton* had been extensive: *Princeton* was withdrawn immediately for repairs in Bahrain and she never rejoined. But the top priority was *Tripoli*; her command

414

and control were less important than her ability to operate the heavy Sea Stallion helicopters. I visited her by Lynx and toured the explosion areas with her charming and composed Captain, Bruce McEwen, admiring the extensive shoring holding back the flooded compartments around the gaping hole. He was candid: any increase in sea state would 'work' the ship's hull, collapsing the main collision bulkhead and allowing millions of gallons to flood the rest of the ship; she would go to the bottom. I was delighted to meet his request for engineers and divers from *Diligence*, noting that our willingness to take the Royal Fleet Auxiliary to the front line was once again proving invaluable.

The inevitable decision was made and we recommenced our creeping approach to the Kuwaiti coast, whilst the USN tug *Beaufort* started the long slow tow of *Princeton* back to Jebel Ali, over 400 miles south. The tow soon shifted to a Dutch salvage tug, allowing *Beaufort* to return to the fray. I was later to find out that the repairs to *Princeton* were to cost in excess of US$50 million.

The Hunts had detected several mine lines of six weapons each moored 200 yards apart in the *Tripoli* strike position; they and *Princeton*'s ground mine were *east* of the alleged outer limit of the minefields. We had no choice but to recommence minehunting much further east than our initial starting position: the delay would have to be accepted. It was only good fortune that there had not been great loss of life. It was also clear from my radio discussions with Peter that serious damage to a billion-dollar *Aegis* cruiser would see us being offered a somewhat less sophisticated form of air defence in lieu. And so it proved. *Jarret* — the same class as the dispensable *Nicholas* and possessed of but a fraction of *Princeton*'s capabilities — was ordered in to join us.

As we inched back closer to the coast, I was disappointed at the increasing number of areas declared as banned from Coalition attack around the Kuwaiti coast. Although in many cases this merely showed where the USN Seals and other Special Forces were engaged, in some cases it was clear that the risk of collateral damage was the cause. Many Iraqi defensive emplacements positioned amongst stylish coastal houses made the desired softening up of the coastal strip impossible. Modern war is indeed a complex business of infernal bloody compromise.

Meanwhile, our divers were proving outstanding. Having spent twelve years myself as a mere ship's diver, I knew something of the demands upon our infinitely more experienced clearance divers. Either jumping from their Sea Kings or operating from their own boats, they had to get down through the thick oil contamination on the surface, often simply by spreading washing-up liquid to clear a submerging apron. Once in the water, they had to contend not only with high explosives and oil pollution, but also with sea snakes and occasional sharks — more than one diver found himself to be not the only one circling a mine.

The discovery of some unexpected types of

ground mines meant that John Scoles needed approval for these brave men to recover them intact for investigation — 'exploitation' they call it — thereby improving our future chances of combating the weapons. The delights of embracing hundreds of pounds of high explosive by night amidst oily sand and in nil visibility whilst laying a small explosive counter-charge were not lost on my fertile imagination: it bordered on the suicidal. Having been brought to the surface, the weapon then needed to be winched up on to the deck of *Sir Galahad* or dragged ashore. I duly requested the appropriate approval from the UK for such mine recoveries to commence. It was agreed and our divers went to work in the oily gloom with my continued admiration. I wondered sardonically whether they did not feel they already had enough challenge.

Diving officers have to lead by example as perhaps no other at sea. The three teams were headed by typical extroverts: Lieutenant Commander Mike Leaney; Lieutenant Ralph Dreimanis (of the Canadian armed forces) and Lieutenant Steve Marshall. The latter had been a gifted officer candidate with me in *Alacrity*.

The days which followed were packed with incident. On 19 February, USS *Adroit* discovered two floating mines tied together by an extended length of line — ostensibly to snag around the bows of the unwary — and more free-floating mines were found in the Dhorra. An A6 Intruder aircraft engaged some enemy rigid inflatables transiting the Bubiyan Channel — hardly a fair

417

fight. Manchester's Lynx rushed in to finish the 'lilos', as I deprecatingly called them, with his heavy machine-gun pod, but by the time he arrived they had either deflated or had run for shelter. *Atherstone* recovered another Iraqi body; *London* Lynx detected a radar contact just off the Kuwaiti coast and called in aircraft to prosecute; and one of the Pioneer remotely piloted vehicles from *Missouri* splashed into the sea near *Gloucester*. Down to the south, divers from *Exeter* and *Diligence* discovered that the legs of the oil-rigs had been booby-trapped with more than 1,000 lbs of explosive. We were in a busy piece of ocean.

That night our divers were trying to identify, then raise, a huge new ground mine from a cold depth of 40 metres, necessitating working in minimal visibility and enduring chilling decompression stops on the way up — one of them was rendered unconscious from hypoxia. Nevertheless, by the following morning, the mine had been countercharged and brought to the surface. Nobody in the Task Group wanted the divers' job.

We spent hours each day changing the positions of our dispersed ships and attending to their separate needs. Simply co-ordinating the transfer of all the anti-submarine high explosive held by our newcomers into the ammunition ships, before the warships came into the risk area, was a major undertaking. Bringing forward fresh stocks of Sea Skuas and squeezing two Lynx into Type 42 destroyers only designed for one presented another headache. Each ship was a small, separate town in itself — with almost as many demands and difficulties. And trying to ensure the coherence of their efforts in support of the war was demanding. On several occasions I had to shoo my adjacent warships back from the edge of suspected minefields: there was a little too much cavalier spirit in the face of uncertainty. One of the heavy Iraqi ground mines exploding under the keel of my flagship would certainly break her back and take several hundred men to the bottom. Perhaps the most timeless and precise summary of the necessary attributes for this type of passionless fighting is a Viking saying: 'Fire in the belly: ice in the mind.'

I conferred regularly on secure speech with Peter Buckeley: he was extremely good at taking comments, giving me the opportunity to challenge or debate before carefully outlining his intentions for the following day. Conscious that he needed full support, I limited my comments merely to major points of anxiety. It was a difficult situation for us both. He was aware that I was a full national commander, highly experienced and well established in the theatre, with many ships under my command. He was also well aware of the friction which had arisen from the ill-conceived planning phases and suspected that I had brought my flagship into this perilous location solely to keep the closest watch upon my ships, rather than out of bravura. For myself, I knew that he was the third incumbent in four weeks to have responsibility for the most fraught part of the maritime

419

campaign; that his priorities seemed not to be getting the high-level attention that they deserved; and that the existing command system was dividing co-ordination of our defences. Poor Peter: he had massive responsibility and insufficient control over his assets — he needed my help.

Other than mines, we shared one common anxiety — missing a Silkworm amongst friendly aircraft departing the Kuwaiti coast by day and night; or, conversely, killing a friendly aircraft in a Blue-on-Blue confusion.

Meanwhile, the Air Tasking Organization (ATO), planned and directed from Riyadh, remained hugely complex, imposing and inflexible. Though a masterly tool for controlling so much air activity, it was ill-suited to supporting fast, reactive operations at sea. Enemy missile launchers and ships could all relocate well within the forty-eight hours it took the ATO to plan and execute an attack against them. Thus aircraft would arrive over their briefed target position only to find their potential victim gone.

Deep in the minefields, tension remained high. By then we had the satisfaction of seeing, hearing and feeling our own forces detonating enemy mines. Every blast seemed to give us a modicum more confidence. Nevertheless, near detonation with no advance warning was an unwelcome surprise to those in the adjacent steel hull. At one stage, Martin Lander appeared back in the command centre claiming to have discovered the first homeopathic laxative: he had been seated on porcelain as a particularly shattering blast erupted close to *London*'s beam, and his own.

Mine clearance set me reflecting upon gallantry, and its recognition. Courage is not the absolute quality beloved of fiction: it is variable — many shades of grey. Some are more inclined to possess it but all can develop the capacity for it: it can be fuelled by motivation, by loyalty, by peer-group pressure, by expectation — even, sometimes, by ignorance or insensitivity. It can be readily eroded by fatigue, by wrong cues, by too long an exposure to risk, or by disillusionment. Some can have courage and then lose it; most men are capable of courage one day and semi-cowardice the next. It is a complex combination of emotion, logic and resolve — and perhaps some irrationality.

Ironically, many acts of courage, particularly those fuelled by adrenalin on the spur of the moment, are launched from a platform of ignorance and confusion. The risk involved is often obscure. It is sad that men can undertake acts of great valour, but when the actual threat turns out to be far less than their original perception of it, then there is no acclaim. And yet is the deed any the less valiant?

Attribution of glory can be equally random, and the recipient would be well advised to take the gift with much gratitude — and some humility. Selection is rarely a measured, objective process. Injustice can be done and assessment can be imperfect, particularly when affected by media reportage or an eloquent reporting officer. Thus many can leave the

421

field of combat bitterly disappointed by the lack of rightful recognition. However, like me, they will probably be unable to offer a better alternative to the imperfections of the honours and awards system. But all should recognize that the gap between those aglitter with medals and those who 'merely' fought is often much smaller than folklore would have us believe.

The Navy, in particular, suffers from another dilemma — that of recognizing individual merit amongst collective achievement. The combat performance of a ship will be a combination of extreme bravery and more indifferent performances, as is that of every regiment. But, on land, there are more opportunities for individual acts to be separated out and acclaimed. So, the Navy can sometimes do no better than decorate the one man in the ship whose abilities and energy should set the standard for all — its captain. The symbol of collective achievement by that ship goes to the man who carries absolute accountability for every failure as well as every success, and only the most egocentric commanding officer thinks the award his alone.

There remains a final quandary for the Navy, and it relates to the proximity of the enemy in modern warfare. The very phrase which governs the criteria for gallantry awards, 'in the face of the enemy', is outdated and increasingly irrelevant to much of long-range naval warfare. Retention of the criteria will progressively see maritime forces disadvantaged in the allocation of gallantry awards. But, as with perception of risk, the courage involved in performing exceptionally for a sustained period in the midst of minefields or under constant threat of long-range missile attack can be every bit as worthy as conducting a short action in close proximity to the enemy. There must be many a long-range bomber pilot from the Second World War who would be inclined to agree. There was certainly courage aplenty on display amongst the minefields off Kuwait in late February 1991.

At this stage, I was advised that USN auxiliaries were not being allowed to proceed beyond 28°30'N: the ripples of *Tripoli* and *Princeton* were apparent. This kept USN supply ships and tankers well south of the Dhorra and many miles away from the hard-working ships amongst the minefields. If our defences were not to be weakened by ships periodically retiring for fuel, then we had to make use of *Olna*. I had no difficulty with this. I was by then entirely satisfied that there were no mines south of the Dhorra, so provided my 'heavies' only moved by day and went no further north, then it would be unlikely that they would catch a floater. Accordingly, I offered Peter Buckeley the services of Captain Stuart Pearce and *Olna*, running an east — west filling station for his ships. Given the chance, Stuart would have continued clear on to Baghdad. Peter gratefully accepted.

We soon encountered another challenge — false alarms of mines due to the sighting of floating rubbish. All British ships had a routine for dealing with the garbage — in naval parlance 'gash' — generated by several hundred men. We collected it, compressed it, and then ditched it overboard, suitably weighted, by night. One or two lucky ships had automatic shredding plants but most were committed to this archaic and thoroughly unpleasant practice. Whether some of our ships were becoming sloppy or whether the US regime was less disciplined than ours, I did not find out. Cautionary signals produced rapid improvement and Peter even nominated a gash ditching point, stepped back from the minefield, so that the highly sensitive bottom-search sonars were not duped by Coke cans. Such are the less glamorous realities of war.

I was also again having difficulty with our embarked media, and I sympathized with their predicament. All around they could see newsworthy events of some drama unfolding but they were constrained by the American and British embargo upon the release of information. I remained obdurate that I would not take a single casualty merely to provide newshounds with satisfaction. So we remained the Silent Service, and I was less than popular. But this situation took on a new twist when the USN suddenly embarked a CNN team in *Missouri* and went for an immediate and massive release of information. Clearly, the information embargo was seen to have outlived its usefulness. Peeved by more lack of consultation, I promptly lifted my own ban and gave COs the selective ability to release information. We were able to put Michael Nicholson and Eugene Campbell on board *Missouri*, a trickle of maritime publicity seeped into the sitting-rooms of Europe and America, and our people at last received some of the credit they so richly deserved. Doubtless the publicity was also giving the Iraqis a logical target area for their Silkworm missiles.

Yet again I was being reminded that, in an image-conscious world, media coverage can never be far from the attention of the military commander. Its ability to deny him his aims is second only to that of the enemy itself. If malevolent, or mishandled, it can rupture security, destroy morale, obscure achievement and transform a minor setback into a national disaster. Ultimately it can fracture the very consensus which sustains action itself. The commander must live with the whims of this capricious mistress and accept her often damaging tantrums in exchange for the many fruits she can bestow.

On 20 February it was the Lynx that was again in the spotlight. *London*'s aircraft made a precautionary landing with an electrical defect on board *Tripoli*, whilst another came under AA fire from Bubiyan as he scoured the coast under the control of a USN ship. I was concerned that a combination of heavily overworked fliers and a restless new Group would soon produce an unnecessary tragedy. My second tough signal was paralleled by one from Peter Buckeley to the tasking units, but neither of us enjoyed back-seat driving.

When I flew back to *Tripoli* for a working lunch with Admiral Arthur on the 20th, I was made aware of the full scale of

425

the Coalition air effort which by now had completed 100,000 sorties, launched 323 cruise missiles, and delivered 88,500 tons of munitions (including 6,000 tons of smart bombs) — an average of 350 lbs for each Iraqi in the Kuwait area. Estimates of 40 per cent Iraqi infantry desertion rates were also coming in: improbable but elating. More certain were sightings of large enemy relocations of tanks and armoured vehicles to the coast. It was thought that Saddam had placed up to ten divisions eastward, against a possible amphibious assault. If it was just a Coalition ruse it was certainly proving to be highly effective.

The weather had grown turbulent. A long, high swell impaired the Hunts' sonar performance, restricted Sea Stallion operations and slowed our advance. The little ships bucked and corkscrewed in the unaccustomed surf which degraded the accuracy of their 'hovering' and thus their sonar. In order to speed up, we agreed to reduce the width of the swept channel from 2,000 yards to 1,600 yards. Although this presented no problem to slim-beamed and agile warships, it would cramp transiting heavy vessels. I also chose to move *Herald* forward under *London* escort to reduce the off-task time taken by the Hunts in backtracking for fuel and material support. But still we lacked the full strip of cleared water. Further delay stemmed from all *Argus* helos being grounded by a Sea King jamming her flight-deck lift. It took some hours to clear.

By 21 February, wind and sea had abated

and it was clear that the main land assault was imminent. My Military Intelligence Officer, Royal Marine Captain Gordon Mackenzie-Philps, was picking up signal snippets which fitted the final preparatory stages. The messages were classified SECRET but only gave vague hints when one piece of information was balanced against another: I was impressed that there were not more clues. Coalition security was good but the Iraqis must have known that the trap was about to be sprung, and no wonder. Predictably, false peace alarms were filling international radio and television: the Iraqi Revolutionary Council had allegedly declared its willingness to negotiate, including the possibility of withdrawal from Kuwait. I put no credence in the offer, though many remained more gullible. We intensified our mine-clearance effort and waited for news.

And then, just before dawn on the morning of 22 February, *Ledbury* conducted us through the swept channel and into the cleared area. We were through and spirits were high. My signal to Riyadh concluded: 'Fine brave Hunts standing isolated at the head of allied maritime forces; undoubtedly one of the sights of the war.'

But anxiety over air defence intensified as we moved even closer to Kuwait — the Coalition aircraft that streamed towards us were increasingly singletons coming low, fast and sometimes without the distinctive emissions of Identification Friend or Foe. Often damaged by AA fire or running short on fuel, they were unaware that they were under an additional threat from over-eager naval missile operators afloat.

Peter Buckeley and David Grieve breakfasted with me on board *London* and we proposed to Admiral March the establishment of a zone around us that would exclude our own air assets and thus ensure their safety. He decided that returning aircrew had enough difficulty without having to route around us: we, and they, would have to take our chances. When we asked for much smaller missile engagement zones around our main block of ships, the answer was the same. Friendly aircraft were not to be given any additional complication on their return journey. I reflected that being shot down inadvertently by one's own side was something of a complication.

Vigilance was heightened still further by an Intelligence report that two Silkworms had apparently been fired to the south on 20 February. Their target had been *Wisconsin*, who had been continuing her shelling of the coast near the border and south of the minefields. So much for US claims that they had totally eliminated the Silkworm launchers. In an effort to counter this threat, we tied together some of our inflatable missile decoys and placed them in the water at the shoreward end of the swept area to protect the Hunts as they worked. It was unlikely that an incoming missile would be seduced by the decoys but their presence would at least give the lonely crews some confidence.

Away in the desert, helicopter gunships had been goading the enemy by taking 15 bunkers and 500 prisoners. There was no doubt that thousands of hours of carpet bombing by the B52s — the equivalent of five Hiroshima bombs — must have shattered enemy morale; sleep must also have been woefully scarce. The international media announced that the Coalition was minehunting prior to conducting landings. Dangle that bait!

We were approaching the Sea Island oil-loading terminal which stretched 10 miles perpendicularly offshore, affording the Iraqis an excellent view of our advancing forces across the mirror-like sea. I suggested to Peter that it also made an excellent target for our destroyer's gun. I received the somewhat sheepish response that our timing was less than perfect — US Special Forces were very shortly going in by helicopter. How much more were we not being told? Nevertheless, I busied myself with the many demands of my own force and the need to support the US efforts as best we could.

Whether or not our efforts would culminate in the amphibious operation being mounted remained a secret known only to the very highest level of the Coalition command. It appeared I had no 'need to know'. I was also still ignorant of the start time for the land assault, but later information indicated that Peter had no more information than I and was similarly frustrated. Clearly our efforts were not to be tightly integrated with the land war, so perhaps we had no need to know. When I returned to *London*, my team briefed me upon a major change of Coalition air-defence fighter positions over the whole of the northern Gulf. We had our first solid indication and warning that something was up, but as nobody had provided me with some solid information I felt that flexibility was becoming a somewhat overworked principle of war.

On 23 February, the Iraqis engaged in an appalling tantrum. With defeat looming, they wantonly set fire to oil wells throughout Kuwait; more than 100 were lit in the first twenty-four hours. As a piece of spiteful ecological sabotage, it could not have been more destructive. That same afternoon, our long-awaited debutante arrived: the great *Missouri* slid into the swept apron of water and unleashed the immense destructive power of her guns upon Faylakah Island. 'Mighty Mo' was on station. The shockwave ran through all the ships, psychologically and physically. At last we were attacking the enemy directly. I was grateful that we were behind the huge belching guns rather than waiting in a trench, watching the circling of the Pioneers radiating video pictures to bring the next shattering explosion: the Iraqis rightly called them 'buzzards'. It was brutal sea power at its most devastating. They would soon be bringing down fire upon the entire coastal strip up to 10 miles inland and there would be no more sleep for the enemy in that corridor. It was hardly surprising, therefore, that subsequent capture of many Iraqi maps showed large-scale amphibious assault as part of the Coalition attack plan. All the pieces of the Coalition maritime effort were at last coming together and my nightly signal relayed the charge it gave us: 'The battle being carried to the enemy overcomes fatigue and anxiety alike.'

As if trying to match the efforts of the battleships, the US Air Force had taken to dropping huge bombs, nicknamed 'Blues Brothers', on the troops occupying Faylakah Island. Each of them contained 12,000 lbs of explosive.

The Americans had withdrawn *Tripoli* to Bahrain for her delayed repairs, she having done her job by sustaining the Sea Stallion helicopter effort. The Hunts were by then no more than 16 miles offshore, extending the fire support areas even closer. I took the opportunity to be helicopter-winched down to *Cattistock*, where Mike Shrives and his team were in vigorous form. Our divers too had had a bumper day, destroying five mines. I watched them leaping from the 826 Sea King, swimming to the bobbing, lethally spiked globe, attaching plastic explosive, carefully paying out the cordtex fuse and then, from a safe distance, blowing it joyously away.

That same morning it was confirmed that the Sea Island Terminal was in the hands of Coalition Special Forces. In the afternoon, *Jarret* reported a missile impact in the sea close to her starboard side: no other ships had any evidence of a missile flight and subsequent post-war analysis gave no clue. Nevertheless, the report did little to settle pulses, particularly as our interceptions of enemy targeting radars had increased markedly, indicating a possible firing

431

sequence by Silkworm. Radar and missile crews were intense in their concentration and as edgy as they had been since we had first entered the minefields. We were at near point-blank range for Silkworm.

Briefly that afternoon, we pulled back all the Hunts and the US minesweepers *Adroit* and *Impervious* to secure — 'raft up' — alongside *Herald* for the final restock of fuel and water. By this stage I had brought *Hecla* close to the front line, intent upon changing her with *Herald* at the first sensible opportunity. I also invited *Fort Grange* to accompany *Sir Bedivere* and come forward to the edge of the minefields. Though I had declared the provisional aim of changing my flagship to *Brave* on 3 March, subject to external events, I was determined that the time had come to replace *Gloucester* with *Exeter*. The latter clearly had a handle on events and was now ready for anything: she should be given her chance. And *Gloucester* had paid all her dues, though she was to mount her greatest performance just before she left centre stage.

In the meantime, General de la Billière had been teasing our Admirals at home, wanting to know when they were going to show some high-level interest and make an operational visit. In truth, I thought my high command had been wonderfully restrained in giving me my head without supervision. Nevertheless, Rear Admiral Peter Woodhead made a flying visit from High Wycombe on 24 February. Having taken over from the dynamic Roy Newman in early January, he had tracked all Gulf naval business for CINCFLEET. An excellent listener and a very bright man, his short visit was a motivating tonic and he went out of his way to reassure us that we were doing well.

He picked a good day to visit. At 0100 that morning, we received Codeword Ripper transmitted by an airborne early warning aircraft from the carrier *Roosevelt*. The land war had started. The thunder of *Missouri*'s heavy guns increased in cadence — answering the call for fire. Our land forces numbered 540,000 troops from thirty-one countries. Though they had 3,400 tanks and 1,600 pieces of artillery, they were still well short of the 3:1 numerical advantage favoured by military textbooks when moving against well dug-in defenders. Nevertheless, we did have total air domination: 1,736 combat aircraft and 747 support aircraft from twelve nations, backed by sixty B52s, had the skies to themselves. Afloat, there were 170 ships from fifteen nations, which included six Carrier Battle Groups, two battleships and several cruise-missile firing submarines. Perhaps the ratio of 3:1 was not that important.

The US XVIII Airborne Corps, together with the French Daguet Division, had been positioned in the far west. On their right were placed the main attack force of the US VII Corps, with the British 1st UK Division on their eastern flank. Islamic Forces had been divided into two Corps, with the two US Marine Divisions between them; their orders were to advance along the coast.

After initial reconnaissance probes, the US and

French to the west produced an irresistible surge to secure the left flank. Meanwhile, the US 101 Air Mobile Division launched a 300-helicopter assault of their 'Screaming Eagles' to take a future operating area about halfway to the River Euphrates. To the east, the Arabs and the marines overcame co-ordination difficulties and made a rapid advance.

The main allied attack was then launched fifteen hours early to take advantage of such momentum, after a reduced period of bombardment to soften up opposing forces. Following some highly effective feints, the US 1st Infantry Division breached the enemy defences, allowing the 1st UK Infantry Division to roll forward. The Divisional Commander, General Rupert Smith, alternated the efforts of his two brigades in a series of punches, each brigade replenishing in between attacks. The two Brigade Commanders, Brigadiers Patrick Cordingley and Christopher Hammerbeck, achieved great success, destroying large numbers of Iraqi armed vehicles and guns.

Throughout 25 February, the XVIII Airborne Corps commenced a dynamic advance into the Euphrates Valley and cut off the Iraqi escape route to the north-west. This allowed divisions to thrust east towards Basra in a pincer movement, rolling up the enemy defences. The eastern advance met little resistance and soon found itself up on the Al Mutl'a Ridge and in a position to dominate retreating Iraqi columns.

Whilst the land forces were punching through Iraqi defences, out at sea during the entire night of the 24th and the following day, the reverberations of the 16-inch guns shuddered through all ships. Endless thunder. *Missouri* had no need to economize on her huge ammunition stock: Pioneers were giving bombardment co-ordinators a precise view of the fall of shot and thus they only needed to fire a single pulverizing round every few minutes, right over the top of the masts of the Hunts. Targets were tank and gun emplacements on Faylakah, and ammunition dumps, supply centres and armoured units around Kuwait Airport. I could envisage the effect on morale at the other end of the arcing trajectory of shells. Notwithstanding their destructive power, the psychological warfare being waged upon tired and tense men as they huddled in their inadequate defensive fortifications must have been devastating. But the enemy was far from toothless.

At 0151 on the morning of Monday, 25 February, 20 miles directly to the west of our position, a group of Iraqis wheeled their mobile Silkworm missile launcher out from cover and prepared a pair of 22-foot-long, 6,000 lb Silkworms for launch. They wanted allied blood as vengeance for the whistling death that was destroying their troops. In the deep dead of night, twin tongues of flame burst from the missile tails and they ripped themselves from launch rails into their flat attack trajectory. Though one malfunctioned and ditched into the sea shortly after launch, the other continued at a little less than the speed of sound and at 1,000 feet straight towards *Missouri*. Our missile crews thus had only a small radar contact coming off the coast at high speed without any identifying emissions. The radar contact was exactly similar to many hundreds of other such echoes from returning allied aircraft over the previous forty-six days and nights.

Gloucester's weeks of hard-won experience paid dividends: Little Glo was about to defend Mighty Mo. She alone of the air-defence ships detected the missile, correctly identified it, allocated it to Sea Dart, ensured that no aircraft were in the vicinity, and obtained command approval to engage. Petty Officer John Roberts hit the button, and two Sea Darts ripped into the skies above us at Mach 3. It was a perfect shot, and the big Silkworm erupted amidst a bright blue flash. Our missile warheads were the expanding-rod variety: they scissor out as they explode, chopping their target to pieces. The entire process had taken no longer than three minutes from Silkworm launch to destruction, all at the lowest ebb of vigilance in the small hours of the morning and after innumerable false alarms. There was confusion as ships heard *Gloucester*'s engagement call and a massive fall of debris cascaded into the water close to *London*'s stern — giving us a moment's anxiety that a long-range multiple rocket-launcher firing was also underway.

I ordered the Hunts to withdraw in column formation and Peter called down immediate retaliatory air strikes on the launch position. As there had been no radar emission from the missile, it was likely that it had been fired solely on the basis of radar detections from ashore. Indeed, there was a possibility that the Iraqis thought we were further east than we were, therefore programming the Silkworm homing head to commence its search further out.

Philip Wilcocks was far from confident about his target and naturally concerned that he might have 'taken' an allied aircraft by mistake. We talked at length over secure speech and I reassured him that he had done exceptionally well. Whatever was by then sinking into the oil-blackened waters beneath us, I was entirely happy that Philip had acted correctly: I recalled Admiral Woodward's similar reassurances to me as I returned to his force after sinking the *Isla de los Estados*.

Philip felt better when Riyadh confirmed that no Coalition aircraft had gone missing in our vicinity and better still when we got confirmation from *Cattistock* — Sub Lieutenant Rob Burford had been working on the sweepdeck when his gaze had been caught by a streamer of orange flame flying arrow-straight at low level towards the big ships. It was a Silkworm. *Gloucester*'s peerless performance was hugely admired subsequently, by the Americans in particular, and merited rightful acclaim. Philip's award of the Distinguished Service Cross on behalf of himself and his men was so very well deserved — for this and many other achievements. It had been *Gloucester*'s swansong. *Exeter* came up the swept channel at 0530 and took her place whilst *Gloucester* turned her battered bows away. I paid her ringing tribute by signal as she slid wearily east and then south to offload her equipment and spare ammunition before starting the long road home. No ship could have done more. Following on behind *Exeter* came *Wisconsin*, *Lasalle* and *Raleigh*. The swept area was getting crowded. And then we were ordered to punch the last 10 miles direct to the nearest port — Mina Al Shuaybah.

The US Marines had taken Kuwait Airport after heavy fighting, allowing the Pan-Islamic forces to push right through to Kuwait City. Meanwhile, the main US VII Corps punched their big left hook through increasingly demoralized Iraqi defenders, finishing astride the main road between Kuwait City and Basra — soon to be known as the infamous 'Highway of Death'. The Corps had covered over 150 miles, destroyed 8,000 vehicles (including 1,300 tanks) and taken more than 22,000 prisoners — all in less than two days.

Visibility had, by this stage, become atrocious. Burning oil from 500 blazing oil wells ashore tainted the air as ships slid silently through the gloom. Days were all the same beneath the oil smoke: chill, foul-tasting and dark. Even the searing tropical sun could not penetrate the dense layer that was covering hundreds of square miles. On occasions, an eddy of offshore breeze would push a block of truly impenetrable darkness over us and we would enter instant night. Rivulets of brown slid down once-immaculate grey paintwork, and flags hung, heavy and foul, from their halyards. Jagged rivers of crude oil latticed their way from horizon to horizon as sunken oil was stirred from the bottom, discolouring and tainting the shallow waters. We had no more than 30 feet of bottom clearance below the whirling propellers of our bigger ships which continuously stirred the glutinous pudding of filth. Evidence of man's inhumanity to his planet was all around.

By night, the blanket of smoke would lift just enough to show us the carnival death-dance of the oil fires ashore. From horizon to horizon, the entire coast seemed ablaze, with only the silhouettes of the Hunts etched defiantly against the flickering amber glow. On this satanic stage, the elevated gun barrels of the battleships traversed back and forth, seeking fresh prey, before erupting their own torrent of flame — as if hungry to join the inferno. We were at the edge of hell amidst the thunder of gunships.

7

Sour Fruits of Victory

26 – 28 February 1991

'When thousands weep'

AT dawn on 26 February whilst an electrical storm raged away to the north, the Hunts worked closer to Shuaybah; battleship gunfire pounded enemy targets around the airport; and US Marine helicopters streamed in upon Bubiyan Island.

The amphibious 'ruse' was being dramatically enhanced by 18,000 embarked US Marines poised at sea — the biggest amphibious gathering afloat for fifty years. Marine Corps General Alfred M. Gray rightly employed the timeless wisdom of Sun Tzu when he told his men after the war that: 'To subdue the enemy without fighting is the acme of skill.'

A different kind of subjugation was undertaken by Les Port and his 846 aviator brigands from *Argus*. They executed the long-planned Operation Trebor, winching Royal Marines SBS on to the roof of the British Embassy in Kuwait City to safeguard the building against looting or reprisals. The US were doing the same a few blocks away. After the war, the British Ambassador, Mike Weston, confided in me that

440

he had been less than delighted at the endeavour as they had kicked in his magnificent doors in their rapid envelopment: but his Embassy stayed safe. I felt very sorry for the SBS; in contrast to the Falklands, they had been precluded from undertaking operations such as the superb achievements of the SAS in harrying Iraqi Scud sites.

Good pugnacious *Exeter* pleaded for clearance to close just a little further to allow her gunfire to join with that of the battleships. The Hunts seemed to be moving faster still, with the spur of a coastline clearly visible in between the oil clouds.

At just this inopportune moment, *London* developed a major interference in her Sea Wolf radar, which meant that she was virtually toothless until the problem was cured. I had no choice: bitterly disappointed, I had to pull her back a few miles out of Silkworm missile range and bring *Manchester* up to defend *Hecla* and *Sir Galahad*. Was I always to be doomed to miss the finale of any war I fought?

Pioneer pilotless drones and Cobra helicopter gunships went sniffing around Shuaybah at first light on 27 February — except that first light no longer existed. Offshore breezes from Ahmadi had by then turned day into constant night. Our helicopters cautiously probed Kuwait Harbour, returning to report that the city was quiet and there was no small boat traffic: there had been concern that the enemy might try to evacuate their secret police to seaward — atrocities against the population of Kuwait City made retribution likely. As we had no idea of the Coalition casualty rates on land, I had brought *Argus* and *Fort Grange* forward to exploit their operating theatres and flight-decks in support of mobile surgeries ashore; the ever-adaptable *Sir Bedivere* came up in support. When the amphibious group started its heli-borne raid against Faylakah, I sensed we were winning a stunningly fast victory.

That night we had unconfirmed reports that Kuwait City had been abandoned by the enemy: the Coalition had an emphatic military victory on its hands. Over the space of 100 hours, it had neutralized thirty-six divisions of the enemy and taken 86,000 prisoners. Kuwait City was indeed in allied hands and, on 27 February at 1200 Eastern Standard Time, President Bush told the world that Kuwait had been liberated and that the 100-hour offensive advance was suspended. We had a ceasefire.

The BBC then gave us the announcement we had spent nearly seven months waiting to hear — an astonishing victory had been won. By a bizarre coincidence, both the Falkland and the Gulf War had lasted for almost the same period of time — forty-three days and forty-two days respectively.

Responses in the flagship certainly varied. 'Damn,' said Gordon Mackenzie-Philps. 'Bang goes my chance of a VC!'

'Mines don't surrender,' responded the dour Scottish tones of unexcitable Bill Kerr. Psychological profiling of my staff would have been illuminating.

I felt precisely nothing; indeed anti-climax

was much more dominant than elation. We had spent so long anticipating a protracted and bloody struggle, it was hard to readjust. I felt weary. War is a young man's game: stamina, aggression, resilience and adaptability all start to wane once you pass the age of 50, and the much-trumpeted compensator of mental strength is overstated. I was four months short of my fiftieth birthday.

I was also cynical about the durability of any ceasefire, having become intensely suspicious of any Iraqi negotiating position. The slaughter ashore set me thanking God that we were to be spared such massive losses afloat. Was I actually to complete two combat commands in the thick of the action without incurring a single casualty? I ceased my speculation and merely concentrated upon maximizing the odds that it would be so.

Of course, we all wanted our land forces to finish the job of war, destroy all Iraqi armour, drive to Baghdad and eliminate Saddam. Our wish was simplistic and naïve: the Coalition had no international support to go any further than it already had. In the Falklands, a remarkably firm national resolve had endured throughout, with the sole exception of reactions to the sinking of the *Belgrano*. In the Gulf, an unprecedented Coalition had been constructed and retained with great diplomatic skill: to have exceeded its mandate would have been to risk massive world approbation and fracture of the all-important consensus.

Democratically elected governments must

continually remember the limits of their powers: national approval for the use of arms has to be retained. In the future, increasing demand for the United Nations to act as 'world policeman' will need to be moderated by recognizing the implicit limitations of its freedom of action.

Nevertheless, there are two factors which always seem to be capable of disrupting such a consensus. In the dying days of the Gulf War, it was these same two factors which combined to ensure that the watching world would countenance no more fighting, irrespective of any military logic. These factors were the media and the taking of large-scale casualties, albeit by the enemy.

At 0600 on the morning of 28 February, I resumed full control of all UK maritime units. Staking claim to part of the swept waters, *London* and then *Manchester* came to single anchor within a few hundred yards of each other, neither ship looking pretty in the gloom. I signalled details of the flagship changeover and we started preparing for it. Peter Buckeley confirmed that he would shift with his staff to *Lasalle* and that *Missouri* would then pull out to refuel. I relaxed clothing restrictions, allowing people to shed their combat coveralls and cease taking NAPS, to the relief of all. An irreverent member of my staff reflected that the relaxation would certainly keep our peckers up — rumours about the tablets' bromide qualities were widespread.

Although suitable cautions were signalled and command teams pushed very hard to avoid complacency, there was no escaping the feeling that it was all over. The only remaining threats were maverick or suicide attack, or proxy mines. Indeed, fresh concern was generated when *Avenger* detected a Manta mine actually in the swept channel. All movements were cancelled and *Ledbury* and *Avenger* went to investigate. *Avenger*'s diving team identified the supposed mine as an ammunition box discarded by some sloppy warship, but at least the accuracy of our mine detection sonar had been proved. We re-opened the channel with relief.

The Kuwaiti naval commander stated his understandable wish to make a spectacular entry into Kuwait Harbour in his one remaining patrol craft through the, as yet, uncleared waters. I wryly suggested he might like to do so by helicopter rather than risk making his entry more spectacular still.

To the south, some Saudi patrol boats had anchored inside an area declared by us as still being unswept and there they remained, despite reminders. I wondered whether they were working from different Intelligence or were simply foolhardy. The area was indeed confirmed as entirely clear of Iraqi mines when we received enemy mine-laying charts a few days later. I still speculate on whether the Intelligence held by the Saudis and the US and British forces was the same. Saudi boats had appeared to operate with abandon in a number of 'risk' areas during those last days and nights.

Thirty miles north-west of our position lay Kuwait City. I remembered from my earlier visits the city's towering minarets, its breeze blocks, dust and parking lots. Amidst its buildings, industry had thrived and profits had soared whilst Yemenis, Pakistanis, Bangladeshis and Koreans had toiled at their manual labour. Virtually all of them had gone — as had the very face of the city itself.

The US Marines afloat evacuated 1,400 Iraqi prisoners of war from Faylakah whilst *Wisconsin* and *Missouri* departed. The two great gunships had fired a total of 1,000 rounds in support of the land advance, *Missouri* alone firing 1 million lbs of ordnance. Nearly 70 per cent of all their targets had been severely damaged or destroyed.

I summoned *Brave*, *Hecla*, *Diligence* and *Sir Galahad* to advance down the swept channel and we started our own command shifts in the first really bad weather of the campaign — blustering winds of up to 40 knots. I had intended that *London* should secure alongside the ugly bulk of anchored *Diligence* with *Brave* secured on the other side, so that staff could readily transfer publications, charts and personal gear, but it was not to be. The combined tonnage of the three ships was way in excess of *Diligence*'s ability to hold her position and she started to drag her anchor. Thus we had to disgorge myself and my staff swiftly to *Diligence* whilst slipping the two frigates in quick succession, as we drifted at an alarming rate towards the boundary on the chart that marked as yet unswept water. I reflected ruefully upon the headlines that would appear if I contrived to blow up my flagship and Fleet

446

Repair Ship simultaneously within 24 hours of the ceasefire because of a squall. Control was restored but the weather did not improve. As *Diligence* was buffeted unrelentingly until nightfall and as I was not prepared to spend the night marooned from my communications, I summoned an unfortunate Lynx to transfer David and myself. The aircraft lacked back seats and we crouched uncomfortably on the floor, trying not to think of the hazards of collision with overhanging cranes and to ignore the massive turbulence and thunder of rain on the canopy. After one missed approach to the wrong ship — mistaken in the oily blackness — we eventually and gratefully flopped on to *Brave*'s greasy flight-deck.

Torrential rain laden with oil had fallen throughout the transfer and my staff, once immaculate in their white overalls, looked for all the world like a herd of zebra when we finally gathered in our new flagship. Transfer to *Brave* had taken six edgy hours. I bade farewell to the splendidly loyal *London* and watched her turn south at last.

The Coalition navies faced a massive clearance task that was to last for another six months, despite remarkable subsequent estimates that more than half of the Iraqi mines had been maldeployed as they were laid. Whether this was due to Iraqi haste to complete the task under cover of darkness or whether out of sheer incompetence will never be known. Either way, it probably saved more than one ship and several hundred lives. Nevertheless, the final tally of Iraqi mines was formidable. They had placed 744 moored mines, 303 ground mines, 90 beached mines and 146 set free as drifters — a grand total of 1,283. I recalled with wry amusement the initial Intelligence assessment in the Maritime Tactical School — a total of 300.

I asked for signalled operating statistics from the Task Group, which I correlated and passed back to them to savour the Royal Naval effort. In total, our twenty-six ships had steamed 93,000 miles, had played a key part in establishing the embargo, had led the penetration of the minefields, had provided unceasing support in the very front line, and had destroyed the only missile attack against Coalition ships. Our helicopters had eliminated more than 25 per cent of the Iraqi Navy and had helped supply our foremost vessels. All had been achieved without the loss of lives, ships or aircraft. I had much for which to give thanks.

The detail of our naval aircraft achievements was similarly impressive. Over forty-seven days and nights of war, 846 helos had flown 1,350 sorties, totalling more than 2,000 flying hours, and had conducted 1,100 deck landings and 120 mine searches. Their Lynx colleagues averaged more than 100 combat flying hours each: *Gloucester* Flight alone flew more than 190 hours. Though the naval Sea Kings in the desert had not been under my command, or even view, final analysis of their contribution to land operations was comparable to the massive flying effort afloat: 845 Squadron (Lieutenant

Commander Mark Salter) and 848 Squadron (Lieutenant Commander Nigel North) flew more than 1,000 sorties between 5 January and 31 March, totalling 1,800 flying hours, and carried more than 60 tons of stores and 600 prisoners of war.

And now I and a majority of my ships would be committed to a much longer stay — clearing mines, sustaining the embargo, and restoring stability to the region. I flew round to all my forward ships to convey my thanks and — in some cases — goodbyes before they started for home. It was time to make my most important visit of all — to view the fruits of victory.

* * *

Beating rotor blades spill dust all around the square in front of the British Embassy. My reception party arches into the downwash, blending inconspicuously in their camouflage uniforms against the sand-blasted background. The Landrover looks as if it too has fought the length of the Arabian Peninsula; battered to a veteran-like weariness, it is much in keeping with the scarred face of Kuwait as we start out along the beach road.

Ironically, the tall, smiling blond giant who has come to greet and escort me is none other than Ian Stanley, the young hero of South Georgia who flew so gallantly on to the Fortuna Glacier: typically he has inveigled himself into Riyadh and now Kuwait City. Whilst it is good to see him again, it is a misery to see the

449

battered face of Kuwait. Once white sands are all contaminated and a meandering trench-line scars the shore for mile after mile, coiling back and forth behind its line of barbed wire. Creamy oil froth laps at the tank traps jutting from the shallows; broken hulks of shattered boats are everywhere. Virtually every structure along the promenade is daubed with graffiti, and garbage drifts forlornly along the tarmac, patrolling the deserted city on the sweaty morning breeze.

'They used the ice rink as a bloody great morgue, but of course it couldn't cope. Stuff melted. Ghastly.' I grunt in acknowledgement; braced against the jarring suspension; eyes never still, mind appalled by what I see. No electricity means no traffic lights. But there is virtually no other traffic; just us and a ghost kingdom. On either side of the road, only uniforms are in evidence — and always weapons. God, or Allah, alone knows what scores are being settled in the suburbs. Thankfully there is no visible bomb damage; the Iraqis alone had the monopoly of mayhem in Kuwait City. Dogs prowl everywhere on the once-gracious streets, shop-fronts are either desecrated or boarded up, the walls and pavements are filthy. Could it be just seven months since this glittering city, symbolic jewel of a vastly affluent land, was invaded by Saddam Hussein's tanks? We lurch on and I feel relief as we clear the suburbs. It is short-lived — the spreading dark mushroom of the burning Ahmadi oil fields tower ahead of us.

The temperature drop is distinct and I shall

450

not see the sun again today. We curve along the pitted, oil-soaked road, with the first of the blazing pyres gouting up into the billowing blackness overhead. Incandescent amber and scarlet columns, pressure-fed from far below, are roaring up in vast towers with the intensity of a hundred forges. Sudden heat sears the lungs and burns the skin as we hasten to wind up windows, often passing within one hundred yards of the blazing towers. Dense smoke is everywhere, visibility often down to less than 30 yards. Well-fires come and go, looming out of the blackness. It is impossible to imagine that there are hundreds more of these spewing, molten fountains across the length of the coastal kingdom; that they will take nearly two years to extinguish; that the lost revenue amounts to £60 million each day; and that the environmental cost is going to be unquantifiable. We don linen facemasks, nobody talking in the oil-laden air as we jolt our way through the impenetrable gloom. We are re-entering hell.

And then we are through the worst, back on to the battered highway, with the air still chill and foul but visibility improved, the green motorway signs directing us on to the port of Shuaybah. We swing between the steel gates to see sabotaged cranes lying toppled and half-immersed in the foul thickness of what was once water — like the skeletons of prehistoric creatures preserved in their death throes. No doors and windows have survived in the administrative buildings, and glutinous hooked fingers of flotsam gleam blackly in the docks and basins of the harbour.

451

Our divers have transferred ashore to work with the American and Australian divers, living out of shipping containers on the docks in Shuaybah Port, shrouded in the icy gloom. Their only light relief is when they are allowed to blow up the massive stocks of light ammunition left behind by fleeing Iraqis. By the time the detachments return to the UK on 23 April, they will have countermined or made safe forty mines.

My team is working just inside the main harbour wall; those not diving or supervising are huddled around a brazier in whatever layers of clothing they can fit over their uniform. They look like a group of down-and-outs surviving inner city decay on an English winter's day. I am met by their CO, Lieutenant Peter Williams, once a carefree Sub Lieutenant with me in Avenger. He now looks drawn and a good deal older — but I dare say so do I. His exploits will rightly win him a Distinguished Service Cross. The temperature should be 30° centigrade but is less than half that as I join the fireside circle, wishing I had brought something more substantial than my thin action working uniform — and something equally substantial in a bottle. I inspect their 'goodies', row upon row of Iraqi ordnance: booby traps extracted from dark corners; abandoned shells and grenades; flares and machine-gun bullet bandoliers and weapon cases. They are all stacked neatly into little symmetrical pyramids along the jetty.

'What visibility distance have you got down there?' I enquire of a recently surfaced diver as

452

I gesture out across the glutinous basin. The response is succinct: 'What visibility, sir?'

He has just dived beneath the gun emplacements that were attacked by Coalition aircraft. Feeling his way along the foul slime of the harbour bottom, he found himself embracing a tumescent, bloated Iraqi corpse which disintegrated beneath his grasp. A report comes in that a Sergeant on the US clearance team has just lost his hand in an explosion whilst working the adjacent shallows. The cheerful banter of the team, though welcoming, leaves me marooned in introspective reflection. I stare morosely through the harbour entrance. Curving ribbons of contamination ripple away out to sea, to where our ships are just visible, working their way towards us through the mines, and re-opening Kuwait to prosperity. The symbolic first entry by a British minehunter is only days away, but there are four more major ports still to be cleared by this weary team.

I suck despondently at the thin air, still rancid with burnt oil. Bodies, blazing wells, desecrated buildings, burnt-out trucks, charred flesh, tragedy — it is a maimed country. I shiver as again I taste the fruits of victory, with their familiar bitterness. All the glory fades and all the vigour drains. I am intensely weary.

Epilogue
May of '91

'He that outlives this day
and comes safe home'

IT was 22 May, nearly six months since I had first flown into Dubai. We had been admiringly received in the littoral states and by our allies for our disproportionate contribution to the success at sea. Admiral Arthur had personally and kindly presented me with the US Bronze Star just before his return to his command in Japan. *Brilliant,* girls and all, had lived up to her name in saving a merchant ship from a large fire. *Brave* had carried me for a gruelling succession of port calls to the littoral states. Harbours were open, mines nearly cleared, Coalition co-operation was winding down — I could at last go home.

My fellow major military commanders had all long since departed for the UK; to receptions, lecture tours, presentations and rightful adulation. Letters and newspapers from home had left me feeling as I had after the Falklands, but worse: public perception seemed to have overlooked our Navy's presence in the Gulf. I was unduly sensitive over the achievements of 'my' people.

The same Arab band played on the jetty

as my successor was piped on board and we completed the ritual brief turnover that our Service demands before I was led out into bright sunlight for my final departure. The haze had cleared for me, as had the men of HMS *Brave* who were lined along the upper deck. I had addressed them some minutes earlier, thanking them for their many achievements as busy flagship during the most difficult performance, that which follows the Lord Mayor's Show. I reminded them that they had helped in part to change the face of history — defeat for the Coalition would have left the world a far uglier place. It was something of which they could always be proud. I concluded with the same words I had used to the men of *Alacrity* in 1982: 'My abiding memory is of the quality and character of our people."

I bade Bob Williams goodbye and was pleased to note that the final pipe by the gangway staff was precise and clear. On the jetty was a mobile Iraq anti-aircraft battery, its tow lines manned by personal staff, all immaculate in fresh whites. Saluted into the bucket seat, I was towed away to cheers from the men of *Brave*. At the end of the jetty I dismounted, shook hands with my team and paused for a moment, looking back across the elegant bow of my former flagship. Gulf waters and clear heavens merged into one glittering bowl which dazzled my eyes — the same blending of sea and sky which had given me a glorious, exciting thirty years. I acknowledged last salutes and was proffered into the sumptuous interior of an enormous stretch limousine, obtained from heaven knows where. Settling into the velvet cushions, I was driven to Dubai Airport accompanied by the wailing tones of Arab music on the hi-fi. I had finished. For me, war was over.

When finally I arrived at Gatwick, there was nobody on the hardstanding to meet me. As I fought with the sweaty crowd jostling for taxis, I recalled a fragment of a recently read poem by G. K. Chesterton:

> For I also had my hour; one far fierce hour
> and sweet;
> There was a shout about my ears, and palms
> beneath my feet.

I went home to dig the garden.

Chronology

The Falklands

1982

19 Mar.	Argentinian scrap-metal workers hoist the Argentinian flag at Leith, South Georgia.
20 Mar.	HMS *Endurance* and a force of Royal Marines are dispatched from Stanley to South Georgia.
1 Apr.	Preparations begin to form a British Task Group to sail to the Falklands.
1 – 2 Apr.	Argentinian forces invade the Falkland Islands.
3 Apr.	Argentinian forces take Grytviken, South Georgia.
4 Apr.	The British aircraft-carriers *Hermes* and *Invincible* sail under escort from the United Kingdom.
11 Apr.	Three British nuclear submarines arrive off the Falkland Islands.

12 Apr.	The British Government declares a 200-mile Maritime Exclusion Zone around the Falklands.
16 Apr.	The main vessels of the British Task Group arrive at their half-way staging-point of Ascension Island.
18 Apr.	British aircraft-carriers sail under escort from Ascension Island.
25 Apr.	British warships under the command of *Antrim* recapture South Georgia.
1 May	British ships and aircraft launch first attacks upon Argentinian forces on East Falkland.
2 May	The Argentinian cruiser *General Belgrano* is sunk by the nuclear submarine *Conqueror*.
4 May	HMS *Sheffield* is disabled and abandoned following air attack by Exocet.
21 May	British forces conduct the main landing at San Carlos Water in Falkland Sound. HMS *Ardent* is sunk.
23 May	HMS *Antelope* explodes and sinks following air attack.

25 May	HMS *Coventry* and MV *Altantic Conveyor* are both sunk in separate air attacks.
28 – 29 May	2 Para take Goose Green after fierce battle.
8 Jun.	RFA *Sir Galahad* and *Sir Tristram* are bombed at Bluff Cove.
11 – 12 Jun.	British land forces take Mount Longden, Mount Harriet and Two Sisters Ridge.
13 – 14 Jun.	British land forces take Tumbledown Mountain and Wireless Ridge.
14 Jun.	The formal surrender of Argentinian forces takes place at Stanley.

The Gulf War

1990

2 Aug.   Iraqi forces invade Kuwait.

3 Aug.   The United Nations Security
                Council votes 14 – 0 for immediate
                Iraqi withdrawal.

6 Aug.   The United Nations Security
                Council votes 13 – 0 for sanctions
                against Iraq.

10 Aug.   The Arab League agrees to send
                forces to Saudi Arabia.

17 Aug.   The first Iraqi vessels are
                intercepted by the Coalition.

25 Aug.   The United Nations Security
                Council votes to support a full
                naval blockade.

30 Sep.   General de la Billière is appointed
                as British Joint Force Commander
                in the Gulf.

29 Nov.   The United Nations Security
                Council approves the use of

force if Iraq does not vacate Kuwait by 16 January.

10 Dec.   1 (BR) Division units arrive in Saudi Arabia from British Forces Germany.

1991

17 Jan.   The Coalition starts offensive action, codename Desert Storm, against Iraq under United Nations Security Council provisions.

29 – 30 Jan.   The Iraqi Navy is largely destroyed by British naval Lynx helicopters and Coalition fixed-wing aircraft.

15 Feb.   US and British naval forces move into the coastal minefields off Kuwait. Iraq issues a statement claiming her readiness to negotiate; this is subsequently proved to be a hoax.

18 Feb.   USS *Tripoli* and USS *Princeton* are struck by mines off Kuwait.

21 Feb.   Iraq allegedly accepts a Soviet-proposed peace plan. President Bush demands immediate large-scale withdrawals.

23 Feb.	After non-compliance by Iraq with the withdrawal terms, the Coalition commences large-scale ground assault.
25 Feb.	Following rapid advances by the Coalition, their forces enter Kuwait City. Large losses by the Iraqis prompt Baghdad radio to announce a fighting withdrawal from Kuwait.
27 Feb.	The Coalition suspends further offensive action.
3 Mar.	Iraq formally accepts a ceasefire.

Glossary

ATO	Air Tasking Organization.
Chaff	Radar echoes deployed to confuse enemy radars or seduce their missiles.
CINCFLEET	Commander-in-Chief Fleet.
DOPC	British Defence and Overseas Planning Committee — political forum used for crisis management.
GPS	Global Positioning System; a precise satellite navigation system.
IFF	Identification Friend or Foe; an automatic interrogation system to identify air and surface radar contacts.
JFHQ	British Joint Forces Headquarters at Riyadh during the Gulf War.
MCM	Mine-countermeasures; these embrace minesweeping, mine-hunting and supporting diving operations.
MCMV	A mine-countermeasures vessel.
MOD	The British Ministry of Defence in Whitehall; the overall command centre of the British Armed Forces.
NVG	Night Vision Goggles; light-enhancement device to allow visual flight by night.
LSL	Logistical Landing Ship; British utility Fleet Auxiliary used in

	both the Falklands and the Gulf (the *Sir Galahad* class).
Lynx	Multi-purpose embarked helicopter operated by British destroyers and frigates.
MEZ	Maritime Exclusion Zone.
NAPS	Nerve Agent Prophylactic Tablets; issued to British Armed Forces to protect against military nerve agents.
ROE	Rules of Engagement; the political control of the military in time of tension.
RFA	Royal Fleet Auxiliary; the Service which provides the Royal Navy with tanker, storeship, repair and amphibious support.
SHAR	Sea Harrier; Royal Navy single-sea jet aircraft, used primarily as an interceptor.
SNOME	Senior Naval Officer, Middle East.
TEZ	Total Exclusion Zone; the 200–mile radius area declared around the Falklands by the British in April 1982.
USN	United States Navy.
WEU	Western European Union.

Bibliography

The following books provided me with useful selective background reading:

Algosaibi, Ghazi A., *The Gulf Crisis*; *An Attempt to Understand*, 1991.

Brown, David, *The Royal Navy in the Falklands War*, Leo Cooper, 1987.

Central Office of Information, 'Britain and the Falklands Crisis — A Documentary Record', Reference pamphlet 176, HMSO, 1982.

Coll, Alberto R., and Arend, Anthony C., *The Falklands War — Lessons for Strategy, Diplomacy and International Law*, George Allen and Unwin, 1985.

de la Billière, General Sir Peter, *Storm Command*, HarperCollins, 1992.

Department of the Navy, Office of the Chief of Naval Operations, 'The United States Navy in DESERT SHIELD/DESERT STORM', Washington DC, 15 May 1991.

Ethell, Jeffrey, and Price, Alfred, *Air War South Atlantic*, Sidgwick and Jackson, 1983.

The Falklands Campaign — The Lessons, HMSO, January 1982.

'Falkland Island Review', Report of a Committee of Privy Counsellors, HMSO, January 1983.

Friedman, Norman, *Desert Victory: The War for Kuwait*, The Naval Institute Press, 1991.

Godden, John (ed.), *Shield and Storm*, Brasseys, 1994.

McCausland, Lt. Col. Jeffrey, *The Gulf Conflict: A Military Analysis*, Adelphi Paper 282, Brasseys/IISS

Middlebrook, Martin, *Operation CORPORATE*, Viking, 1985.

— *The Fight for the Malvinas*, Viking, 1989.

Pimlott, John, and Badsey, Stephen (eds.), *The Gulf War Assessed*, Arms and Armour Press, 1992.

Record, Jeffrey, *Hollow Victory — The Contrary View of the Gulf War*, Brasseys, 1993.

Schwarzkopf, General H. Norman, with Petre, Peter, *It Doesn't Take a Hero: The Autobiography*, Bantam, 1992.

Smith, Gordon, *Battles of the Falklands War*, Ian Allen, 1989.

Strange, Ian, *The Falklands Islands*, David & Charles, 1972.

Thompson, Julian, *No Picnic*, Leo Cooper with Secker and Warburg, 1985.

The Times Guide to the Middle East.

Ward, Sharkey, *Sea Harrier over the Falklands*, Leo Cooper, 1992.

Woodward, Admiral Sandy, *100 Days*, HarperCollins, 1992.

Other titles in the
Charnwood Library Series:

PAY ANY PRICE
Ted Allbeury

After the Kennedy killings the heat was on
— on the Mafia, the KGB, the Cubans, and
the FBI . . .

MY SWEET AUDRINA
Virginia Andrews

She wanted to be loved as much as the
first Audrina, the sister who was perfect
and beautiful — and dead.

PRIDE AND PREJUDICE
Jane Austen

Mr. Bennet's five eligible daughters will never
inherit their father's money. The family fortunes
are destined to pass to a cousin. Should one
of the daughters marry him?

THE GLASS BLOWERS
Daphne Du Maurier

A novel about the author's forebears, the
Bussons, which gives an unusual glimpse
of the events that led up to the French
Revolution, and of the Revolution itself.

CHINESE ALICE
Pat Barr

The story of Alice Greenwood gives a complete picture of late 19th century China.

UNCUT JADE
Pat Barr

In this sequel to CHINESE ALICE, Alice Greenwood finds herself widowed and alone in a turbulent China.

THE GRAND BABYLON HOTEL
Arnold Bennett

A romantic thriller set in an exclusive London Hotel at the turn of the century.

SINGING SPEARS
E. V. Thompson

Daniel Retallick, son of Josh and Miriam (from CHASE THE WIND) was growing up to manhood. This novel portrays his prime in Central Africa.

A HERITAGE OF SHADOWS
Madeleine Brent

This romantic novel, set in the 1890's, follows the fortunes of eighteen-year-old Hannah McLeod.

BARRINGTON'S WOMEN
Steven Cade

In order to prevent Norway's gold reserves falling into German hands in 1940, Charles Barrington was forced to hide them in Borgas, a remote mountain village.

THE PLAGUE
Albert Camus

The plague in question afflicted Oran in the 1940's.

THE RESTLESS SEA
E. V. Thompson

A tale of love and adventure set against a panorama of Cornwall in the early 1800's.

THE RIDDLE OF THE SANDS
Erskine Childers

First published in 1903 this thriller, deals with the discovery of a threatened invasion of England by a Continental power.

WHERE ARE THE CHILDREN?
Mary Higgins Clark

A novel of suspense set in peaceful Cape Cod.

KING RAT
James Clavell

Set in Changi, the most notorious Japanese POW camp in Asia.

THE BLACK VELVET GOWN
Catherine Cookson

There would be times when Riah Millican would regret that her late miner husband had learned to read and then shared his knowledge with his family.

THE WHIP
Catherine Cookson

Emma Molinero's dying father, a circus performer, sends her to live with an unknown English grandmother on a farm in Victorian Durham and to a life of misery.

SHANNON'S WAY
A. J. Cronin

Robert Shannon, a devoted scientist had no time for anything outside his laboratory. But Jean Law had other plans for him.

THE JADE ALLIANCE
Elizabeth Darrell

The story opens in 1905 in St. Petersburg with the Brusilov family swept up in the chaos of revolution.

THE DREAM TRADERS
E. V. Thompson

This saga, is set against the background of intrigue, greed and misery surrounding the Chinese opium trade in the late 1830s.

BERLIN GAME
Len Deighton

Bernard Samson had been behind a desk in Whitehall for five years when his bosses decided that he was the right man to slip into East Berlin.

HARD TIMES
Charles Dickens

Conveys with realism the repulsive aspect of a Lancashire manufacturing town during the 1850s.

THE RICE DRAGON
Emma Drummond

The story of Rupert Torrington and his bride Harriet, against a background of Hong Kong and Canton during the 1850s.

FIREFOX DOWN
Craig Thomas

The stolen Firefox — Russia's most advanced and deadly aircraft is crippled, but Gant is determined not to abandon it.

THE DOGS OF WAR
Frederic Forsyth

The discovery of the existence of a mountain of platinum in a remote African republic causes Sir James Manson to hire an army of trained mercenaries to topple the government of Zangaro.

THE DAYS OF WINTER
Cynthia Freeman

The story of a family caught between two world wars — a saga of pride and regret, of tears and joy.

REGENESIS
Alexander Fullerton

It's 1990. The crew of the US submarine ARKANSAS appear to be the only survivors of a nuclear holocaust.

SEA LEOPARD
Craig Thomas

HMS 'Proteus', the latest British nuclear submarine, is lured to a sinister rendezvous in the Barents Sea.

THE TORCH BEARERS
Alexander Fullerton

1942: Captain Nicholas Everard has to escort a big, slow convoy . . . a sacrificial convoy.

DAUGHTER OF THE HOUSE
Catherine Gaskin

An account of the destroying impact of love which is set among the tidal creeks and scattered cottages of the Essex Marshes.

FAMILY AFFAIRS
Catherine Gaskin

Born in Ireland in the Great Depression, the illegitimate daughter of a servant, Kelly Anderson's birthright was poverty and shame.

THE EXPLORERS
Vivian Stuart

The fourth novel in 'The Australians' series which continues the story of Australia from 1809 to 1813.